Don't Seek Trophies

A letter of confirmation from the past

I took a book off my grandmother's bookshelf not 30 minutes after her funeral. The next day, I put it on a shelf at home and forgot about it for years, but after I finished typing this book (08/08/2021), I decided to open it.

There was dust encasing the book that seemingly had not been opened in decades. I couldn't remember why I decided to not to open it, but it was probably due to the fact it brought up the memories of my favorite person passing away.
When I opened it, I noticed it belonged to my grandfather whom I never met. Inside the cover was a letter from him I was clearly meant to find, as the book had not been opened since before my birth…

The letter was there in the untouched book for at least 40-50 years, unknown to the world.

Here are those words:

"**Fear** is lack of **faith**. **Lack of faith** is **ignorance**. Fear can only be cured by vision. Give the world vision, it will see. Give it ears, it will hear. Give it a right arm, it will act. Man needs time and room. Man needs soil, rain, and sunshine to have a chance. Open all your doors and windows. Let everything pass freely in and out, out and in. Even the <u>evil</u>, let it pass out and in, in and out. No man hates the truth. But most <u>men</u> (people) are afraid of the <u>truth</u>. Make the <u>truth</u> easier than a <u>lie</u>. Make the truth more welcome than its counterfeit. Then people will no longer be <u>afraid</u>: being <u>afraid</u> is being <u>ignorant</u>. Being <u>ignorant</u> is <u>being without faith</u>."

I'm giving the individuals of the world, eyes to see, ears to listen, a right arm to act, and making the truth…more clear to see.

We all individually can be greater in any or every chapter of this book. The problem is, like the first domino that knocks over the rest; bad patterns in one can affect you <u>when</u> life happens. Thus, making them all essential to be greater in the end. So, for a greatness driven life, they are all needed to some degree on your journey to become…a <u>True</u> Champion.

Why <u>True</u> Champions Don't Seek Trophies

By: Joshua Rose

100 Fold Publishing LLC

Content start to completion: 03/03/2021-08/08/2021
Edit completions: 12/15/2021
First Publication date: 03/25/2022
ISBN (Paperback): 979-8-9856661-2-0

Copyright ©, 2021 by POC (Point of Contact) for Joshua Rose: Calvin Rosinbaum

All rights reserved. No part of this book may be reproduced without written permission, except for brief quotations in book and critical reviews. For more info, email jrose@lifeofpatterns.com, and a representative will be with you as quickly as possible.

Everything in the universe from science, physics, medicine, and study of the mind have patterns that derive from greater patterns. The scary part is, they are all tied together with non-random interwoven patterns.

The problem with today's world is individuals apply their flawed patterns of life to the world, through reaction emotions to label their personal world. When in reality, pattern driven greatness <u>for the world</u> is right in front of their closed eyes as they face a mirror.

OTHER THAN A HANDFUL OF PEOPLE WHO KNOW THE MEANING OF <u>JOSHUA ROSE</u>. I HOPE TO REMAIN ANONYMOUS UNTIL I DECIDE OTHERWISE.
IF YOU DO WANT TO FIND OUT WHO I AM. THEN TELL OTHERS TO READ THIS BOOK, AND MAYBE ONE DAY YOU'LL FIND OUT MY TRUE IDENTITY.

FOR NOW, THE PERSON OF CONTACT FOR ME AND ANY SOCIAL MEDIE I DECIDE TO USE (IF ANY), AND TO CONFIRM IF THE POSTS OR ACCOUNT ARE OF MY DOING; WILL BE THE OWNER OF 100 FOLD PUBLISHING:

CALVIN JORDAN ROSINBAUM

Don't Seek Trophies

TABLE OF CONTENTS

Letter from the past: 2

Prologue: 12-15

Part 1: Pattern-allistic mentality and keys of life we can all be greater in

    Chapter 1. Intro to Pattern-allistic Mentality: 18-64
- Pattern-allistic Mentality: 18-56
- Sliding Door of Wisdom: 58-64

    Chapter 2. Simple keys anyone can work on for greater pattern-allistic mentality: 65-143
- DETAILS: 65-74
- ADAPTABILITY: 75-82
- PERSISTENCE/DETERMINATION: 83-91
- DISCIPLINE/SELF-DISCIPLINE/ACCOUNTABILITY/SELF-ACCOUNTABILITY: 92-104
- TRUE LOVE/HONOR: 105-114
- HUMBLENESS/SWAGGER: 115-132
- RESPECT/INTEGRITY THROUGH HONOR/RIGHTEOUSNESS: 133-138

Part 2: What to expect…

    Chapter 3. Respect the Failure: 145-195
- Relationships: 147-165
- Why you should be afraid to fail: 166-173
- Why you are going to fail in life: 174-179
- Why you shouldn't "care" what others thinks if you fail and mentalities between the lines: 180-187
- Why you shouldn't be afraid to fail: 188-191
- *The Mountain* made of mountains: 192-195

    Chapter 4. Why the world doesn't like True Champions: 196-237
- What's wrong with the world today as a whole: 196-217
- Why the world doesn't like a greatness pattern mindset: 218-224

- Why the world will love your greatness pattern mindset: 225-226
- The truth of why a true growth mindset is starting to disappear: 227-237

Chapter 5. Look to something Higher: 238-269
- As proven by patterns of the world: 251-269

Chapter 6. The weight of the Great Journey: 270-307
- A Good, "Good", and Bad person: 273-289
- Greatness for humans at the core today (giving/care): 290-307

Part 3

Chapter 7. Why True Champions Don't Seek Trophies: 309-366
- True Empathy: 311-317
- The Gravity of the situation: 318-321
- Anyone can be a Phoenix: 322-326
- True Empathy, Sliding Door of Wisdom, Biblical Understanding of real-world Patterns: 327-338
- Forgiveness: 339-351
- The Bible: 352-359
- Joy, Peace, Favor, and Blessing: 360-361
- Why True Champions Don't Seek Trophies: 362-366

Chapter 8. My final incites to you (Using this book): 367-377
- The wisdom of an apple: 372-375
- One Last Thing: 376-377

Letter to you, the Epilogue, and more: 379-399

Letter to the Church: 400-401

Sources: 403-406

<u>The task at hand</u>:

Goals:

Can I make the situations in my life greater:

How do I become greater:

Obstacles in my way:

What can I control in myself when going through these obstacles:

FIRST OF ALL, I WANT TO THANK THE PEOPLE THAT TAUGHT ME WHAT IT MEANT TO GROW:

- THOSE WHO DID/DIDN'T SHOW ME FAVOR
- THOSE WHO SAID I WOULD/WOULDN'T AMASS TO ANYTHING
- THOSE WHO SAID I COULD/COULDN'T DO ANYTHING
- THOSE WHO SAID LIFE WAS EASY
- THOSE WHO SAID LIFE WAS HARD
- EVERYONE WHO INTENTIONALLY/UNINTENTIONALLY DID ME WRONG
- EVERYONE WHO HELPED ME AND THOSE WHO LEFT ME TO SINK IN THE OCEAN OF LIFE

<u>YOU ALL MADE THIS POSSIBLE</u>

To cover my backside (You'll see why ☺)

Legalities:

All sites, sources stated, and companies are not associated with the complete opinions of this book.

PROLOGUE

<u>EVERYTHING</u> IN THIS BOOK HAS MEANING AND PLACEMENT, BECAUSE WE ALL STRUGGLE IN ANY SECTION NOW OR IN THE FUTURE AS WE GO THROUGH LIFE. **EVEN THE ORIGINAL PRICE OF, $29.24. SEE MEANING OF THOSE PROVERBS CHAPTERS**

<u>You'll either love this book, or you'll hate it. But we all will eventually struggle with the things in it.</u>

This book is going to draw attention to your blind hypocrisies and show you what it takes to be greater, according to your own pattern-allistic mentality.

I know some, if not most people don't like the truth, and you're mentally weaker than you give yourself credit for. As time has passed, you've sought and been given some kind of trophy for being your base self, which in the end has hurt your mentality and ultimately, your life. I want you to be something greater than you see yourself now, because if you continue on your current track, you <u>will</u> one day fall into stagnation of the mind. So, in order to achieve greater, I believe it means you keep on reading, and take everything to heart.

Dive deeper than you ever have in yourself and the pattern-allistic mentality that you have, in order to become, the True Champion you were and are meant to be.

The greatest champion endeavors either start with **baby steps** you decided to take on your own, or you are/were free falling into a dark pit that has no end, and now you're looking for something to grab on to. That being known, I don't want you to feel the full weight of experience or have to continually go through the "fall on your face" wisdom, without having the ability to properly grow through it all. So, I wrote this book because I'm absolutely fed up with seeing people fine, with being mentally and physically "fine".

If you're perfectly fine with being perfectly fine, then you've never been pushed to the limit of your capability and will more than likely one day, regret not finding out about your limitless potential for greatness.

If you want respect, then you must know respect is not taken…<u>it's earned through self-validation first</u>.

Self-validation is a simple concept that can set you a part in any room and is also what gives you the ability to respect what you see in the mirror when you wake up, and right before you go to sleep.

I respect what and who I am. People who are seen as successful, unsuccessful, victims, bullies, cheaters, those who have been hurt, those who will be hurt, musicians, sports teams, family, champions from the past, and my savior Jesus Christ have all put me on the path for greatness today.

I hope this book changes your mentality by learning from mountains I've climbed, but also seen and heard others climb as well.

THE HIDDEN MENTAL DETIALS ARE MORE IMPORTANT THAN YOU COULD EVER IMAGINE.

<u>Let's get started</u>

You turned the page after that last paragraph!! That's great!!

Now you might think I'm crazy, but you have to see things from my perspective. I've seen schools, media, other religions, and people who claim to be Christians, take Jesus (my King) out of my life with a smile on their face. All while saying it was for the "benefit" of other people, even though it led to no true benefit for them in the end.

Furthermore, I've seen people openly bash and spit on my King for no reason, other than people don't want to hear an opinion, or from people associated with it.

But what about my benefit? Why does no one seem to care more about me?

To those questions, I respond with:

I have to keep fighting for what has happened to me and my generation (the weakest, biggest complainers of them all). Eventually, I'm going to receive compensation for what happened or change the way people think of me; while not needing to add to myself, because everyone/the world needs to change for me!!

You might not see what I did there. But whether you know it or not, that one paragraph can tell me exactly the type of person you are or are on your way to becoming.

Wanting to mentally elevate yourself into a champion, is not for the faint of heart, but is easier than people realize. So, I'm going to do my best to assist you over the mental mountains that your parents might have never taught you, and mountains the world doesn't want you to learn to climb.

Now let's get started!!!

Part 1

Pattern-allistic Mentality (my new word)

Keys we can all individually improve upon

These sections/chapters are absolutely necessary for you to understand for a greatness led life.

Important note

I can't wait until the end for you to discover why this book was written this way. *Hint: It might take a little reflection*

Trust me, I could put a sad back story into everything, but wisdom in any aspect of life is not just learned from a personal failure situation(s). So, this book will relate to life in such a way, that everyone can associate with on some level.

If I wanted to have pity contest like what most influential motivational speakers or writers use, then I could. But how relatable to everyone is some 1% chance of happening terrible problem that basically says, "I made it over this one huge, ginormous mountain, so you can beat your smaller problems." Especially, when they don't completely understand the how or Who, got them through that problem.

This world needs to stop comparing someone's life to another, and that includes circumstances of how we individually grew up. We instead, need to look inwards at ourselves to understand the generalities of life's mountains, and the knowledge of how to find the keys that unlock our hidden potential greatness ourselves, with pattern-allistic help.

Trust me, you will not win in a pity contest against me. I've either seen or experienced pretty much everything. I'm not saying I do not want to comfort you, but any pity party you want to have, I know how it feels and how to get past it. And I know, eventually, you're going to have to move on from your present-past, to step into your greater future.

The ability to change our life is entirely in our own hands. No one (especially in America) has the ability regardless of skin color, economic situation, or family background, to take away your greatness that lies deep within.

So, the only one who can be to blame for not achieving greatness, is the person staring back at you in the mirror every day.

CHAPTER 1: Intro to Pattern-allistic Mentality

But first my "Why?"

    I wrote this book because I heard of an 18-year-old kid committing suicide, due to this young person not knowing what they wanted to do with their life. Nor did it seem like they were provided any direction to their potential.

    I know it's in some way selfish to feel other's pain. But had I been there in some capacity, maybe I could've walked them through their pattern-allistic blueprint. That being known, I can't be everywhere at once, so this book is a way for me to see everyone's blueprint all at once. So even if all you do is read the book without writing in any of the sections, I believe it will raise anyone's level of thinking.

    This book has been written in a very specific way for <u>YOU</u>. In fact, I didn't even use my real name, because this world needs to know someone out there truly loves and wants the best for it, without seeking their own glory, honor, or accolades. My reasoning for doing this, is so I could in a sense be <u>anyone and anywhere</u>. But I will give you several hints over the course of the book of who I am. I even provide a couple hints at the end of where I spend a good portion of my time today, when I'm not traveling across the nation, spending time in various places or cities.

<u>There is one thing I do know for a fact</u>: *consistent action and application must be put in through your own life first.*

Otherwise, how can you expect anything great to happen through you? Whether you realize it or not in life; for every action, there is an equal and opposite, reaction.

Pattern-allistic mentality of tasks:

Let's start off simple, then work our way up regarding this topic. Take a look at the below:

<u>As most you probably know, this is a basic pattern in terms of numbers:</u>

<u>1, 5, 10, 1, 5, 10, 1, 5, 10</u>,……..etc.

<u>Patterns of this type can be compared to bigger more broad things you do in everyday life. Such as:</u>

- <u>Wake up</u>
    - Breakfast
    - Participate in work or school
- <u>Lunch</u>
    - Finish work or school
    - Dinner
- <u>Go to sleep</u>
- Repeat

Now let's take it a level deeper, so the pattern becomes a little more complex when you add various smaller tasks that you participate in the in-between.

<u>So instead of:</u>

<u>1, 5, 10, 1, 5, 10, 1, 5, 10</u>,…… etc

<u>The pattern becomes:</u>

<u>1</u>, 2, 3, 4, <u>5</u>, 6, 7, 8, 9, <u>10</u>, <u>1</u>, 2, 3, 4, <u>5</u>, 6, 7, 8, 9, <u>10</u>, <u>1</u>, 2, 3, 4, <u>5</u>, 6, 7, 8, 9, <u>10</u>,……..etc.

<u>Thus, the pattern of life then turns into:</u>

- <u>Wake up</u>
    - Get out of bed (difference between waking up and getting out of bed to start the day)
    - Get dressed, brush your teeth, shower, etc
    - Make food or coffee
- Breakfast
    - Eat
    - Get out the door (Because I know how difficult it can be to get out of the door LOL)
    - Drive to work or get dropped off at school
- Participate in work or school
    - Individual meetings or classes
    - Work on tasks or do schoolwork
- <u>Lunch</u>
    - Come to a stopping point in work or class
    - Eat for a designated time period socialize if presented
- Finish work or school
    - Leave work or get finished with school
- Dinner
    - Make food or work on homework (both sometimes)
    - Relax
    - Get ready for bed
- <u>Go to sleep</u>
- Repeat

Next, we apply time to the overall pattern board. Meaning, over the course of the day, all of those smaller tasks are spent doing something to prepare for the next smaller task, for the overall broad task. Which results in making what was spent, represented by a given amount of time. That being said, there are some things we as individuals are more efficient at than others (or so some may believe), because of a deeper understanding.

This time efficiency and smaller tasks, represent how we handle time over the course of any given moment within the bigger tasks, and/or our life in general.

Look at the things or area around that you personally have control over. Are there singular or multiple detailed attributes? In what you can control are you really doing your best with what you have? (ex: dirty car, dirty house, etc)

With this pattern information, let's take a step back to make our pattern picture bigger, and look at grouped individuals in a country

<u>Those in High School, College, or School in general time map:</u>

When you map out the total time spent of someone in school for a 24-hour time period, it should represent anywhere from 10-14 hours day of non-negotiables that include homework, classes, and/or possibly sports. 7-8 hours should be applied to sleep, and almost every weekend these people should to some degree have time off.

Meaning, total time spent doing non-negotiables is anywhere from 17-22 hours. Which leaves about 2 to 5 hours during the day, and around 16 hours on the weekend to spend time doing other things. (Sports are a privilege, not an entitlement. If your grades are lacking, then use the extra time to study.)

This one is pretty straight forward. When I was working on this concept in college, I understood why my parents always said, "You have it easy right now." (LOL)

The biggest problem with the type of individual we are talking about, is they are never taught the pattern of being efficient with their time. So, when they move on to the next type/step of person (real life) they struggle... <u>MIGHTELY</u>!!!

Those working (the real world), while possibly in College or School at any capacity time map

When in college and working at the same time, it is important to make conscious pattern decisions regarding the time needed for studying.

I'm going to introduce you to someone who is on the furthest end of the real-world spectrum in order to get you to think about your patterns of efficiency:

Based on a 24-hour time period: those who regularly work 12 hour shifts every day, have about 3-4 hours of free time daily, and 21-28 hours a week of free time. Granted, the workday can vary, but even those working 12 hour shifts every day, have the ability accomplish more if they chose to do so.

Don't think so??....Watch this ☺

A 12-hour shift, 7-8 hours of sleep, and making food 1 hour a day; equates to 20-21 hours of non-negotiables any given day. So, you have 3-4 hours of free time a day, which equates to 21-28 hours per week.

In order to level up your growth bar in your career (thus minimizing stress), you first need a strong base in which to build your current life up from.

Now guess how much time online classes take.

An average of a little more than 1 hour per day a week, per online course. (source: http://learnmore.uncg.edu/blog/bid/157407/how-much-time-should-one-commit-to-online-degree-coursework)

Can you guess how much time on average a day you still have even if it's one online course, work a 12-hour shift, and cook food for yourself an average of 1 hour a day?

About 2-3 hours per day, or 14-21 hours a week of free time. Kids can be a varying factor of the time spent. But, once again, how time efficient are you or your household if you find ways waste 2-3 hours a day, and are constantly inefficient in the small tasks? (You can still have family time too)

Now let's take Pattern-allistic mentality in this specific arena a step further by diving deeper into the mentality portion

Your efficiency of time depends on how well disciplined <u>you</u> are in getting tasks done.
Trust me, I know the importance of taking a break every once in a while. But if you are constantly taking a break, then are you in any way being efficient with your time? No…

Wasting time for the sake of wasting it and recharging your batteries for a brief moment, are two totally different things.

When anyone asks me how my day has been I reply, "Productively busy!!", instead of the normal "Busy!!". You might be wondering what the difference is between, "productively busy", and "busy".

Well, anyone can be "busy" doing anything. I could be "busy" looking at social media, watching television, or "busy" not doing anything. But when I'm productively busy, that means I've been getting things done for any range of tasks at hand for the day. So, when I say, "productively busy", it sets a precedence in my mind for a pattern of getting things done, because it holds my subconscious accountable in the realm of time efficiency.

<u>Application of patterns to the day as displayed in mentality:</u>

<u>1</u>, 2, 3, 4, <u>5</u>, 6, 7, 8, 9, <u>10</u>, <u>1</u>, 2, 3, 4, <u>5</u>, 6, 7, 8, 9, <u>10</u>, <u>1</u>, 2, 3, 4, <u>5</u>, 6, 7, 8, 9, <u>10</u>,……..etc.

The numbers represent the tasks throughout any given day, but the individual task (number) is represented by the efficiency level at which we perform each said task.

What causes any amount of additional effort to be factored in at the end of the day, or to move to the next task in the moment, is directly correlated by our **mental understanding** *of the task at hand.*

<u>For example:</u>

<u>1</u>, <u>5</u>, <u>10</u>

<u>Top level efficiency numbers for each task:</u>

1. -25+125
5. 0+100
10. -50+150

<u>So as you can see this person had to apply additional effort in 2 of the 3 tasks, so overall they had a:</u>

Level of understanding for efficiency: (-25) + (-50) = -75

Overall effort having to be put in moving to the next big task(s) (1, 5, 10): 125+100+150 = 375

-75/375 = -.2 efficiency level of the day, as 75 more units of effort needed to be exerted to in order to complete the broad task at hand

<u>The goal of pure efficiency in a task is, 0/100 = 0</u>
The additional 25 for number 1 and 50 needed for 10, represent the time taken away that could be spent towards other possible smaller tasks, or tasked numbers depending on the schedule of the day.

<u>The cool thing about this top-level efficiency is:</u>

However efficient you are in a small task leading to the next small task, all contribute to the efficiency factor of moving from each bigger task to the next, and ultimately the overall efficiency pattern of your day. Thus, also reflecting <u>your life</u>.

So, if you care (time efficiency) about the small things, you'll carry that care (time efficiency) over to the big things.

Now I know what you might be thinking, "What? How can I be purely efficient in everything? I can't control some tasks." I get there, keep reading.

For instance (example above continued):

> Tasks you can solely control = **

> Tasks where you cannot control what happens = ++
> Tasks we participate with others where we can control what we do, but not someone else = *+

- Wake up (Broad task)

    o **Get out of bed (difference between waking up and getting out of bed to start the day) => Efficiency factor -8

    o **Get dressed, brush your teeth => Efficiency factor -2

    o **Make food or coffee => Efficiency factor -4

- Breakfast
    o **Eat => Efficiency factor 0

    o **Get out the door (Because I know how difficult it can be to get out of the door LOL) => Efficiency factor -3. (Can be *+ For parents because well…you know…kids)

    o *+Drive to work or get dropped off at school => Efficiency factor -5

- Participate in work or school

    o *+Individual meetings or classes=> Efficiency factor 0

    o **Work on tasks or do schoolwork => Efficiency factor -3

As you can tell, there are tasks the person in this example can control (represented by **). If we can control these particular tasks ourselves, why can we not reach pure efficiency, or get closer to it?

Not being more efficient in smaller tasks, can lead to more potential stress in the overall bigger task at hand.

There are some tasks that require more than just you the individual, to contribute to the efficiency of the task (represented by *+). Which could be for example: meetings we need to attend, classes we participate in, getting kids out of the door, or driving to work.

We as individuals cannot control everything over the course of every task, but we can control how we act during that particular task. Which means we are the biggest contributors to the efficiency, or overall caring of how well those tasks go in what we can control. So ultimately, it's on us as individuals to adapt using what we learned in the past to further understand how to be better at the task at hand in the future.

As we as individuals go through life, there is no task we participate in which we can/could not control ourselves in some way before any variety of situations occur(ed).

You know what else is awesome about this concept?
In <u>small</u> or <u>big</u> tasks, you can control how you personally can work to be greater in terms of self-efficiency in order to relieve the once normal everyday stress of life you used to experience.

But whether you can truly be more efficient, depends on how well you <u>understand</u> the task at hand. And if you truly are efficient, someone around you will take notice, thus recognizing what you do as a skill. In turn, if one person recognizes a skill, then 100 people can recognize a degree level of that skill. But it is on you to use your pattern-allsitic mentality to hone said skill, or become greater in areas you need growth in, in order to potentially turn it into money.

As you begin to understand the pattern-allistic mentality going on in your mind, adapting yourself to become more efficient (or show care) will contribute to becoming closer to pure efficiency in the overall scale of your day to day, and ultimately……<u>your life</u>.

This change in yourself to become greater from an efficiency standpoint is represented by the, <u>understanding percentage factor</u>, to adapt, and raise your level in that given task.

<u>For instance (example continued)</u>:

- **Get out of bed (difference between waking up and getting out of bed to start the day) => Efficiency factor -8

    - Percentage change based on how well you adapt your pattern-allistic mentality (Alarm goes off):

1. Getting up at the alarm = 50% Efficiency factor => 0

2. Hitting snooze any number of times = 30% Efficiency factor => 1-10 (for example)

3. Not getting up = 20% (highest # of previous option)

4. Unknown = ??? (can increase the likely hood of any of the known tasks)

This concept can become a little trickier to explain, as it is one of the deepest portions of any task. But the efficiency of a task you start always begins at 0 and goes down from there. So how well you perform that task, varies in percentages based on the <u>understanding</u> of your <u>pattern-allistic mentality</u> such as: **getting up when the alarm rings, hitting snooze, not getting up, and an unknown factor that can bring to the table any number of known tasks (unknown is always potential in any task).**

So, if this person recognizes the need to start the day on time, their efficiency is pure 0 for this small task (lying in bed is not starting your day, so it decreases the efficiency). From there, those smaller tasks can possibly maintain, or decrease the average efficiency of the overall broad task, for any number of reasons (i.e. not knowing what to wear, undecided on whether to take a shower or not).

This example of simply starting your day can be applied to any number of tasks we can solely control. So, if you are in a task that you participate in along with someone else or group of people, remember: <u>The efficiency of the task at hand will more than likely never be pure.</u>

It is important to want to be more efficient in the time you have, but do not let it make you emotional when things don't work out exactly how you envisioned.

It's understandable to let something irk you, but when it bothers you emotionally, it can affect how efficient you personally can be. And as a result, you're giving that other person, or situation control over your life. Which only causes more effort to have to be exerted on yourself in the end, to remain at a level of efficiency in all other tasks, because you're mentally allowing that problem to bleed over mental stress into the rest of your life.

If you have a pattern-allistic mentality of becoming greater in the small tasks, the bigger ones will follow suit. But you need to be mentally prepared in understanding the recognition of preparation first. So, you can then adapt in all areas you can control, whether that be emotionally, or performance wise in yourself.

Simply completing something fast does not mean it was done in an efficient manner that displays your full capability to perform said task. In the end, if you did not <u>understand</u> the task at hand, the more effort that will have to be exerted as a result to go back and complete the task to a higher level of completion. So do not be afraid to humble yourself in the time efficiency realm in order to raise your level of understanding in your pattern-allistic mentality.

<u>Example</u>: cleaning your room in the proper way. (Don't do what I did and throw everything under the bed or in the closet. Because that means I had to later clean under my bed or organize my closet, exerting more effort in the end than when the initial task was at hand.)

A few things to remember:

Dependent on your upbringing, we as individuals are more inclined to have higher odds of making any particular choice, due to inherent pattern-allistic mentality, unless we are so driven to change it. But whether or not the choice we make or are driven to change raises our potential life factor, strictly depends on the <u>understanding</u> of the task at hand.

Once we know how to truly listen, and how well we use our, "sliding door" of wisdom, all in conjunction with understanding you can possibly become, truly more efficient.

We can never achieve pure efficiency as the average of life, because (as you could tell from the example) there are factors we personally can never control. Yet, that does not mean we cannot hold ourselves individually more accountable to get as close as possible to pure efficiency (showing care) in ourselves as we can. For this is the truly honorable/respectable thing to do for yourself and others, when real life is at hand, and thus will also benefit you even more over the course of your life.

However, it is ok to turn off this deep efficiency/care need when given the opportunity to briefly recharge your batteries. But remember, too much of a good thing can be bad, and a little healthy randomness within your life is beneficial for you to build upon your pattern-allistic mentality.

<u>*Controlling everything is impossible. So why let things you have no control take hold of your life, mentally, emotionally, and ultimately, what you do in the real world.*</u>

*Saying that, "(**blank**) is hard", <u>can be</u> **false**, because anything <u>can be hard if you make it hard</u>, by <u>not being consistently disciplined efficient</u> in anything. Thus, making the statement of, <u>"If (**blank**) was easy, then everyone would do it.",</u> **true**.*

Please take about 10-15 minutes to think about the concept in the previous section, because this next topic of how pattern-allistic mentality can be seen in subconscious thought patterns, has the possibility to absolutely nuke your mind.

I really hope you took that break ☺
Let's do this!!

Pattern-allistic mentality, and how or why you think the way you do/do not

The simple definition of Pattern-allistic Mentality as determined by thought patterns:

Everything we say/don't say, hear/not hear, see/not see, do/not do, can subconsciously and mentally affect us on any given level, in any given way, depending on how many times we potentially associate ourselves with any specific topic/thing, based on our own individual experiences to create patterns in our own mind that lead to what we say/don't say, hear/not hear, see/not see, or do/not do.

Yeeeeaaaaaahh…..if you didn't take that break, you might want to now….

Remember what I said about the patterns of life and efficiency/care factor? Well……the same pattern of how efficient we are, can be applied to how we go through life in our own mind. Though the terms do change, we individually have a whole trunk full of separate mentalities dependent on emotion, intellect, wisdom, and experience that come into play for our overall potential life factor.

As for the factors of why/how, the percentages of what you will/could do, are indicated by mental choice and the unknown factor still plays a significant role. As the individual, you have certain, "non-negotiables", or life standard standpoints that play a direct role in the odds of doing something. But we all have options within anything that can be subject to change whenever we so choose or are led to.

Yet, prior to change, we as an individual must decide within our own pattern-allistic mentality, to add a pattern (we so chose) to be greater than our current mental pattern approach, and then add baby steps that lead to strides within that desired pattern. This baby step and then stride approach, is what helps us as the individual evolve over time.

So, it can be said that pattern-allistic mentality, is literally what makes us as individuals different from each other no matter how many patterns of life we associate with someone else. Because just as everyone is not the same, the patterns in which we experience those things are never the exact same for anyone else.

We all have differing factors of our past and present, that form(ed) our individual future. But it is natural instinct of humans to want to associate our mental approaches with others in order to form communities.

Bonus time: A major problem today is we are too associative in the world of communities and are now label driven. So here is a question I want you to think about: <u>What happens when the thing you associate yourself with the most, provides a pattern into your mind that is not beneficial to your overall growth as an individual or a nation?</u>

<u>Similar individuals, but different pattern-allistic mentality choice example:</u>

Two people whose backgrounds involve the divorce of their parents, truly only have one major thing in common: the divorce. The circumstances and things experienced, are never the exact same.

So, while it might seem as though one never lets the divorce affect their life or pattern-allistic mentality too much, and found joy or importance in relationships with people, it was because of the choice they mentally made earlier in life to not let what someone else did in a situation they could not fully control take over their life in detrimental ways.

Meanwhile, the other kid who experienced divorce, allowed the pattern-allistic mentality of it to stick with them, causing them to develop a pattern of leaving a range of situations at the slightest sign of trouble thinking it beneficial for their life. When in fact, it only hurt their mentality in a variety of ways in the end, such as giving up on school because it was seen as an inconvenience. Which means, the now pattern cannot be fixed until that individual so chooses to get rid of the patterns haunting them from the divorce.

The depth of severity concerning affect in life for either individual can differ. But all levels of severity caused by certain types of situations can be *seen in both cases of hurting someone mentally or causing greatness to occur in another. Meaning, there are those who in <u>comparison to another</u> rose above worse situations than another person to achieve greatness. The only difference was in their pattern-allsitic mentality.*

Everyone has the choice to let something affect (trigger) them for no reason other than to let it do so, because it is easier than raising the standard within themselves. So, these types of people tend to show unreasonable emotion, and lash out when they do not get their way. When in fact, the only way to bring about lasting change around or within said person, is to let the light shine from their individual life to show the greatness within, whether disrespect is/was "felt" or not.

Sometimes staying quiet in disrespect, is the most honorable/wise thing you can do for yourself.

There are a number of things that can happen with both of these individuals in this divorce example, but I'm trying to keep it as simple as I can.

<u>Group real-world example:</u>

<u>3 workers walk into a meeting with someone, who for this example, knows how to perfectly do a task with a pure efficiency rating of 0.</u>

After hearing the explanation of how to get the best results and exiting the meeting, each worker is then asked to explain how to perform said task to their best ability, based on what they just heard. Even though they all might explain the task in similar ways to the person who explained perfection. The workers will never use the exact word for word explanation when describing it to someone else.

Why does each worker not say the exact same thing word for word when they were taught/told how to perform the task perfectly?

Simple, each worker has a different pattern-allistic mentality of how they approach the task when performing it. They might get to the same result from a passing or failing point of view. But they all have different filters or pattern-allistic mentalities behind how to accomplish the task. So, they will

never reach pure efficiency/care. Instead, they will get as close as their mentality will allow.

<u>End of example</u>

Pattern-allistic mentality is what makes you……well, you. All of the good, bad, ugly, and everything in-between. It's the reasoning for the mental filter of choice you have in anything and everything. That being known, you can instill <u>any</u> pattern through application that you so choose.

Think supercomputer, except the only person who has the passcode to get in and out on command, is the person who owns the computer (<u>you</u>).

We all have a supercomputer but are limited by the amount of access we <u>believe</u> we have. So, the only way to increase the belief of access to understand the genius we all are, is by comprehending the hidden password built into ourselves within our pattern-allistic mentality.

<u>Here are some simple factors that can play a key role of the filter in our minds as soon as we become cognitively able to understand what is going on around us:</u>

- Parents or Parents of choice
- Book(s)
- Friends
- Marketing (the biggest one in today's world)
- Social media (the biggest one in today's world)
- News (the biggest one in today's world)
- Any type of experience (good or bad)
- Circumstance you were born into
- Obstacle or mountain in life
- Teacher
- Video(s)
- How you live life currently (yourself, stop blaming everyone else)
- Person you look up to
- What you're currently going through

- The future everyone tells you, you will have, without the knowledge of the **potential life factor** they are steering you towards (be careful of whose words you take to heart)
- Family member
- Etc.

<u>A little about pattern-allistic mentality:</u>

Aspects or talents of life are coins (talents) with given worth that anyone can attain, with varying levels of value, as your hone those aspects or talents. So, the only other coin that can even compare to knowledge of pattern-allistic mentality, is pattern processing. Which in today's world, is used by marketing companies, social media, the news, therapists, psychiatrists, and psychologists. But if I'm going to be frank with you, this comparable coin is definitely not as valuable, because comprehension of your pattern-allistic mentality will change the game for the rest of your life. As it has the potential to add value to all of the other coins you may/can attain.

Don't get me wrong, pattern processing is an extremely valuable coin to have, but it pales in the potential value of pattern-allistic mentality.

Pattern-allistic mentality has everything to do with anything of individuals, groups, and nations all at once. Whereas pattern processing, tries to make very few things about everything in our lives. Which might have worked to benefit growth in individuals for before the age of technology, but has now diminished in value, due to the complexity of the life individuals live.

If pattern processing is an individual or computer coding throwing a bunch of darts from one point at a dark wall hoping to hit the target. Pattern-allistic mentality can see the target behind the darkness using the conscious and subconscious in conjunction, to hit the bullseye every time.......and guess who's throwing the darts? You....the one with the passcode for your supercomputer, but first, you have to understand what to hit.

Pattern-allistic mentality connects all the dots at once to in order to understand the greatest outcome. Whereas pattern processing, goes from dot to dot to discover the reasoning why someone thinks the way they do, then alters that thought process for the greater...or not. But as you know, people are flawed in many aspects and whether you realize it or not, the processing anything/anyone wants you to go through, cannot be meant for the most righteous, or greatest version of yourself in the end.

I do have a coin in my deep collection of gifts that is so special I cannot talk about it, because it is so ultra-rare, and the world is simply not ready for it yet. This coin is so rare, I have only met one other person with this gift in my long life of searching and constant research.

For instance, pattern processing:

The media, marketing, politicians, and social media in the hopes of making a connection, will increase the ability to hit the target by narrowing down the number of variables (patterns) that play into the target placement on the dark canvas in an attempt to find where it is. All in the hopes to get you to react how they want, which is started by getting your attention with eye catching things. That being said, another reason for me writing this book is because all of those listed earlier, have reached a higher level of knowing how to have individuals associate with a certain aspect (aka: manipulation).

So, it's time to raise the level of the individual's mentality to avoid destructive end goal patterns.

How do you raise the level of everyone out of perceived stagnation in an ever-changing world, and limit manipulation?

Easy, you give everyone the potential to access the keys, and get the ball rolling in certain areas to create momentum using the baby steps needed for growth.

What happens when you give anyone the ability to raise their level in discovering their pattern-allistic mentality and prepare them for what this world will throw at everyone, to get them off track? Once discovered, you will see manipulation and darkness of the mind decrease. Resulting in the potential for greatness in anyone to increase.

With this book I'm going to show you your individual target for many, if not all aspects of life. I truly believe I'm giving you the pen and paper to your personal life greatness, and the best part is...all you have to do is provide the ink (literally in some cases). Then apply it to your current life, and consistently work on continuing your personal greatness potentially, surpassing what even you thought using action.

This book will help you by starting with the pieces of your future older-self that will say, "If I only knew this earlier.", or "I wish I would've known this prior to (blank)….". I cannot give you everything in life that will happen, but I do my best to pinpoint areas we all eventually struggle <u>when</u> life hits, and have you more prepared. This book will help stir thinking into your own patterns for greater, long-lasting change.

*With the opinions of this world, how the way life can seem to switch on a dime, and so can the unknown factor of events. I say it is never, if something bad will happen, but <u>when</u> something bad <u>**could**</u> happen, within any given aspect of life.*
That being known, there is no reason to live in fear, because as long as you understand how to subconsciously prepare and navigate your <u>pattern-allistic mentality</u>, you can <u>mitigate the bad things that can potentially happen in what you can control</u>.

Now for the numbers example as seen in efficiency:

Here is an example of a small sample size of a pattern-allistic mentality choices, before and after you recognize it in yourself. (You have to understand, I am trying to make this incredibly hard topic as simple as I can.) The decisions or emotions we feel, all play an important factor in the decision-making percentage, and in how we perceive the life factor results right now.

You have to think about what plays big rolls in your life as seen from the variables and evaluate if they are truly beneficial for your current or future life.

Definitions:
- **Life factor** – the way you pattern-allistically think in a situation, and how you believe it will benefit you or not, going into a situation

    o Always is seen as a plus or negative in our minds depending on the pattern-allistic mentality we have in that moment

- **Potential Life Factor** – the true-life factor that determines how you will view life after the decision and follow through

    o Always the true number <u>when</u> life happens

    o When doing some things that are/can be bad for you, the potential life factor always goes even lower when you do not understand your pattern-allistic mentality to some degree. So, based on our comprehension to break a cycle we put ourselves in, the highest number of the <u>potential life factor</u> for the bad will always outweigh the <u>life factor</u> you give that bad choice.

    o **So a pattern-allistic mentality for growth can pull you out of the worst situations faster, once you understand your pattern-allistic mentality for growth. Thus, making the potential life factor be higher after comprehension, had you not known.**

- **Odds of doing it (follow through)** – this is where the variables above play a factor

    o Dependent on your life and what you spend the most time associating with, you might need a re-evaluation of the current standing of association in your current life

- **Unknown factor** – could change the odds of doing something good and above higher, and can potentially lead to a greater Potential Life Factor

- For ex: something extra you did not expect to happen from your pattern-allistic mentality of growth, so this factor of addition is subject to change, depending on your current mentality

Before discovering your pattern-allistic mentality:

1. Decision that seems beneficial now, but is bad for yourself => **Life factor** for right now = **+20** => **Odds of doing it = 55%**

    a. But lead to something bad later causing an increase in problems in any way => **-25 to -75** for <u>when</u> it happens **(potential life factor)**

2. Decision that is <u>good</u> => **Life factor** for right now = **-5** => **Odds of doing it 25%**

    a. <u>Could</u> lead to something <u>good</u> causing => **+15 (potential life factor)**

3. Decision that is <u>best</u> => **Life factor** for right now => **-20** => **Odds of doing it 10%**

    a. <u>Could</u> lead to something <u>great</u> if you apply yourself => **+75 (potential life factor)**

Unknown factor that could change the mental percentage that could affect the **odds of doing something for the better and above = **+5%** => **+10 (potential life factor additions)****

<u>The ultimate life factor of this situation including unknown:</u>

35% of having a **potential life factor** of **+15 to +85**

<u>Even by just reading this book guess what happens to your pattern-allistic mentality with a growth mindset:</u>

1. Decision that seems beneficial now, but is bad for yourself => **Life factor** for right now = **+10** => **Odds of doing it = 40%**

    a. But could lead to something bad later, causing an increase in problems in any way => **-15 to -50** for <u>when</u> it happens **(potential life factor)**

2. Decision that is <u>good</u> => **Life factor** for right now = **+5** => **Odds of doing it 35%**

    a. <u>Could</u> lead to something <u>good</u> causing => **+15 (potential life factor)**

3. Decision that is <u>best</u> => **Life factor** for right now => **-10** => **Odds of doing it 25%**

    a. <u>Could</u> lead to something <u>great</u> if you apply yourself => **+75 (potential life factor)**

Unknown factor that could change the mental percentage that could change the **odds of doing something good and above = **+10%** => **+20 (potential life factor additions)****

<u>The ultimate life factor of this situation including unknown:</u>

70% of having a **potential life factor** of **+35 to +95**

    This is as simple as I can make it, because it is such a strenuous concept. Mainly due to the fact, that even though we as individuals subconsciously know we have an infinite number of choices, our current pattern-allistic mentality will not allow most of us to think on a higher level of understanding. Which results in a limiting of choices within our own mind.

So, in all cases of life decision making, we will have more than one option, but the number of choices stems directly from the current understanding of our personal pattern-allistic mentality; when used in conjunction with our, "sliding door" of wisdom.

Not only that, but the realms or aspects of your life, have varying decisions that use this exact same format. So, as you go through life, and I believe as you make greater choices working towards the greatness in your life; the decision making for the greatest outcome in your subconscious become the norm for all realms or aspects of your life. (Including the tasks of efficiency in the previous section!! ☺)

Dependent on your upbringing, we as individuals are more inclined to have higher odds of making any particular choice due to the inherent pattern-allistic mentality, unless we are so driven to change it. But whether or not the choice we make, or the patterns we are so driven to change, cause a rise in our potential life factor, is strictly dependent on:

The comprehension of the options at hand, while in conjunction of understanding what it means to truly listen, and how well we as the individual know how to use our "sliding door" of wisdom.

The higher the level of understanding for the factors above, as led by non-biased factual examples; the greater the potential life factor for greatness anyone can be destined to have.

Why pattern-allistic mentality?

We all know of, have seen, or heard of honorable/respectable/detailed/determined/truly loving greatness patterns. With this being understood, only you have the choice to practice, develop, and hone them. But the age you understand of how to hone your greatness patterns will determine how much potential greatness you left on the table, because time is of the essence, and you only get one life.

Greatness patterns are not subject to race, gender, or background. So, simply blaming the past events of your previous self-patterns, family, people, or background, means you don't fully realize your freedom in greatness of choice, and don't yet fully understand your mental, then actionable greatness within.

Only <u>you</u> have the choice to break <u>all</u> of the inherent <u>patterns</u> displayed for your life. And by <u>all</u>, I mean <u>all patterns</u> on both sides of the <u>spectrum of bad and great, in both the physical and mental realms</u>.

<u>Like I recently told my mother when she asked if I turned out the way I did due to the way I was raised:</u>

Parents and parents of choice (or lack thereof) do play a huge part in all the patterns displayed in someone's life, which do correlate to how much perceived greatness someone can achieve. Yet, so do influences, friends, and actions of life presented by other people. But it is on the individual to decide what patterns to practice or break, according to the patterns they understand to be beneficial when working towards their honorable, respectable, and integrity-based purpose in life.

You can have nice parent's or parents of choice, but without a growth/competition mentality, your pattern-allistic mentality will be bent away from greatness, because the intentionality for great beneficial patterns will never take root.

Meaning, an individual's pattern-allistic mentality for their purpose, is the direct result of their emotional connections to patterns upon first cognitive recognition as seen through actions, words, tone of voice, and reactions when extremely young, and continues to develop over the course of their *life as more emotional connections are built. But the individual ultimately has to choose for themselves what patterns to follow.*

Here is a short example of pattern-allistic mentality that could've been waaaayyyyy longer, trust me. The understanding of the mind in conjunction with current life, is not easy to explain. Unless you comprehend various patterns in the big and small aspects, with a truly empathetic sliding door of wisdom that can move across the bar of life with ease.

Someone was told they can't do something (bad at), or see people doing what was told is not beneficial (good for).

Step 1 reality in action:

Controlled discipline or lack thereof, with/without respectable/honorable reasoning for why that pattern is or is not beneficial, or even when the pattern was/is seen or practiced by other people.

Step 2 searching subconsciously and intentionally (development of patterns as life lived):

Subjected to opinions about the reasoning why that control in step 1 was displayed, or why they can't do something that was based on what previously happened. So, they develop <u>emotional ties</u> to those opinionated truths, because they "see" themselves. As more emotion or influence relates to the experience, the stronger the tie. Today (as opposed to before the age of technology), individuals expose themselves to everyone else's opinion pattern (good or bad).

<u>Possible emotional connections of opinions that play the biggest factor behind step 3 in the person's pattern:</u>

➢ Resents authority or discipline in that pattern of life.

➢ Understands what was said and grows from it. Thus, not allowing for insecurity emotions to take hold when deemed appropriate timing.

> Resents the idea of there are patterns they should not follow, because they connect the perception of authority over one's life choices.

> Has insecurity (fear) about the thing they were told they are not good at or cannot do. Then relates that emotional feeling to other aspects of life.

> Sets unachievable expectations for themselves or others when interacting, because they want to feel as though they have authority over their destiny and/or someone's life.

Step 3 pattern base for step 1 and bleed over in other aspects of life based on comprehension that lead to step 4 reactions (later in life after initial cognitive recognition). ****Stay the same from the above understanding all-encompassing life example, because they are applicable to all emotional ties in pattern choice application decision making****

A. React in insecurity patterns for certain situations relatable to what they went through by hanging onto the emotion, because they do not deem themselves good enough to hardly attempt that realm and let the most emotionally perceived power influence in their life to decide the action for them (most seen: social media).

B. Standup for themselves or choose to follow the pattern, because the individual is currently set in their pattern(s) that were based on previous emotionally connected influences and are backed to some degree by perceived emotionally beneficial results of the pattern(s). These subconscious emotional patterns will not be broken until a blatant factual truth disproves this current mental or physical pattern. Dependent on the strength of the emotionally developed bond determines the tipping point of the fight, respectfully fight, or flight reaction. (Reaction depth is dependent on how well someone understands the pattern mindset to truly love themselves and others in the most honorable way.)

C. Seek to find the benefit in performing a pattern unless provided a beneficial result from someone they emotionally trust (influenced by).

Then the understanding of action will be determinant for how to partake in the pattern if found beneficial.

Step 4 <u>impulse mental pattern reactions through action are based on mental ties of subconscious emotion dependent on perceived understanding:</u>

    A. <u>A lack of understanding the benefits of statement in step 1 (without respectable/honorable reasoning)</u>

        a. Allows <u>great</u> possibility for others to control patterns of emotions and actions

        b. Allows <u>great</u> possibility for others to control opinion patterns

        c. Lacks the deeper reasoning behind the aspect of the pattern, <u>so will not practice with accountability. Nor, will practice many other aspects with accountability based on step 1</u>

    B. <u>A decent understanding of benefit from top-level pattern recognition in step 1 statement (with & without respectable/honorable reasoning)</u>

        a. Allows possibility for others to control patterns of emotions and actions not as strongly emotionally tied to

        b. Allows for others to control certain opinion patterns, not as strongly emotionally tied to

        c. Understands the deeper reasoning behind the aspect of the pattern, so will practice with some accountability. But will choose to not translate the pattern to other aspects in life they are not strongly emotionally tied to, or will not be as successful as they could be

    C. <u>Potential great understanding of top-level pattern in step 1 statement (with respectable/honorable reasoning)</u>

a. Allows themselves to understand the benefit of patterns they associate emotionally with (so can still become greater in all aspects) if chosen to adhere to it using the previous step 1-3 pattern

b. Attempts to stick to pattern aspects they know to be beneficial for them in the end, if chosen to adhere to it using the previous step 1-3 pattern
   i. Willing to break pattern to insert a greater pattern

c. Understands the deeper reasoning for a pattern and practices in great efficiency. If the individual chooses to adhere to another pattern, they will use the previous step 1-3 pattern when applying it to their life
   i. Willing to break pattern to insert a greater pattern

<u>Real world example</u>

<u>Step 1</u> reality in action:

All decisions of life were/are made by (blank)

<u>Decisions</u> - different from rules that represent honor, integrity, and respect

<u>Blank</u> examples: parents, government control, boss

<u>Step 2</u> searching subconsciously and intentionally (development of patterns as life lived):

Subjected to opinions about the reasoning why that control was displayed or why they can't do something that was based on what previously happened. So, they will develop <u>emotional ties</u> to those opinionated truths, because they "see" themselves. As more emotion or influence relates to the experience, the stronger the emotional tie. Today (as opposed to before the age of technology), they expose themselves to everyone else's opinion pattern.

Possible emotional connections of opinions that play the biggest factor behind step 3 in the person's pattern. ***Stay the same from the above understanding all-***

encompassing life example, because they are applicable to all emotional ties in pattern choice application decision making**

<u>Step 3</u> pattern base for step 1 and bleed over in other aspects of life based on comprehension that lead to step 4 reactions (later in life after initial cognitive recognition). ****Stay the same from the above understanding all-encompassing life example, because they are applicable to all emotional ties in pattern choice application decision making****

<u>Step 4</u> impulse mental pattern reactions through action are based on mental ties of subconscious emotion dependent on perceived understanding:

- **A.** <u>Potential great understanding of top-level pattern in step 1 statement (without respectable/honorable reasoning):</u>

    a. As time progresses kids, people of nation, or employees will not be able to think for themselves or discover the balance of developing greatness patterns

    b. Leads to patterns of excuses and complaining <u>when</u> life happens, or <u>when</u> problems occur and looking to others to fix <u>when</u> those things happen

    c. Creates patterns of weak mentality that can easily be controlled

- **B.** <u>Decent understanding of benefit from top-level pattern recognition in step 1 statement (with & without respectable/honorable reasoning):</u>

    a. They will notice blatant hypocrisy unless they themselves live in hypocrisy and become emotionally subjected to others as they build on those emotional ties

    b. Opinions are easily manipulated depending on the development of those emotional ties

c. Certain patterns will be practiced in high degree through actions that have the most emotional ties built in

C. <u>Potential great understanding of top-level pattern in step 1 statement (with respectable/honorable reasoning)</u>:

a. Individual(s) will understand the benefit of the pattern emotionally associated with and seek to become greater within the pattern

b. Individual(s) will then apply it to other patterns that are within a value reasoning of their other valued patterns

c. Will mentally attempt to stick to certain pattern aspects they know to be beneficial for them in the end, if they chose to adhere to it using the previous step 1-4 pattern
   i. Willing to break a current pattern to insert a greater pattern

---

The A, B, C in step 4 are percentages of decision-making actions, because decision making in the pattern impulse, is also subject to other valued patterns in life. Hence the name, pattern-allistic mentality, because it encompasses all life aspects that can be translated back to a few emotionally tied instances that were recognized cognitively, then developed to a point of action through reaction.

*In life, by not being accountable to growth in great life patterns, perceived stagnation lies dormant in <u>lack of understanding</u> and waits for <u>when</u> life happens to explode into frustration, then quickly the mentally worse beyond. So, those types of individuals will <u>choose</u> to stay in the rubble around them and <u>choose</u> to stay in the mentally worse beyond, slowly cleaning up and in the end, gain **little** wisdom because they choose to not care about the details of the flume.*

*Those who <u>understand to some degree</u> great life patterns, but do not inhibit greatness accountability to all life aspects, prolong the explosion by elongating the fuse when the flame gets close to the powder. But eventually <u>when</u> life happens, there will be a certain event making the flame impossible to control, resulting in an explosion of perceived stagnation, frustration, and the mentally worse beyond. They will slowly bring in tools to clean up the mess and **might** gain wisdom.*

*Those with <u>great understanding</u> in a life aspect, will know how and when to put the flame out on the fuse. If the flame is too hot, they will seek to take as much explosive powder out as they can and bring in the tools to clean up as best as possible. Then, they will learn how to better handle the flame through creating greater patterns because they **did** gain wisdom in the details. These people still go through perceived stagnation and frustration, but rarely reach the final stage of the mentally worse beyond as often as others.*

In any scenario, the bomb of life explodes <u>when</u> the fire on the fuse becomes uncontrollable (and it will at times think story of, Job). When it does, all types of people perceive stagnation and frustration, but only one chooses not to linger too long in the mentally worse beyond if at all. So, it's up to you and your pattern-allistic mentality alone, to decide if you want to linger in the mentally worse beyond.

Do you want to add a growth mindset? Or will you wait until so many bombs go off, you're stuck in failure, and are forced to understand the hard way?

<u>Wow…that even makes my head feel kind of weird still, but the real-life part of that section above is:</u>

<u>Pattern-allistic mentality is the master key or passcode, to access your life coding behind the programs of your supercomputer!!</u>

Adhering to comprehending your pattern-allistic mentality, potentially gives you the ability to block the backdoor virus coding manipulators use.
I want you to have the ability to think for yourself, but that doesn't mean you shouldn't adhere to others either. So I'm going to help you along the way. This book is not done yet!!!

Please go back over the examples of the before and after, in the prior sections one more time. Then point out various differences below. You'll start to recognize some very interesting things.

Patterns are……EVERYWHERE (DUN DUUUNNN DUUUUUUNNNNN)

But for real though….

Patterns are probably one of the most un-seen/underrated things about people, nature, the world, the universe, etc.

Some may call patterns predictability of individuals or life. Which leads others proclaim, the only way to achieve greatness is to follow the exact mindsets of people who have made it.

But like I stated, just as no two people are alike, no two mental patterns can or will be exactly the same for greatness. And if all we as a species did was look to people that are successful today for how we should think (creating clones), then how would we ever collectively grow to greater heights?

Many people will say things in direct, but also very general and vague terms, to allow individuals to decide how to react. Which means, those who connect with a certain speaker, will tend to follow them in many aspects of life. But the problem is, many people who speak over life have severe mental patterns that are flawed in significant ways when it comes to portraying the mental avenues towards greatness on a real-world personal level (that tends to come with being human, we are all flawed in some way).

As for most speakers within a particular realm, there tends to be a lot of cursing and/or telling you how you should act, to try to invoke justification in your mind of their words. Then at the very end when an individual made some kind of vague connection (if they didn't already do so) the speaker will ask for money to be given to them in some way when they really <u>didn't present any kind of pathway that would last</u> **(This is key for chapter 7)**.

<u>It's not their fault, and I am not judging people for trying…but:</u>

<u>One</u>: *I understand emotions can get the best of you sometimes. But <u>consistent cursing</u> is an insult to intelligence and displays a major flaw in your ability to lead others through life.*

There is nothing more hypocritical in showing how to live a greater life, than listening to someone curse every other word, or every other sentence

for that matter. Because the entire group listening will relate that pattern to success, and in the end, allow that pattern of vulgarity (pride) to spread into the rest of their life aspects. (It shows why you should not be followed.)

Two: It is understandable not to be able to walk everything through with everyone, as the speaker is just one person, and walking through mentality can be time consuming

****Let alone pattern-allistic mentality which is a level even deeper. So I made a book so you did not spend thousands, tens of thousands, or even hundreds of thousands of dollars trying to dissect hypocrisy.****

<u>**Living or leading in constant hypocrisy of what honor/respect is, is just as bad as not saying anything at all.**</u>

<u>Business types of speakers/leaders (most speakers or motivators) are essentially practicing the same thing the military does (which from a mental change standpoint is smart…but…)</u>

When boot camp starts for the military, it is meant to completely break down your old pattern mentality and build it into one that is completely different. Which is great for a military setting, <u>when</u> life and death hang in the balance (I fully back the military, anyone who is willing to die for another deserves the utmost respect). But then when those men and women get back from war, most experience a range of difficulty levels for adjustment to what can be considered, "normal life", because of a lack of comprehension of why others do not have the same pattern-allistic mentality as them.

Where the military does get things right about life mentality, is the notion of if you take care of the small things in excellence, via understanding the objective. The big things will not seem like a mountain, but more like a prolonged and tedious workable hill, taken one step at a time.

<u>Motivational impartation boot camp:</u>

When you inject life with what is considered a great mindset to have through the business of life; adaptation and fluidity basically go out the window.

Because business is very stubborn, so people only get good at a select finite group of things. When in reality, life is more complicated, and bleeds into business life as a whole.

Thus, meaning all life aspects translate into business, but not all business aspects translate into life for lasting personal growth. So those who know how to use their "sliding door" of wisdom are the ones who understand the variety of disconnects between the comparisons of life to business, and business to life.

Those who hear words of business into life, that led back to life for business from the speaker, struggle in many other areas mentally with no initial pattern base to grow from, because they "changed" themselves so much, and only see greatness in a certain pattern of thinking that someone else instilled in them.

Furthermore, that person seeking more was just given a pattern-allistic mentality of someone else, which is partly conducive at best, and only if the subconscious pattern-allistic mentality hypocrisy is sorted out (which it never really is). And on top of it all, the person listening does not know how to add to their pattern-allistic mentality, because they were told to ignore it for someone else's.

The patterns of mentality are totally different and are not fluid, so the change wanted does not last. Meaning, when the listener tries to go back to the same well (motivational/speaker's words) they will only find out the speaker does not know either, because they have no personal pattern proof, and/or live, in hypocrisy.

So in the end, the person who listened so intently, unknowingly created a confusion of pattern-allistic mentality within themselves. Resulting in not knowing how to adapt their life or adding greatness to any aspect coin unless told. Which then creates a pattern of searching to find someone else who seems to relate more to their pattern-allistic mentality in some way and will never find a way to build themselves. Which means, they will eventually repeat the entire find, search, and find, process all over again when they discover another problem that the current life speaker does not seem to solve.

<u>By that translation:</u>

- You have people who interjected business thinking into life mentality, and only know how to grow things from that standpoint, <u>when</u> in reality they struggle in many other areas in life.

    o   Most people take what they say at face value with little understanding of application of how this pattern can benefit their life in many if not all ways.

    o   Then the speaker asks for money (or more money) as the only way for someone to have full access to the people around them. So, there is no real way to know how "successful" they are, due to the fact those people could be in hypocrisy, because they chose to associate with blatant hypocrisy. So what is the point of paying them more money?

- Said speaker makes a brand based off of growing your life when you grow from business, and money. The biggest attractor being money, which "leads to a better life.", (which is true to a certain degree) <u>without being greater in an array of other aspects of life (wait until chapter 7)</u>

- People don't <u>truly listen</u> to <u>noticeable hypocrisy</u>, and do not realize it is affecting their subconscious pattern-allistic mentality (unless it is corrected <u>by a bigger greatness</u>)

    o   Which leads them to wonder why said person cannot solve the rest of their problems

    o   So most people go on not to achieve greater things in life, and wonder who could possibly have all of the answers so they search for more speakers/motivators

- This searching for other people causes a stagnation of the mind, because of the pattern-allistic mentality they unknowingly self-implanted

---

Smaller impartation sessions

In the beginning of someone's growth path, these smaller sessions do help more, because of the greater emotional personal connection.

Then you have those speakers who do things in smaller groups trying come from a life perspective. Which only ends up in directly telling you exactly how to act in order to get specified results. But they don't comprehend that everyone's pathway is not the exact same. So, they try to mitigate the variables by offering some kind of personality test without knowing the deeper parts of an individual.

But, do you remember what I said about the pattern-allistic mentality of everyone being different due to varying situations? So, this imparted mentality of life will not work either, unless the speaker has the ability and availability to access the special coin I told you about (Which is highly unlikely, because I've only met one other person who has this same gift in multiple decades of researching).

I'm not saying these imparters/people have not done great things. I'm merely saying there is an inherent, giant, and glaring flaw in how they portray most things in today's world.

<u>One thing to comprehend when following the impartation of others</u>:
All life growth applications can be translated into the business patterns, but not all growth business patterns SHOULD be translated into real life applications, as pertaining to the absolute growth of the individual in the end.
<u>***Whether we believe it or not, individual life, and life of everyone as a whole is made up of nothing but patterns, upon patterns, upon even more patterns***</u>***.***

This book has the potential to raise one person, group of people, or mindset of an entire country all at once. Through using the simple method of raising the pattern-allistic mentality way of life in every individual person towards higher levels, to potentially overcome anything, using something so simple.

So, what happens when you grow an individual's mindset who can overcome, while adapting to anything/everything, while finding wisdom at the same time through connecting the dots of strengths, that can come from any situation, and all while learning about themselves even more without being told what to think?

<u>Through pattern-allistic mentality for growth, the individual has the ability to attain what I call, the "sliding door" of wisdom, through true empathy.</u>
Resulting in the creation of an unfathomable person, deriving from their own pattern-allistic mentality that works out many life aspects at a consistent greatness level path higher than any motivational speaker can instill.

You also get someone who can raise the level of greatness in every room they step into; no matter the topic, because their true empathy level is so high from their "sliding door" of wisdom. So, solving problems comes easier to them than anyone else, and provides LASTING BENEFICIAL CHANGE that will prove itself in time. Without the need of detrimental emotions or mentalities stepping in.

Wisdom can be found in the details of the facts using any background. But the findings need to be paired with the ability to know how or why people think, based on patterns that this world provides with <u>true</u> empathy, and then injected with wisdom that is derived from a constant growth mentality (chapter 7).

<u>Don't worry, I know what you might be thinking, "That makes sense, but its' hard to wrap my head around it all." I know it might seem scary now, but as you continue to read and meditate on your own pattern-allistic mentality, it only gets easier and easier to understand.</u>

Please take about 10-15 minutes to wrap your head around this concept. Close your eyes, process, and mentally download it if you have to. I highly suggest starting this chapter over after you mentally process what you've read to this point. This concept is of a doctorates level condensed and communicated in a way to make sense in your mind. (I should know, I had a psychologist ask me how I understood this concept to the extent I did, when I don't have a doctorate, after I had them look at a curriculum I helped develop.)

<u>Now for your part: What's your, "Why?"</u>

Everyone has a "<u>why</u>" for everything they've done, will do, said, didn't say, thought about, etc. Without this "<u>why</u>" we as humans are merely wandering from place-to-place, living in either perceived stagnation or are walking around in a ticking mental time bomb of <u>when</u> that perception occurs. So, no matter how significant or insignificant, a "<u>why</u>" in today's world is very much a must have in order to take the first step in true empathy discovered within yourself, needed to become something greater.

<u>Baby steps</u> are key, and no matter how insignificant it may seem, write your "<u>why</u>" below for picking up this book. **After writing it down, say your "<u>why</u>" out loud, because saying anything out loud holds a place in your mentality longer than just having an idea (thought). Which is exactly why you need to be careful in what you speak over yourself in any aspect.**:

The Sliding Door of Wisdom
Visualization first

I want you to visualize a door that is not attached to hinges, and instead is attached to a bar above the door allowing it to slide. At the top of this door, is your full name, and on it are webs of bracket type patterns that stem from one singular point at the bottom (your birth) and work their way up.

The golden web stemming from one point are actually tiny inscriptions of all the decisions, situations, problems you did/didn't solve, bad times, good times, things seen, things heard, and everything in-between. Then you take a closer look at this door, you notice that it, and the golden webbing are slowly growing in height and width by the second.

It is growing, because the previous sections are used to spark debate of mental patterns within yourself, which causes a subconscious download to happen. That being said, anything you take in mentally over time, or grow from, can cause a growth of this door.

After downloading the vision of the door. I now want you to mentally group all the events on this door into bucket categories of your choice (example: hurt, joy, embarrassment, hard work, love, been let down, confidence, anger, and humbleness). From there, put the label, "Wisdom", below all of those categories.

Why did I want you to do this?
Well, there is wisdom/intellect in literally everything you've been through, that can apply to any variety of life aspects as long as you comprehend how the sliding door of wisdom works.

There is wisdom in everything for building your "sliding door" of wisdom, but first, some stories:

After using one of my gifts to serve others. I remember asking a young person who was given $100 what they planned on doing with the money.

This person said with a joyful smile on their face, "Well, I was thinking about it. My friend and I have a business. So, I'm going to print a bunch of flyers, and if I can get even 10 jobs, I'll make about $3000!!"

And after the group finished complimenting this person, I quickly contemplated this person's pattern-allistic mentality, then stated, "That is good you made this connection. But I'm assuming you already have more than enough money saved up from the previous jobs. So, if you knew the benefits, why did you wait until money was given to you in order to make potential greatness happen?"

In an instant, this person's face and mood went from joy to a sudden feeling of humbleness. So, with a smile on my face I said, "Don't feel bad about just now realizing it. That was the reasoning for this. It's to expand your pattern-allistic mentality towards a greater way of thinking. So, from now, it is on you to not be afraid of the greater potential pattern-allistic mentality you could achieve."

<u>Another example from my childhood:</u>

My aunt was in the military for years and understands the noticeable differences in military personnel and civilians. The military and civilians are two different breeds of people, because they have opposing pattern-allisitic mentalities.

One of those differences is of getting things done and following through with their word with little to no excuse. While the other, mainly runs based off emotion with a subconscious "why" when a task is/was not completed.

Anyways, she knew I loved playing sports and being active, so she would allow me to get on base with her to go to the gym. But most times that meant she had one condition.

I had to wake up when she did and leave with her.
(This is when everyone who's ever been in the military starts laughing, because of how early they know I had to wake up. LOL)

Even as a young kid, I was used to waking up early, but no one would want to wake up early after a night of hanging out with their cousins. Yet, low and behold my aunt woke me up as she said she would, and (as many would expect) I questioned my love for being active, because of what I just did to myself.

After bouncing a few excuses around in my head, I managed to roll over out of bed to get ready, because I wanted to follow through with what I asked for her to do. Then as I began to brush my teeth, I started to question if anyone would actually be at the gym this early, so I thought about telling her I was going back to bed. But I let the thought go as she came back to make sure I was ready, nor did I bother to ask it on the way, mainly because I was asleep (LOL).

When she dropped me off, she playfully let the person in charge of the complex know, that if anything happened to me, it was on them. To which they smiled and replied with a resounding, "Yes ma'am". (My aunt is pretty awesome. Not only is my aunt well respected for her ranking but is a respectfully firm leader that respects herself on the job.)

Short story shorter. I had a lot of fun and couldn't believe how many people were up that early?! (But I guess that's the military pattern for you!!)

<u>There is wisdom in the simple things if you truly know how to listen:</u>

So why do we give up on something? Is it due a situation we went through that caused doubt? Then instead of realizing it in our-self we find ways to blame others, or a specific reason because of our personal laziness.

I could've blamed what happened in the past (the night before, and/or is applicable to even further past happenings) for why I could've acted the way I wanted to, and ultimately blame someone else as a reason to not live up to greatness standards that garner respect in someone else, through respecting yourself.

<u>Wisdom of life using the sliding door:</u>

It's normal to think about what can happen when taking a leap of faith until you have little to no reason to worry, and/or know what happens as you get into a situation. But even if you know what can happen within a calculated decision, there is little to no reason to worry, when you know, all you have to do is execute in the situation through effort and have the understanding you've done your best in order to yield the highest results. From there, growth <u>can</u> happen in any situation or circumstance, but you need to be willing to recognize it.

<u>So, there is where the real test lies in everyone's pattern-allistic mentality:</u>

What <u>could</u> happen if (blank) doesn't work, or live up to my expectations?

Well, I assume for mostly everyone, a sense of failure and anger would set in that all of the time and effort, was wasted on expectations.

<u>Yet, here is how you need to see it:</u>

In certain respectable life scenarios (that do not involve someone whom you deeply care about) it is important to do your best to prepare for scenarios that are (within reason) unlikely. You need to use your "sliding door" of wisdom to better understand life through a variety of aspects. **You should not let yourself get too high on life without understanding the lows that lie along the same route. Yet, know that at the end of the day, the goal of greatness lies in your pattern-allistic mentality of growth, by persevering through things you did or did not anticipate.**

<u>I can translate the wisdom in the first example scenario then add it to my own "sliding door" of wisdom:</u>

- Do not let your highs get too high, and your lows too low

- Patience is key when working towards something higher than yourself

    o Flyers take time for calls

    o This can be associated with other life aspects that require patience such as, relationships

- Learn to plan while paving multiple roads at once

- Do not let your own fear get in the way of life when you know all it takes is <u>one time</u> to work to see immediate results

- The mindset of a young person can be one of greatness while needing encouragement in another way to elevate their overall mentality

    o Parents need to encourage their kid to be independent, while realizing they can provide loving encouragement in all things for

- their kid(s). Not just when they feel like it. This is one aspect of a good parent, because they are allowing independence with real world experience.
  - <u>For example</u>: Simply having a young person in a room, or on vacation over the summer sets them up for failure in the real world, because it creates a pattern of laziness

- When doing anything, make sure you find a way to keep pushing for greater

  - When working with friends, there needs to be a precedence of the task of life at hand. So, choose wisely whom your friends are.

- Overall greatness is a road someone cannot pave alone. We all need someone to help in some way

- The idea and action of giving up, is nothing more than how you see a situation or circumstance. Just as the young person from the example was not seeing the possible failure when given money, it's best to try and then gain wisdom for the next time of, "how to…better", than live in fear

I could go on and on and on. But the worst part about life that you'll come to learn, is some people believe the only way to gain wisdom/intellect in an area of real life, is through major personal failure.

Anyone who thinks that way, is not as wise as they believe they are, because wisdom can be found in anything and everything. Wisdom after failure is just the obvious half of the coin.

We have ears, and can understand language for a reason, right?
Those with an understanding of their pattern-allistic mentality can find wisdom all over the place if they choose to use it for growth in greatness. All you have to do is learn to <u>truly listen</u>. Knowing how to <u>truly listen</u> will

use the wisdom of real-life scenarios, to understand where everyone comes from. Thus, separating the bias from the factual truth, in order apply it to your own pattern-allistic mentality for greatness, to be used in anything using your "sliding door" of wisdom.

What I displayed at the end with the list of bullet points was a small example of the sliding door of wisdom using pattern-allistic mentality from the first example. Through a simple conversation, I was able to ascertain simple wisdom truths that I could carry with me, and one day possibly use or put into practice.

This "sliding door" uses your ability to truly listen through true empathy. So, as you learn and raise your ability to truly listen through true empathy to an even higher degree, the "sliding door" of wisdom that was once stuck in one place, will all of a sudden slowly gain the ability to slide on the bar of life with ease.

The result will be the door can possibly open up completely higher levels of greatness, by being able to unlock multiple realms of life using the gained pattern-allistic mentality in various realms. Thus, allowing you to add even more wisdom/intellect at a higher level to your door, as growth continues to occur.

Doesn't that sound pretty awesome?!?! Inside of you is the potential to become "fluent" and master multiple realms of life!!

So, your potential end result is that you can add more valuable coins to your account, but you must understand the baby steps, then comprehend the key to attaining the coin.

Once you've wrote down and said your "why" out loud, it's time!!!

As you go through the rest of this book, keep in mind this "sliding door" and pattern-allistic mentality.

<u>LET'S GET STARTED DOWN THE ROAD INTO YOUR OWN PATTERN-ALLISTIC MENTALITY, AND YOUR UNTAPPED POTENTIAL GREATNESS WITHIN!!!</u>

CHAPTER 2: Simple keys everyone can work on for greater pattern-allistic mentality

DETAILS

Remember what I told you in the epilogue?
The details are more important than you can imagine.

If you don't recall, then you either think there is no reason to read every page, or details aren't your thing. In this case, it's not a problem, but on the path most-true winner's face, it will be. You look at any great winner or any successfully person in any field or walk of life, and they will tell you to some degree, details are absolutely key. That being known, this is the last time I pinpoint something like this.

*If you show a hungry man how to fish, he has the **possibility** of eating for a lifetime.*

One person who taught me to pay attention to the details was my middle school 7th grade math teacher. I cannot remember exactly what we were going over (ironic), but it was a specialized math formula to solve a specific type of equation.

But me being the "great" student I was, I wanted to see if I could come up with something better. So, I began vigorously going through calculations to discover my own way of doing things. When I finally found what I believed to be a faster way (20 minutes later after ignoring the teacher), I raised my hand to answer a question on the board and was immediately called upon.

After getting up to the board, in one confident breath, I explained the answer, and wrote out the steps using the process I had discovered on my own. To which she looked at me with a face of bewilderment as I answered correctly. Yet, reminiscing back on it now, her response was something that only a master in their field would say.

"Wow!!! That's really impressive...but how many examples did you use to prove this new way of doing this type of math?"

In less than 5 seconds, she left me in utter contempt. I wanted to feel a sense of accomplishment, but I just couldn't. So, me being the great student I wasn't, I spent the rest of class trying to figure out if I could permanently use the process I discovered.

So instead of later in tutoring using the aid of someone (my teacher) I knew could help me in my process, I ignored the lecture, and solely focused on proving my new way of doing things.

To my demise, at start of the very next class, there was a pop quiz over what she taught using the steps she went over, and I ended up not performing to the best of my ability.

I ignored what she was trying to teach me, because I thought I could come up with my own way, and in the end underperformed when I should've been paying attention to the details of the task at hand that was her class.

I did not pay attention to the details of the current process being taught, that could have benefitted me overall, because I wanted to prove all my ways in my new pattern, correct.

Don't get me wrong, having the initiative to do something on your own is a great trait to have. But when the task you are performing is something you do not have complete control over (like being in a classroom), it causes you to lose track of the important details you could have used to perform at a level beyond what you were capable of at that point.

Had I decided to wait to put my new way of solving the problem to the test, I could have used the steps my teacher was currently using, applied them to my own, and really cemented my theory down.

<u>Here is the lesson I want you to learn:</u>

If you get caught up in your own details or way of doing things, you could end up ignoring someone with more experience (train of thought) and will more than likely underperform in any variety of tasks at hand.

I bet you didn't see that coming did you. How could someone in the 7th grade, who was coming up with new formulas underperform? You see the on quiz the next day, we were asked to use the formula the teacher had provided and was trying to teach us about.

Sometimes you don't have total control over a situation. So, that makes the details of someone who has more <u>PROVEN</u> experience than you in any situation, absolutely key.

You might be a little disappointed, and probably wanted me to say something to the degree of: "this is what is wrong with schools today…"

Though schools can adjust simple things that would help with building growth in young people in situations like this, I could have studied this new way after class. Instead of ignoring the time someone else dedicated to helping me be greater.

It takes two to tango in relationships like this, and though schools need to understand that they are now seen as more of a "prohibit-or" of determination through imagination. It is important for parents and parents of choice, to instill a right place, right time, and then seize the moment impartation on kids too, in order to maintain the determined imagination in the realm of academics.

<u>Another wisdom filled example:</u>

After getting off work extremely late in the evening, my father used to seemingly have on repeat the statement, "A true athlete performs both on and off the field, court, or track. You can do anything you put your mind to…".

As a kid I always knew what the first part of that statement meant, but the second sentence used to always throw me a bit. It seems like such a normal statement that everyone says now-a-days. But the problem today, is no one applies it, or they make excuses as to why they can't, "put their mind to it". So thankfully, I learned very quickly as a kid, exactly what he meant.

This next example is a sport's backgrounded story, but whether people want to believe it or not. A sports mentality (even playing casually) towards life are a fundamental gauge in how well someone can handle a variety of situations in life, because at its' core…life is competitive.

<u>A sports mentality towards life has taught me and can teach anyone so much.</u>

My dad always used to tell me, "No matter how big someone (life) is. If you can move quicker and lower, you will always win (understand what it takes to become greater)."

So, before I started playing football, he would tell me stories of how even though he was under-sized, he discovered techniques and ways to beat the best players in the state and nation.

I always loved hearing him tell those stories, because I was never the biggest, the fastest, or the strongest. But I succeeded many times over using those very same techniques he talked about.

That being said, this story isn't about football. Well…kind of. It's mainly about basketball. The one sport you need to be taller and more athletic, in order to really succeed…unless…

…I'll never forget the summer my basketball coach brought in a couple of ringers from out of state to help the team in statewide tournaments. And as always, at the end of practice, he would have us play, "King of the court". It was a game where one person would start with the ball at the top of the 3-point line with a defender in front of him and would have 3 dribbles to score.

The coach for some reason liked me (I guess), so he always matched me up with the best defender to start the games. Except this time, it just so happened to be someone that was 6 inches taller and was already dunking. So, me being as big as I wasn't, I knew that I just couldn't use my current ability to beat this defender who had more God given physical abilities than myself. And as expected, I lost every time we squared off that summer.

What I felt that entire summer was new to me. I wasn't used to being so easily dominated, as every move I went through didn't work, and he beat me at every step. So naturally, (as anyone would) I became more and more frustrated with every failed attempt. And slowly over time, I felt like in my mind I failed myself. It translated to games, and then slowly leaked into life outside of sports as time went on. But thankfully, basketball ended, and a month later it was football season.

But if you think that's where the story ends, you have another thing coming. (Hang with me, everything in this book has a purpose).

As you know, in my father's stories, he would tell me the techniques he used. So over time while playing football, I taught my body to instinctively use various tactics to get past someone or use my opponent's own body against them.

Along the way (before gaining such an instinct), in practice and throughout games, I began to mentally study myself. I learned how to play the chess match in my head of how to beat me. Overtime, I learned how I became the player I was (what life events made me, me), the type of players I struggled against (life obstacles), and what their attributes were, so I knew how to adapt (how to become greater). I found my flaws in football against any opponent. Then as the game or practice went on, I would recognize their rhythm, and adapted my patterns where necessary.

What happens if I do this? How does my opponent react? What rhythm of patterns can I use to manipulate the game in a way where I set myself up for winning no matter the situation of patterns I'm thrown into? I stayed in this mindset in football for so long, I didn't realize I subconsciously began to test many things, and apply this, "serial testing", in all walks of life.

I already had a knack for subconsciously running through patterns in my head through trying to read people since I was in grade school, due to constantly being around liars, thieves, and a variety of morally bad people, but now I began doing it with intention.

This is in no way something healthy when/if its' not controlled. So ultimately, I became a quiet kid and let my mind constantly run at 1000 mph. I'm trying to help you on your journey. When running at 1000 mph music helps A LOT, because it takes the whole brain to process. (source: http://www.ucf.edu/pegasus/your-brain-on-music)

As the football season came to a close. I became known as the most coachable, and one of the most dominant players in the league. Not even kids several grades higher could understand how I did it. Even parents and coaches would try to figure me out, but patterns and reading situations faster and faster became my world.

Not even my own father could fully understand how I did things, so he always chalked it up to my pure determination, but that was only partially true.

When football season ended, I set my sights on basketball…

…In the few months I intentionally spent putting this new way of thinking into practice, I hadn't even come close to completely translating it into other areas of life yet (sliding door). The only aspects I could translate were across three sports; in the fact that the defender in football, the offensive player in soccer (My father pointed this relation out to me), and the ball handler in basketball all have the same goal.

<u>*Get past the person in front of you. (Rise above the life obstacle.)*</u>

So, in the days leading up to the first summer basketball practice, I began "scrolling" through what little mental data I had collected, but still couldn't figure out what I could use against this new opponent the coach would inevitably bring in. My dad wasn't a basketball player, so he didn't have many things that could help.

Inevitably, the day of the first practice came, and as usual I asked my father to take me early. Upon walking into the gym, I noticed grown men playing a pick-up game. There was one player in particular I took notice of who was small, not the most athletic, but did play D1 college ball.

I had seen him before, but I never really analyzed what patterns he went through. So, with my newfound ability, I began to watch what he would do when being guarded by certain people. I clipped every piece of mental information I could. From his individual hand movements to his feet, to his eyes, and head.

Then when he did get guarded by someone that could scale to the player I would go against, I would watch with even more intent. After several attempts to truly open my eyes, something finally it clicked. <u>It was his feet!!!</u> The smallest detail that no one below a certain skill level would ever notice.

Usually, the statement went, "As the mind goes the body will follow.". But for this case, as the feet go, the body will follow. The foot positioning chess game creates all of the patterns anyone could ever need in order to read a defender. Once the proper foot placement is achieved, a defender only has two options.

One, completely open up their hips to try and stop the offensive player, thus putting him off balance, or two, foul. Most defenders do not want to give up a cheap foul. So, they will open their hips, leaving themselves in precarious situations with little to no leverage. Which is just like when a defender is trying to get past a blocker in football. Once someone is forced to adhere to the patterns of the aggressor, the chances of stopping them becomes almost impossible.

Needless to say, after some testing of patterns over the course of a few practices. I knew exactly how to beat the player the coach brought in a good portion of the times we went head-to-head, and the coach knew exactly what I was doing. After every basket scored all he could do was smile and say, "See! It's that easy!!".

From that point on, I became a basketball player that knew how to use his head. In fact, in all of the college basketball camps I went to when I was older, every coach wrote down on the camp sheet that my IQ was high, and I was extremely crafty.

(During this, I was about 10-12 years old)

The richest man to ever live (roughly about $2 trillion) asked for wisdom. With the PROPER use of wisdom comes power, riches, and influence beyond belief. (Name: King Solomon). Wisdom is found in the details behind the facts of patterns in conjunction with a sliding door of wisdom.

<u>Details</u>:

I became a "serial mental tester" in sports, and in the end, came to comprehend details of patterns for anything or anyone, in life. I didn't know it at the time, but I unknowingly developed my sliding door of wisdom, and didn't realize until just right before writing this book the potential value of coin I had unlocked.

Why did I use two seemingly simple stories from my childhood that didn't present some huge back story of failure and redemption?

Wisdom can be found anywhere and everywhere. But requires you to know how to truly listen (both know when to be quiet and know when mentally process life). If you always need a horrible thing to happen before gaining wisdom, then you don't understand yet what it means to be wise.

<u>*Pay attention to the details, so you can either reassure yourself in what you do, or realize what you or someone else is doing, is only hurting in the end.*</u>

<u>Pattern-allistic mentality learned</u>:

It is good to try and find your own way of doing things. But eventually you're going to be put into a situation that you won't know how to break through. So, pay attention to the details presented from your teachers, from those around you who have the experience, and the past. I could've used the detailed help from my teacher for my own theory while also performing like I should have in the class, and still created an entirely new way of solving a problem for everyone else to potentially use.

This ability of knowing how to truly listen, shows how coachable you are to yourself, and the people around you.

<u>Wisdom is the gathering of details found within the facts.</u>
So, your level of wisdom depends on the number of details you are able to gather within the facts from any situation and ultimately use, when applying them in either a healthy or toxic way, on your sliding door.

BABY STEPS ARE KEY

What are ways you can be more detailed? (ex: thinking, listening to others, reading, etc)

What areas in your own life do you believe require more attention to detail?

What has occurred in your life where you've done your own thing only to fail? Did you learn from it? How do you know, did you go through a similar situation, and do something different for a greater end result?

Write down 2 examples of wisdom gained for each category: simple (learned from a young age), situational (wisdom when in a circumstance or situation of school, sports, or parents), life (wisdom learned when life hit you)

ADAPTABILITY

How well do you perform in certain situations? What happens when you are suddenly thrust into a situation or circumstance? How well do you adapt yourself to turn something from bad to good, or good to great?

You look at a group of good tennis players on the planet, and every single one of them has a signature hit; their "ace in the hole". But those considered greatest in the sport, are the ones who are best capable of adapting to other's signature strengths and returning the volleys with precision.

Then there is the game of golf. If you know anything about golf. Golf has many factors that may cause individual players to prove how adaptable they are. Outside of just hitting a golf ball correctly, there are the elements of the weather factored into the ever-changing courses. Such as bunker and hole positioning, which can change daily for tournaments. So, the champions for that tournament are always the ones who understand how to best adapt along the time-consuming individual courses in order to receive the best score they can.

How well can you adapt to the course of life <u>when</u> the elements whether known or unknown, come your way? Are you adaptable enough to raise the level of any room, do you keep it the same with lack of input, or do you bring it down?

Adaptability is an extremely important key to have, because as many of you know, life has many signature hits. So, adapting in order to volley back with precision, is necessary.

<u>**You can cave under the pressure or learn to adapt to the punches and keep moving forward.**</u>

My grandfather on my father's side was the epitome of adaptability. He was born during the great depression into generation that was if anything, adaptable.

The generation saw everything from fighting a war for the sake of saving the planet from supreme evil, changing the way society sees race as based upon character, winning the race to put a man on the moon, and developed computers from being the size of entire rooms, to seeing them being put in the palm of the hand.

That generation as a whole, was one that knew what they had to do, because they understood they needed to learn to adapt through anything and everything, as best they could, in order to achieve greatness.

That being said, my grandfather didn't have much growing up (as was the norm for many families, probably why adaptability became a necessary). His father left during the depression, and the family struggled more than most could ever imagine. In fact, at one point as a kid, his family had to live in a cave in order to find shelter. Then as a child/teen, he found himself working in the cotton fields to help provide for his family, because they had very little to eat and had no normal place to call home.

Thankfully for me, my grandfather would not end up becoming the example his blood father was.

He did drop out of high school to help his family, then a few years later he married my Mamaw, and began what I believe is the ultimate adaptive journey my family has ever seen.

After marrying my Mamaw, he trained to become a boxer. He had enough talent to spar with professional boxers, and even sparred with one of the greatest ever known, after no one else would step into the ring with him. But there were a few small, but significant problems. He couldn't afford to train full-time due to the family he started, and (I believe) he didn't want to do anything remotely similar to what his father did, by being gone all the time away from his family by fighting.

So, as his dream to become a boxer faded, he adapted to becoming a pastor. Now there are many, many, stories I could tell you my father told me about his dad while being an evangelist. But I'll leave you with one story to show how deep he went into ministry, and how much he tried serve others.

People can go their entire lives without seeing someone possessed, and I pray you never do. That being known, one of those people was not my grandfather. In fact, he saw many things that will make any person believe there is a God, because he witnessed everything from someone coming back to life, to demon possession.

Though he did his best to serve during huge conferences back in the second half of the 1900's, once again, time and his family were of the essence. So, after coming to the conclusion that being a minister was taking up a lot of time from his family and making enough money to buy a house; he and my Mamaw finally decided a neighborhood so bad that my father used to go to bed to the sounds of gun shots, was home.

In this newfound paradise, he began trying to find a job (as what anyone should do), but not having a high school diploma naturally made finding one pretty hard. So, every day he went to town hall in downtown in the hopes that a job was available, in order to provide for his family.

One day, on his way to the town hall, he noticed a man's car was broken down on the side of the road, and in the pouring rain no less. So, my grandfather being the man he was, pulled over to help him, and went on his way to see about a job.

By the time my grandfather made it to the town-hall, the rain had stopped, and he once again sat on the steps with little to no luck of finding what he desperately wanted. When all of a sudden, he saw the man he had just helped not 45 minutes ago walking up the steps. The man (still soaked from the rain) looked at my grandfather and thanked him once again for the help. And after some light conversation, he right then and there, offered my grandfather a job.

My grandfather turned a bad situation into a good one, through the greatness within himself.

But that's not the end of the story. My grandfather ended up working for the water department of a major city, and once again found a way to adapt to the situation he was thrust into, by turning a good situation into a great one.

With not even a high school education, he noticed the only way to move up was to educate himself higher than he ever thought possible. So, he began studying and working on higher level mathematics without the need to be told to do so. He eventually taught himself what others in this field had to know, in order to have the possibility of moving up, and ultimately achieved the highest level he could without a formal education.

In fact, he was given a certificate from one of the current top engineering colleges in the nation for his field, in recognition of his abilities, became 2nd in command of his group, and even led those who had college degrees teaching them the real-world math lessons they weren't taught in school.

<u>Adaptability:</u>

I can't help but feel that if it were not for all the <u>choosing</u> to adapt to the situations over the course of life in both my grandfather and grandmother; I would probably not be here today. So, what you by reading this book, and what others could fail to realize is:

There is no such thing as coincidence. We all have a purpose in the grand scheme of life. But you individually have to choose to volley back the hits life gives you and if you don't (let's be honest),…life is going to suck unless you comprehend adaptation for your greatness within.
Adaptability is the ability to be flexible in any situation, event, or set of events within your values.

<u>Adaptability can take many forms:</u>

<u>In school, it can take the shape of being thrust into a group you did not see yourself being in, for a project or learning to adjust to a specific teaching style of a teacher in any given subject.</u>

<u>In sports, it could be the coach asking you to take on a situation or role you're not accustomed to.</u>

<u>In work, it could be knowing how to better perform a job or taking on a task that you don't normally handle.</u>

<u>In relationships of all kinds, it could be adapting your understanding that people are not perfect.</u>

<u>Adaptability in life is key</u>. The earlier you learn how to be adaptable, the better chance you have of being successful.

Why True Champions

<u>The story of a young man I heard for a long time named, Joseph, definitely comes to mind when the topic of adaptability comes up:</u>

<u>He was sold off into slavery by his brothers</u> (who told their father Joseph had been killed by a wild animal), to a caravan that eventually sold him to a minister under the Pharaoh in Egypt.

But that did not stop Joseph from finding success and favor. He was eventually put in charge of his master's estate because of adaptable leadership in himself.

One day, the wife of the minister took notice of the younger Joseph and tried to seduce him. But when Joseph refused, the minister's wife became angry and accused the young man of forcing himself on her. <u>Given the situation of Joseph's word against his wife, the minister took the side of his wife and had Joseph thrown in prison.</u>

After some time in prison, and the continued growth of the young person in the qualities first learned at the estate. The young person's talents had been noticed by the warden of the prison, and eventually Joseph was appointed as the right-hand man.

One day, the young person met two strangers and used one of the gifts he was born with, to help provide insight to both regarding their current situation. As it goes both men were accused of a disrespectful deed against Pharoah. Short story shorter, one was found to not be guilty and returned to the Pharaoh's side, while the other was put to death. (As correctly spoken by the young person.)

A couple years later, the Pharaoh had a problem none of his advisors could seem to solve. But the person that was let go from prison remembered the young man that helped him with this same problem only a few years prior and told Pharaoh of the young person's correct insight.

After hearing of the potential to solve the problem the Pharaoh had, Joseph was then taken to him, provided an answer to the conundrum, and then suggested how to fix the upcoming problem. Upon answering, the Pharaoh recognized the wisdom this young, former slave, unrightfully turned prisoner had, and promoted Joseph to viceroy. (Which in title and power was second in command, only to the Pharaoh himself.)

One day, while in the middle of the problem Joseph foresaw and helped prepare for, he saw a few familiar faces. His brothers had come to Egypt in order seek aid from the viceroy (Joseph) by hopefully purchasing much needed goods.

Joseph, knowing they did not recognize him as the viceroy decided to test their hearts by accusing the younger sibling (Joseph's now younger brother birthed while he was enslaved) of stealing. To which the brother's stood up for their younger brother offering their life instead if deemed guilty of the offense. But after seeing the change of heart in his brothers, Joseph decided to show them who he really was, and proceeded to love them as if nothing happened.

<u>The problem Joseph solved:</u>

A 7-year famine hit the nation of Egypt.

When the life events Joseph went through hit him, he had to learn how to adapt to his situation and in the end, he saved his family even after what happened. After revealing himself to his family, he was given a section of Egypt to live in. Then, even further down the road of time, this set of events eventually played a vital part in one of the greatest promises ever known.

<u>Let's recap:</u>

1. Sold into slavery by his brothers => <u>*became in charge of the estate*</u>
2. Wrongfully accused and thrown into prison => <u>*grew his abilities to become the right-hand man of the warden to lead the prison, and helped someone without expecting anything in return right off the bat*</u>
3. Was remembered for a talent, and showed that talent when the opportunity arose=> <u>*became the viceroy saving not only the country, but his family*</u>
4. <u>*All of this led to the greatest promise ever kept*</u>

Do you get it? Just because you are put into a situation does not mean you should stoop to the level you, or someone else sees that situation as. The pattern-allistic mentality of adapting to take a bad situation to a good one, then to a great one, is becoming a lost art because it requires you to find gratitude in where you are at but adapt for growth at the same time.

Adaptability to greatness through application of your own life starts with your mentality towards that specific life aspect itself. Meaning, a change or adaptation in your pattern-allistic mentality is absolutely necessary for a great life, but it starts with consistent <u>baby steps.</u>

If you're angry or frustrated concerning where you specifically are at in life...good. So, in <u>conjunction</u> of having <u>gratitude</u> for what you do have, and what has happened, <u>use the anger as motivation</u> to become something <u>honorably/respectably/righteously filled to reach integrity backed greatness.</u>
Mold the patterns of your anger/frustration and use it as an energy creator to adapt in life. But do not use let it control you because it will slowly become a necessary for you to keep growing. Remember, adaptable growth is a choice, but one day we will all wonder if we did all we could to achieve what we knew we could.

<u>We can't control everything, but we are provided opportunities to adapt for new levels of greatness both physically and mentally. But you need to be persistent in what you are determined to do in the end...</u>

BABY STEPS ARE KEY

Use this page for notes on how to be more adaptive to the situation(s) you are currently in:

What do you want to accomplish in life? How do you perceive where you're at now?

What talents are you growing while in your current life situation or job? (Don't think you're growing in your **job/occupation**? Write out what you do, and the complex verbs will describe the aspects you are growing if you are doing your job. Complex verb ex: organizing, manage, etc) (Don't think you're growing in a **life situation**? Write out what you're growing through, and the complex adjective will be what you can learn to adapt to grow through. Complex adjective ex: communication, lead (ership), understanding, etc)

How can you apply the talents learning above for the betterment of your future (adding to your "sliding door" of wisdom)?

PERSISTENCE/DETERMINATION

After reading adaptability and seeing the title of this section, I know what you could be thinking, "Don't the examples the writer provided apply to this section too? Is the writer about to repeat them self?". Let me answer that with a simple…<u>no</u>.

<u>The definition of persistence</u> -The ability to stand firm, to continue on the course despite difficulty or opposition

<u>The definition of determination</u>- It's the resolve to stand in one's purpose

Persistence/determination, and adaptability are birds of the same feather. But a bird that doesn't adapt can persistently run into the same mirrored window over and over again. Thus, not adapting to the notion, "Maybe I shouldn't do that anymore, because it doesn't feel so good…", meaning that person has unknowingly determined the road ahead is meant to be more difficult than it should have been.

Without adaptation you can't be persistent, but without persistence you can't adapt in what you're determined to accomplish, and if you are not persistent in what you've determined you want to accomplish, you'll never know how to adapt. So, without all three in combination, you can't move forward in <u>ANY</u> of your purposely filled greatness life aspects.

The same process goes for people who think someone is for them, even though that same person leaves them hanging <u>when</u> life happens. You can be determined to believe a person is for you through persistently using your patternallistic mentality to avoid personal adaptation.

This world is full of hypocrites of what true "real world" leaders are, and media of all kinds has proven not to help. So do not be so quick to be persistently determined to believe someone is on your side.

<u>One of the greatest shows of persistence I've ever shown in my determination, is after I hurt my knee playing football:</u>

I'll never forget the drill, time of day, or even how shadows were projecting off the bleachers as I heard what was like a tearing of paper in my knee. I didn't know what happened at the time. All I knew that I was in pain but having pushed my body through so much prior pain, I thought I could play through it. I did finish that practice, and even tried to practice the next day expecting the knee to magically become better. So, it wasn't until after the head coach basically forced me to go see the trainer, did I stop pushing myself.

A few weeks later after the original diagnosis of a torn ACL, the MRI showed I tore most of my meniscus. Which wouldn't be as big of a problem, but it was how I tore it that had the doctor worried.

In less than a couple seconds, I went from having the knee of a normal teen, to one (as the doctor explained) that shouldn't be run on, even after surgery. That being said, the day of the surgery the surgeon did tell me if I wanted to keep playing sports there could be another option.

A band could potentially be put in, but there would be no real way of knowing if, or when it would give out. But the hope was some kind of scar tissue would be formed around the band, and though it was still not conducive for sports, the knee could still be somewhat viable.

The problem with this route was I would risk needing a knee replacement by 25-30 if the band popped. But the only way of knowing if anything could be salvaged was for the band to go in first, and then do even more invasive knee work during the procedure. To which I told the doctor, if they could find a way for me to keep playing sports, then do it.

Short story shorter, miraculously God left just enough on the end of the lateral portion of my knee to put the band in.

Then it was time for the fun part!!! I was put an adjustable leg cast to inhibit movement that extended all the way to the hip for 3 months. Because if I bent my knee or put even a little pressure on it, I would run a serious risk of popping the band and ruining my knee within the next 2-3 years beyond the point of human help without me knowing. While the best-case scenario was putting off another surgery within the next 10-15 years.

The duration of that time was definitely the most brutal physical frustration of my life to date. Every accidental twitch, or twist could lead to me ruining the goal of what I determined in myself long ago to accomplish...playing basketball in college.

Now you're probably wondering, "Why?", and to that I respond with, it was the one sport I couldn't take to naturally and dominate using my mind (mainly due to my size). I also chose to pursue basketball, because I had people always saying, if only I was taller, if only I was this, or if only I was that.

So I long ago made it my personal goal to prove to myself I could do it, and to show I could rise above what the world saw of me. But this knee surgery destroyed all of the progress I made in gaining the respect I wanted from those who doubted. All of the politics I endured in moving to a new school that had been crushed firmly beneath my heel would come back, and unfortunately in an even a more monstrous way after this ordeal.

After the 3 months of me being in a wheelchair as my main way of moving around, the pain from the deep scars, me not being able to sleep properly, and needing help at every turn; it was time for my leg to come out of the adjustable cast.

When they took it off to evaluate my leg, I could literally wrap my hand around what should've been my calf, due to the lack of muscle movement. And it was at this point, I understood the journey that this part of my body would be like trying to completely start over from day one. But in the moment even after seeing the difference between my legs, I was so excited to get out of the cast prison I was put in.

This official removal of the cast signified my climb back up the mountain and it began with me wearing what my dad called, the bionic knee brace, to help me walk, and sleep in. About two months of day after grueling day in physical therapy, and careful not to bend my knee in a way that would cause me to fall over due to it being so weak, was finally breaking me mentally.

One day after waking up in serious pain several times the previous night's even with medication, and a machine trying to numb the pain. The realization that this process was going to take longer and be more painful than expected, hit me all at once. I could hardly walk without having a super brace, and without it I needed a walker for help. On top of everything pain wise, I was not independent at all and had to be monitored in some way at all times.

I'll never forget the day driving to therapy my father looked at me in the hoodie I wore as I was trying to cover my face, and I just slowly began to do the one thing I never really did…cry. It was the first real time I understood pity in myself, knowing the mountain was the size of Everest and in that moment, I could only take one wobbly, cautious step at a time. (I almost lost my leg two years prior in a freak accident I couldn't control. But even then, I understood what could happen next and how to push through.)

After parking in front of the therapy building, my father put his arm around me, looked at me with tears in his eyes, and calmly but reassuringly said, "I know you might want to, but you don't give up now. Don't you ever give up…keep fighting…"

It's amazing what a simple sentence, or two can do sometimes…

That statement rekindled the embers of the once monstrous fire that resided deep within. At the end of this mountainous ordeal, I didn't gain back everything I once had. I lost most of my athleticism and gained too much weight.

I was a shell of myself in all sports from a movement perspective, and through the rest of high school I endured scare after scare of hurting my leg. So, I had to really focus on what I originally did best. I put my mental capabilities of patterns to the test/grind and learned to use my mind more than ever to get the job done. I learned how to adapt my mind to go faster, while remaining calmer in what I was persistently determined to accomplish.

Fast forward four long, hard, and body abusing years to get back some level of what I was before the surgery, and I did it!! I stayed persistently determined and eventually walked onto the D3 basketball team at the college I was attending my junior year.

I proved to myself what I knew I could do. I didn't care it was only D3. I didn't care I adapted myself within hundreds of situations to use my academic abilities to receive a mostly paid college experience at one of the best schools in the nation. I gave myself the opportunity to play basketball in college. I didn't care I had to walk on. I didn't care how many people talked about me while training in college.

Four short years earlier, I was told I shouldn't run, let alone play sports.

I was told all of these things I couldn't, shouldn't, and would never do. But in the end, I was the one who had the final say. By the time I was 17, I conquered many mountains, defeated many Goliaths, and did not succumb to the Mount Everest of my <u>physical</u> body <u>mentality</u>.

Tell me I can't do something I know I have the <u>cap-ability</u> range to accomplish and watch me rise.
You don't know the depth of persistence in my determination of what I know I can handle. I don't care about the words you say if you are trying to keep me down. Watch me put my mind to it, and surprise you with how far I climb…

Even after all these years and fighting back the raw emotion in this coffee shop in typing that story. That example isn't even what I believe to be the greatest show of persistence/determination in my entire family.

This next example is a real emotional one that unfortunately still happens in the world today, but not for the blatant reasoning people claim it as nowadays. People today think just because a little adversity comes their way it is a reason to give a situation, or someone a label. When it's not even remotely close to being what they claim it as. Most of the time, when it comes this next situation labels today are used when someone did not want to adapt within the situation, <u>so instead, they chose to be offended</u>.

This next story is one I have never told anyone. I know I'll cry even more, but this public place is just going to have to bear with me. ☺

People like to talk about the earliest memories they have. Most, if not all are of funny stories, or good times.
Mine……is not.

My earliest memories are something that drives me to this day, and is why I respect/honor everyone, but will not bow to anyone besides God Himself.

My first memories became one of the building blocks of my God given success in life, what it means to be a man, what it means to be a leader, what it means to be a great leader of your household even when things seem grim, and…what it means to stay persistent in your determination.

<u>My earliest memories are of my mother coming home from work, day after day, crying, and my father trying to hold back his anger while consoling her at the same time.</u>

Day after day, my mom was told by her boss, she was nothing.

Day after day, she was told she was worthless.

Day after day, my father wanted so desperately to lay hands on her "leader".

Day after day, they prayed together.

Day after day, she fought back the tears when trying to hug me as she got home.

Day after day, from an extremely young age I studied what a great leader shouldn't do through stories of what happened.

Even though I didn't know it at the time, day after day, I set up a pattern-allistic mentality base that I had to fight every day, to never give up and become something <u>mentally</u> then actionably greater.

With this situation in mind. In some ways I believe my father could sense my latent abilities/talents from an early-age, and I'm grateful he did. Because when he found the time he encouraged and pushed me hard in academics, mental training, and the physical testing of my limits.

By the time I was about 10 years old, I pushed my mind, and body in such ways that most grown men wouldn't attempt to put themselves through. And to be honest at the time, I despised it (LOL). But my father knew <u>how great I could be</u>, so he tried his best to keep up in every aspect.

Reflecting back on it now. All this time I always thought he just wanted me to make it out of the "hood", but he really wanted to set me up to surpass my own limits. Everything I am, is all thanks to my earliest memories of that, "leader", my mother, and my father because pattern-allistic mentality is built around early years of cognitive function.

That fake, hypocritical leader, is the reason why I perfected staying persistent/determined, having faith in what <u>could</u> be done, and led to me to knowing every type of life motivation.

My mother provided the blueprint for the pattern-allistic mentality to remain persistently determined to continue to honor everyone, then rise above, through persistently adapting to go from promotion to promotion. All the while, she gained the respect of every manager and executive she worked for.

Some years later, she ultimately played an integral role in making hundreds of millions of dollars for the company she worked for. It was her persistence/determination that I saw, and thank God was able to comprehend from an early age, that laid my pattern-allistic foundation for the reluctantly-admittedly, unfathomable person I am today (because I've been told).

Persistence/Determination:

<u>*True greatness continues to honor in every situation or circumstance. They do not give up on themselves even when losing, and especially not when there seems to be no hope. For when you start to feel sorry for yourself, that's the day your key of persistence and determination will open the lock of what is truly hidden deep within.*</u>

You were not created to feel sorry for yourself or blame someone else for why you cannot succeed. People now a days <u>blame things of the past</u>, or <u>others even when time has moved forward</u>. Those people decided mentally, they can't or don't, want to put effort in to move themselves along with the hands of time.

Don't be the person who only looks at the hour hand of life, and decides to never start or finish the many, individual, and energy driven ticks it takes by the seconds hand to change the minute hand, and ultimately the hour hand on a clock.

Meaning, you can't completely change your mind about a situation, or person from your past all at once to receive a rapid desired result. It takes effort through baby steps of patterns to eventually take that step back and see major results over time.

<u>*I know not everyone has that one sentence to help rekindle the fire within, so I'll provide one:*</u>
<u>**Everyone has the ability to give up. But the small fact that you are choosing to read this book shows yourself that you can do it. No one will do it for you...so Fight!! Keep yearning to level up the person you see in the mirror every morning and continue to become someone that can be respected by consistently living in greatness!!**</u>

<u>Coming to terms with yourself is key, but it has to start somewhere, and reading this book to its entirety is a great place to start.</u>

BABY STEPS ARE KEY

Are you the type of person who leaves people hanging when life suddenly hits? How do you know?

Provide three examples in which you or someone showed persistence or determination below.

What is something, situation, or circumstance that you believe you can't persist past? Is there a constant pattern within your own actions when involved in things you do not have complete control? (Because you might need to realize that you're letting yourself be controlled by the past.)

What are some ways you can improve yourself after what happened? What patterns either mentally, or physically can you put in place for yourself when those thoughts of insecurity come to mind? (A good place to start is by realizing the good in what you do have, or in what you can do.)

DISCIPLINE/SELF-DISCIPLINE/ACCOUNTABILITY/SELF-ACCOUNTABILITY

Wow, that last section got a little deep, didn't it? Don't worry, this one switches things up. This section can be a major eye opener for many people, because it can be hard to have a healthy view of it today.

<u>Discipline has two different important meanings:</u>

- The ability to <u>*CONSISTENTLY*</u> put yourself in patterns that contribute to pushing yourself to a higher level on a daily basis

- What is used to correct disobedience, can also be used in the realm of criticism

<u>Accountability is one that everyone wants everybody to have, but when it comes back on themselves, most want it to shift to someone else:</u>

Accountability – the ability to take responsibility, and/or comprehend the good or bad contributions for results that derive from the details of facts, within any past, present, or future, situation or circumstance

<u>Types of comprehension that we need to take responsibility for:</u>

- Your own mentality
- Your own actions
- Your need to take a look at yourself before calling someone else out for not having accountability

    o How do you see yourself in a situation that went bad? Did you take responsibility? Do you comprehend what you did to contribute? How? Did you *reeeeally* do nothing to contribute to whatever good or bad went down?

    o Do you still live in the past to blame why it seems like you can't do achieve something now?

I got it!!! You think doing something back that's not worse isn't as bad, and a justified retaliation standpoint doesn't mean you should be held accountable or be disciplined!!
<u>Did I nail it?</u>

<u>If you think you personally don't need help in one of the above words in the title of this section whatsoever...</u>
<u>...CONGRATS!!! YOU'RE LAZY AND WILL FALL FLAT ON YOUR FACE WHEN LIFE HITS!!</u>

    Uh ohhhhhhh!!! Oh yaaa!!! Now it's time to really turn up the heat. I wish I could see your reaction after reading this section. That being known, I personally don't do it to hurt or show that I'm better, but instead do it to show how someone can become greater.

    Reading this section will make you realize you're either a brat who has not had to work for much and needs A LOT of improvement. Or you'll be someone who understands you could be better in many patterns concerning the way you think, regardless of what happened in the past and/or present.

    The problem in the discipline/self-discipline/accountability/self-accountability arena of people, is they never really change unless something drastic happens. Do you want to wait for something bad though? Don't worry, once again, this book was meant to challenge you in a way possibly no one ever has.

Why wait for a chain of events that are bad to happen in order to gain wisdom? Why not do something about it now?

    Discipline is not something that should bring up great memories for anyone. A good amount of people in this day and age have never had their mouth washed out with soap, been spanked, or put in your place, and it shows.

I know because before I was constantly disciplined as a kid…..
...I USED TO DO some of the same things a decent portion of you continue to do as adults.

You're mentally weaker in the end for not getting disciplined when you were younger (in the beginning). For honorable discipline is the fence greatness and leadership are built in.

Meaning, those around you did not do a good job in preparing you for how to be a true-life winner within yourself. And if you had no one to lead you, you might not have known better based on your pattern-allistic mentality, but you did not do a great job at choosing whom you looked up to either. So don't worry, I'll help!! ☺

It's easy to find someone who is going to hold you accountable. *Learn to be a great servant.* Remember the story of Joseph?

He learned how to serve, and gained the respect of everyone in command no matter the situation he found himself in. Then through respect, they helped him grow his talents through **discipline, self-discipline, accountability,** and **self-accountability**. Which all ultimately led to Joseph gaining more responsibility, a higher standing, respect from others, and more power.

You can't expect another person to respect you, if you don't even have the personal self-accountability or self-discipline to show how you honor yourself, or others.

Thankfully, for most of us in the world today all we have to do is seek and then we shall find. But waiting around for someone to appear to show us how to gain accountability, discipline, or respect will more than likely never occur.

So, when you constantly serve another person in some way, you gain the pattern-allistic mentality of helping/honoring, regardless of needing something in return while learning the steps of being a disciplined individual.

That being said, not having this section's way of thinking is still not entirely your fault. Discipline/self-discipline/self-accountability/accountability is not something you can be born with. It's a pattern-allistic mentality you learn over time. Believe it or not, I believe it wasn't even my parent's that showed me how to truly apply this section, and translate the patterns into all non-obligated situations, tasks, or people.

It was my Mamaw, and the human ability to learn from a situation (discernment), that played major roles in understanding discipline and being accountable. Was I perfect kid, student, or even college kid...maybe??..........Ok, NOOO LOL!!!!

As a kid I had my fair share of sprints against my parents to the bathroom I've both won and lost, as soon as I stepped in the house from school.

No, I was not abused. Some of you don't realize it, but there is a difference between abuse and discipline. Though, once your child reaches a level of cognitive ability the need for physically spanking (disciplining) your kid doesn't need to be the main form of how they learn from their mistakes. Instead, learn how to have an adult conversation with them while providing some advice going into a situation.

In college, was I in the wrong place at the wrong time in college? Probably more than I'd like to admit. But did I put myself in those situations due to a lack of self-discipline??? Regrettably, yes. But even today I learn from discipline, and accountability because they are in constant rotation of introducing new patterns to potentially follow in order to become greater.

Life is a constant rotating door of learning about new patterns of discipline and accountability. The more you understand about people, the more patterns you subconsciously add as you comprehend them. So, be careful of who you hang around and understand that all people trying to hold you accountable or discipline you, are not doing it to hurt you.

<u>When on the verge of dishing out discipline, or accountability (in many cases today, are about to start an argument)</u>:
Are you going in with the mentality of, "I know I'm right...", thus throwing away the comprehension of we are all human?

Now for an example:

I'll never forget the days when I went to my Mamaw's house as a kid in the summer. It was such a great time, because I didn't have to work with my dad in the hot Texas heat that week. And instead, spent the week helping her out from about 7-11 am everyday doing her chores. Then afterwards, we played chess, other strategy games, and I helped her cook the rest of the day, while having a variety of conversations. At the end of the day, before she went to bed, she told me <u>I could stay up and watch tv</u>. But she also said **I knew** what time she was going to wake me up at.

After the first couple times of overindulging on the cable television I did not have at home, because I was accustomed to 13 channels. I quickly learned how to be more self-disciplined, because waking up after 3 hours of sleep was not fun, and my Mamaw made sure I was out of bed. LOL

Pause....

Now I know what you're probably thinking, "I was just called out for being lazy. Now the writer is complaining about not helping their dad when he needed it?!". To that, I have this to say:

You try being a 7-year-old working in the hot Texas sun during summer for 8-10 hours a day carrying heavy things around. Then you hear about your friends going on vacation and hanging out all summer. Plus, my dad liked when I went over there, because (as he told me many times) I as a kid, should relax every once in a while.

And I think he told me that because of a running joke. I'll never forget everywhere we went; my father never heard of child labor laws (I was working close to 40 hours since I was about 7). But looking back on it, I'm so glad it happened that way. He did is best to try and make it, so I could have a break every other month to be some kind of a kid.

That being known, the discipline and accountability I learned those summers through hard work, made me twice the person anyone my age would be mentally in life all by the time I entered high school.

I knew what <u>discipline</u> and <u>accountability</u> through labor were, before you knew how to spell those words.

Now back to the story.

My Mamaw, (wife to the man I mentioned in being adaptable) was one of, if not the greatest woman I've ever known. Even being a 7-year-old on, "time off from work", she placed patterns in me of how to maintain a disciplined work ethic in every area of life.

All patterns of this section tie back to my love in serving her. Through understanding how to serve correctly the first time (time efficiency), she allowed me to further practice my many gifts, thus teaching me how to hone them. I believe she knew I was doing it too, so she pushed me even further. As time went on, I like to think I became the closest one in the family to her, because from a young age I could have adult, real world problem conversations.

My Mamaw ingrained in me a pattern-allistic mentality to work hard and get something done right the first time, so I could do what I wanted to later.

She held me accountable in every aspect of life. Whether after she caught me cheating while playing a game, when I was having a hard time listening to my parent's, or anything about life in general. She set the barometer of discipline, and how to hold myself accountable for the rest of my life.

She woke up at 4 am every morning, cleaned her house, tended to her garden, and did her best to keep her land as tidy as possible. Even after having knee and hip replacements in old age, this amazing woman setup various stopping stations within her property, so she could rest on her way from chore to chore.

My Mamaw's discipline and accountability in herself, was to a fault. I'll never forget one Christmas morning after being snowed in the night before, she accidentally woke the entire family at 4 a.m. doing what?........chores!! (LOL)

She was the epitome of personal discipline and accountability through controllable actions.

Some of you still can't figure out how to even pick up your plate every time. Let alone know how to wash it by hand, or even know what it means to do it for someone else. Learning how to hold yourself accountable through self-discipline is what sets people apart in the world today.

When I was pretty young, I remember one time (after not getting much sleep), I had just sat down from finishing the morning chores (my fault in my attitude for not being as self-disciplined), and she asked me to help with one more thing. So, I decided to let my attitude take hold, and I might've… slightly…backtalked. Which I immediately regretted, because it was like the spirit of God awoke within her, and I was about to get a lesson in repercussions, because it was game on!!!

I'd never seen someone that old move so fast. But thankfully, I was closer to the bathroom, locked the door as fast as I could, and stayed in there for a while. Yet even after I got out, she still held me accountable to the chore she asked me to do.

This amazing woman not only helped me. But took in my cousin that was involved with hardcore drugs and set him back on track without the need to constantly tell him he does/did things wrong.

The need to constantly tell someone they are wrong stems from the need to be continually right. Which actually stems from the internal insecurity that you were told that you're never right or were never told you're wrong. Which one could it possibly be for you?

---

let's think about that situation for a little. She was able to completely remove someone from the world of hardcore drugs. Now the road wasn't easy for either of them, and I was there to see some of the bumps. But she used patterns to correct previous patterns and created a system of discipline within him; up to the point that he worked hard to receive a nursing license and is now happily married with a daughter.

The crazy part was, she used a system of patterns to allow for freedoms amidst other things, and eventually led someone who partook in the hardest realm to break out of, to live their life to become greater in less than a few months after conviction.

The respect of the greatness pattern she set, became natural for her friends and family to take part in.

Now you could be thinking, "Wow, that was a lot of discipline imparted by someone. But what does that have to do with maintaining self-discipline, or accountability when someone's not in the room telling you?". Don't worry I'm getting there. This next story/example is to this day one of the most wisdom filled things I remember from my childhood, because it really shows that <u>you</u> make <u>this life what you want</u>.

You can either discipline yourself, grow up, apply this section, and rise to life. Ultimately changing to become something greater than what people or life say. Or you could not rise, and keep doing what you've always done, or seen someone do. Then one day, you'll ask yourself <u>why</u> your life doesn't seem to change for the greater.

My father was a man of the church like his father before him. He was on the board, and a leader of men in the city we lived in. I remember going to several of his one on ones with people in bad neighborhoods, and situations that went to the church. One of those people was in many ways, a genius.

This person I will not name, built their own computers from scratch and worked for a small computer company that would eventually explode as the technology became more prevalent. Unfortunately for them, they would not be able to see that rise to the top because they had one little problem. They were an alcoholic.

This book smart genius eventually lost their job after severely hurting their back in a drunk driving accident, and his wife divorced him because of the drinking. After all of this, he became one of, if not the best car mechanic in the city.

There was only one problem still. He would drink and he couldn't get as many customers as he could have. He tried to quit for the sake of raising his granddaughter whose parents were plain and simple…horrible. But you guessed it, he went back into drinking anyways. Time after time, my father tried to talk to him about the drinking, but he just wouldn't slow down.

On Sunday's he would go to church asking God why these things happened. Then would go home and have another beer.

Do you see what I'm trying to get at? This man could've been a multi-millionaire by the time his granddaughter graduated grade school. He could've retired with his wife and lived comfortably for the rest of his life, but he lacked the self-discipline/self-accountability necessary to do so.

You have to comprehend what self-discipline/accountability are, in order to maintain or do what I want you to, by growing in the potential greatness of your patter-allistic mentality.

As for the little girl (his granddaughter), some of you can relate, can you? A kid caught in the middle of their parent's, and grandparent's problems. Thus, leading to you having no one to look up to at all. But here is the amazing thing about life.

Life has a knack for showing you how to act or react in any and every situation, and each of us as individuals have the ability to choose who we will be no matter our background, or where we come from. But it requires a reflection of events in how you should or shouldn't <u>(re)act</u> as you grow up.
This comprehension and reflection of understanding your life will show you the way to become greater as you mature. Or it will become a reason of why you are as ignorant to discipline, self-discipline, accountability, and self-accountability as you are.

The granddaughter did not let the circumstances stop her. Nor did she blame her father, mother, grandmother, or grandfather for their short comings, or what they put her through. She did her best to truly love/respect them regardless of the situation. <u>In-between maintaining her great grades in school</u>, and she was there for her grandfather, even when he was black out drunk, and tried to be there for her parents when the time arose.

Instead of becoming the examples so blatantly around her, she chose to rise like a phoenix from the ashes to understand discipline, self-discipline, and how to hold herself accountable towards her pattern-allistic greatness. Today, she is practicing in the medical field (a doctor if I remember correctly) and is happily married.

She turned herself into something greater and now she serves people (I'm quite sure as much as she can). In fact, I just recently heard her grandfather (whom she took care of) stopped drinking completely, and I just can't help but know it was all due to her.

Both accountability and discipline are similar, in that they lead down a path that causes a chain of events in how we view them both.

Without discipline, you'll determine how accountable you really are. So the faster you learn how to be disciplined/self-disciplined, and know how to hold yourself accountable; the more successful you'll be in life.

Will you learn to take necessary discipline, and comprehend more from it? Will you compete with your current self, using accountability through discipline? Or will you wait for <u>when</u> **you** feel stagnation, then hope it's not too late, and/or end up wondering what could've been by starting sooner?

<u>Only you can choose to become a product of an environment. Now, whether that means showing why you will be great or why you COULD'VE BEEN GREAT, is up to you.</u>

<u>Discipline(s)/Accountability(ies) for competition:</u>

- Are you going to let a little kid and an old lady, have more discipline and accountability than you?

- After hearing about the granddaughter who should've failed, what's your excuse?

- Your dad or mom weren't around, or weren't perfect…ok? Learn from it. Become the person they weren't.

- "Life never seems to go my way" …AAAAANNND??? I hate to break it to you, that's everyone. So, evaluate your life or talk to someone who seems to have their life together.

    o Who do hang around? Do they help you be greater (this might even be by doing things you don't think help)?
    o How can you make yourself greater?

- Set an alarm for 6:30 am every day, make your freaking bed, and get yourself a workout routine. (Or create a greatness seking pattern in yourself to follow)

- For those of you in school: make sure you study the correct way first before playing video games or enjoy other things life has to offer.

- You want (blank) in life. Ok, what does it take to get there/it? Setup a pattern(s) of planning and a path. Then have the discipline to stick with it.

- You want this out of your job? Show the discipline necessary to go above and beyond to create a difference where you're at right now. Do you hold yourself accountable to keep the job, and/or do you justify more responsibility through consistently being great?

Everyone has the ability to learn and gain the wisdom of discipline and accountability. All it takes is to comprehend the details within the facts to pick up on the mental patterns.

<u>I WANT THE BEST FOR YOU. I BELIEVE IN YOU AND YOUR ABILITIES TO POTENTIALLY BECOME GREATER.</u>

BABY STEPS ARE KEY

(Yes, I evaluated myself like this. It is hard, but absolutely key in personal growth.)

WHAT DO YOU WANT OUT OF LIFE? WHAT DOES IT TAKE TO GET THERE?

WHAT ARE THE DUMB EXCUSES YOU CREATE THAT HOLD YOU BACK? (Don't think you have any? Ok, what causes you to feel anger, or insecurity…BINGO!!)

WHAT ARE PATTENS YOU CAN INSTILL IN YOURSELF TO BECOME MORE DISCPLINED/ACCOUNTABLE?

I'm so happy for you that you decided to stick with this book, filled out the previous page, and didn't just skip it. If you did complete it, go ahead and move on to the next section. If you didn't. Here's a period of awkward, possibly torturously silence from me trying to hold you accountable.

....
....
....
............................all of the cool kids are doing it ....
....
....
....
....
....
....
....
....
....
.... ok no seriously go back and do it ....
....
....
....
....
....
....
....
....
....
....
....

… I double dog dare you to not be as lazy as you have been. Become something more and answer the questions.

TRUE LOVE/HONOR

*True love for yourself or another is not, never displaying emotion. But rather, knowing when or when not to apply emotion **after** truly righteous and/or honorable actions.*

Yes, true love and honor play huge roles in becoming a winner in every aspect of life, and even in sports believe it or not.

"You can't truly love without having honor."

One of the greatest people I've met in my entire life taught me that statement. They are someone not like the rest I've encountered.

Because of the situation's I've grew up in. I am well practiced in knowing when someone is just giving a great pitch and doesn't truly hold them-self accountable. Such a practice of a gift has helped in me knowing when someone is just manipulating another to get a desired outcome too.

Is this person big time? In my opinion, yes. Do they provide insight in a prosperous way? Yes.

Now I know what you're thinking if you've heard of these types of people. In fact, it could be the reason why you don't/will not go to church or gathering of people these days. But I'm confident in my tools enough to know this person loves God and lives it out when they are not in front of the world to see.

One thing you might see in today's world, are people like this person saying you need to give in order to receive. Then you look at what they buy themselves with what their congregation gives. The hypocritical people you have chosen to see, have all these many worldly possessions from the money people give. Then during service tell people they are poor, and certain bad things happen because they do not give as much as they should.

To that point, here is what I have to tell you:
My pastor was a millionaire before he even decided to become a pastor. He doesn't need our money.

Plus, I've talked to people who have worked with/known him on a personal life participant level for decades. I've asked many people about the type of person he was for certain reasons that I only recently told him in the form of a letter, and I have confirmed.

He practices what he preaches. Whether my pastor and now mentor knows it or not; I've used my God given abilities to see into his heart and confirmed it through many people to determine where it lies.
That being known, I will not say I want to be like him, because I AM BELIEVING IN MY DRIVE to surpass his greatness, and all the great he's done in the world.

From the people I've talked to, my pastor gives the most monthly in the church. Yet, he still puts in the time and effort, to come to service every week to give a great message. Now you tell me what kind of person you know does something like that to benefit you? Who spends hours without needing to get paid to serve you in the best way possible? Then on top of all that greatness, he chooses to celebrate others and looks to serve any environment he's in.

He embodies my saying of, "money cannot buy happiness, but is rather the greatest tool in relieving stress…", and he lives it out. From what I know, I can confidently say, his and my heart come from the same cloth.

I don't know about you, but that's in my definition of true love/honor. Someone who wants the very best for you without needing or inquiring why you won't do the same for them. Yet, they still maintain the drive to climb even higher in the world, to become a beacon of what it means to truly love/honor someone else.

He has met several presidents, and even met one that for sure did not know honor, as he couldn't even honor his own wife (I will not mention his name but leave you to research it. I'm not going to spoon feed you everything).

My pastor did not meet the man trying to go in and change his presidential views, and as he stated, it was not his job to. He went into the meeting honoring the president as he would any other man, and then proceeded to pray for him like he would any other person. Now I'm quite sure my pastor could've <u>pushed</u> his views on the president, but what kind of honor or true love for yourself or someone, else is that?

Forcing someone to change to your perspective is not honor at all. It's a childish flailing that shows you do not honor, nor truly love anyone, including yourself. You will see no growth in yourself, or the people around you. In fact, all forcing your viewpoint does, is show why you shouldn't be shown the honor/respect you believe you deserve.

<u>This is something that I am telling you from a human standpoint and want you to put into practice for at least a year. If you work on honoring yourself and work hard to become something greater in the best way possible. Then you will honor the people around you in ways you don't now, and they will appreciate you even more as you do. But it requires a consistent pattern of greatness first, before change can be seen.</u>

I can guarantee you growth if you put in productive effort through patterns. Along the way you'll become more satisfied with what you're personally trying to get accomplished, and you'll see every type of bond become greater.

Things as simple as what I mention completing in the Discipline/Self-Discipline/Accountability/Self-Accountability section, are ways of honoring/truly loving yourself. But it starts with **baby steps** and is on you to grow taking bigger strides from there.

How you honor could be as simple as serving others by holding the door for people with a smile on your face everywhere you go when you get the chance, or genuinely giving compliments to people around you. You don't have to be like myself. Someone who constantly works out to honor my body, pay for others food at a restaurant, or give a range of money to help families as to honor others.

But as time goes on, work your leveling up to working out, because it sets up a pattern of true love for your body. For patterns of money, start by buying random people's coffee every other time you're in a shop.

Create a to-do-list of great **baby step** patterns and complete it within a week or two. Then level up greatness patterns from there doing things that stretch comfortability.

Consistency patterns in greatness of any degree that truly loves or honors yourself or someone else, builds onto your pattern-allistic mentality.

Great <u>baby step</u> patterns build the foundation. But life greatness is cemented when those patterns are not always convenient or comfortable to do.

Will you get recognized every time for honoring or truly loving people? No, but is that truly showing honor or love if you always need something in return?

<u>Absolutely not.</u>

Is it human to want to be recognized for doing good things? Yes, but if you expect it every time, then you need to re-evaluate your heart. Always expecting something when you honor or respect someone, is what leads to pride, which is the root of all bad thing's individuals do to one another on this planet.

You're probably wondering why I stopped it there. It's because pride is going to be covered later in the book.

*If you think you don't need anyone, that's a load of crap, and if you think you know everything, <u>you're the most **prideful** person on the planet</u>.*

If you think you won't get exposed sooner or later, you're the biggest, most stubborn moron ever. If you think you're the smartest in any room, then you're all of those I just mentioned. Being wrong in a situation happens to everyone eventually, or from time to time.

Now for the other side of true love. The side of love no one really likes. Constructive criticism. When your parents, someone you look up to, or someone in charge of your group at school or work who criticized you in some way, what did you do?

- Did you cry?
- Did you talk back?
- Did you storm off?

- Did you stop talking to that person until they apologized?

I'm human, so I know at first, I didn't take criticism too well either.
But I know everything already. I didn't need anyone else's opinion or insight. I knew exactly what to do and am the smartest person ever. (Extreme sarcasm, and for sure a prideful fool's way of thinking that some people still believe.)
Your parent's or parents of choice, truly love you. That's why they provide discipline for you (or they should) because it's for your own benefit. Your teacher's grade you to show you how to be better. Your coach yells because he wants you to be greater. If you show your coach or teacher more honor then your parent's, than you need a reality check. Your parent's (even the worst kinds) or parents of choice, to some degree want the very best for you.
People who truly love/honor and want the very best for you in any situation, will be there for you no matter what. They will not leave you hanging but extend a hand in a way that honors yourself and the people around you, expecting nothing in return.

The most successful people in business and in life I've ever met all show honor. Believe it or not, there is an awesome link between showing honor/true love to someone without always needing something in return, and success in life.

Let me put it to you this way. Who would you do business with? Someone who <u>CONSISTENTLY</u> brings their best, honors everyone, and tries to become better in the process? Or the person who claims to be the "best" and feels offended when someone brings up a VALID/RESEARCHED opinion to the table. Then at the end, the "best" proceeds/chooses to ignore those factual researched opinions anyways.

Let's put it another way. What person has more REAL friends? Someone who works hard in their everyday life, makes time for people, and offers advice in such a way that wants someone to search for greatness. Or the person who says, "I'm living my best life. Why change to become something better?" and proceeds to leave people in a problem all alone. Then says things to people around them they want to hear and talks behind people's backs about how much lesser someone else is.

Could it be coincidence that those who truly honor and love, have a special way of winning?

Maybe, but how many coincidences do there have to be before something becomes more than a theory?

There are no such things as coincidences when it comes to life. Everything happens for a reason, but the reasoning for it happening is up to you.

A GREAT LEADER SHOWS HOW TO HONOR AND TRULY LOVE THROUGH THEIR EVERYDAY LIFE.

<u>*TRUE LOVE IS NOT ONLY COMFORTING AND REASSURING BUT CAN ALSO BE TOUGH. BECAUSE TRUE LOVE IS THE PATHWAY TO TRUE LEADERSHIP!!*</u>

<u>Let me give you a little insight into today's problems and how to fix most of them:</u>

Truly love and honor someone in such a way that it shows why you deserve to be shown true love and honor in return.

You should not always expect anything in return but know that honor will be shown unto you if you have a pattern-allistic mentality for it. So, if someone criticizes you, show honor to yourself by honoring them. Truly love yourself by being open to opinion, and research that opinion for factual truths. (Does the opinion make sense?)

Honor/truly love no matter what. Eventually someone/people will take notice and decide to show the same level of honor in return.

REMEMBER, WE ARE ALL HUMAN, SO ALLOW FOR HUMAN INADEQUACIES TO OCCUR.

If negative, never give in to the example or box that someone puts you in. By doing so, you give into the hypocrisy of wanting to be great, but yet are stooping to the level another sees you as.

True Love/Honor example:

Even in other biases of Christianity, Jesus is looked at as being someone of great importance. Theologians in other religions lay claim that He was great, and atheists who have heard of the Bible, say He was/is great. Those who say, "Jesus still loves me no matter what I do", say He's great.

But where they all go wrong, is He did not love blindly, but instead, truly loved/loves with the intention of wanting people to be greater according to the Word. He was a worldly ruler who did not live to enforce His will on people with an iron fist. Yet, He did want to show you how to be greater by example.

Within the religion that persecuted Him, Jesus pointed out flaws that they had through parables, because though definitions can be changed, the base pattern mentality behind a parable is not so easily manipulated. He came to show people how to be greater, and how did they repay Him? By killing Him.

Yet, even in on death's doorstep He wished them the best, and forgave them in His heart, His words, and His actions.

That's what true love/honor is. I'm not saying to die as an example. But rather telling you to listen to those who display true love/honor, because they don't want to control you and want the greatest for you.

Those who truly love/honor you will want to see you reach your potential greatness and want you to consistently be your best.

That being said, true love/honor does not mean what most people today believe it does. Some people believe there are no consequences to their actions as long as it was done within the parameters of a cause. All those people are doing, is showing that they neither honor, truly love themselves, or consider the people around them.

Those who say they truly love/honor you, will prove it. Yet do not wait to truly love/honor until someone does it for you. Instead, validate yourself and become something this world needs.

Today the nation of Israel is still known as God's chosen nation even after putting Jesus to death. (Which needed to happen to save us all by giving us the opportunity to be with Him. I challenge you to honor yourself by reading why He had to do that. He loves you more than you can imagine).

True Love/Honor is not one sided, saying someone can do no wrong. But instead, putting in the effort to understand each other better, and wanting greatness for one another.

TRUE LOVE + HONOR = <u>SELFLESSNESS</u>
<u>SELFLESSNESS</u> LEADS TO GREATER HEIGHTS (IF YOUR PRODUCTIVE EFFORT IS PUT IN)

<u>My definition of true love:</u>

The ability to see, then celebrate the good/great in everyone and take the good with the bad, while comprehending we all have flaws. All in conjunction with caring enough to respectfully understand that there are ways and habits (patterns) we all can grow in and tell those in an honorable way, how to become greater, even when it seems difficult to do so. So, it is key for you to understand that listening to others who care for you in this way, can create a deeper, more loving connection.

<u>What happens when true love/honor are not at the forefront</u> **WHEN** <u>life happens?</u>

While helping my father with his business in the summer he would tell me horror stories from his home health nursing days of the possible evils in this world. One of which, was about a very kind elderly person whose kids were wanting for them to die, so they could get ahold of the property that was sitting on prime real estate in the city.

One day, before a huge winter cold front came through. My father was talking to the main nurse about the terrible situation going on with the kids regarding their horrible end goals, and lack of care or true love/honor for their parent. He told the nurse about the several times he noticed some bad trends that would occur when the kids were involved. Then spoke of several speculated deliberate attempts to fulfill their heart's evil desire before he left the household that night.

The next day, after the cold front moved through, my father received terrible news from the head nurse. The elderly person passed away overnight, and was most likely due to the cold, because the gas heater was off. It might be speculation, but these selfish kids stayed with their trends, and intentionally killed their parent, by essentially freezing them all for the sake of money….

I am in no way condoning this action, or blaming the elderly parent for what happened, because everyone has the ability to choose in any, and every situation. Yet, I can't help but wonder…how were the kids raised?

In terms of background, they were born into a semi-comparable situation as myself, but I could never think about hoping for the death of my parent's. Let alone play a significant role leading to their death.

If the parent was kind and likeable, not being hated by other family members (per my father). Why did the kids have this selfishly evil mentality?
I may never know, but I believe it was due to true love not being shown through intentional true leadership.

Even though the parent was nice and could have been the likeable parent that anyone would want to have. In the end, the kids were probably <u>never shown</u> how to seek something greater in themselves, through <u>true love</u> and <u>true leadership,</u> to form a <u>true connection</u> with the person who brought them into the world to ultimately show true honor.

Without intentionally imparting patterns of true love/honor through true leadership, only resentment will be born in the hearts of individuals, because they will not understand how to truly love or truly lead themselves.

BABY STEPS ARE KEY

How are you showing true love/honor to people or yourself now?

What patterns can you put into practice to be better at showing honor/true love for yourself? (example: working out and sticking to the routine, setting an alarm and not hitting the snooze button 100 times, be better at showing up 15 minutes early to things)

Others? (example: paying for someone you care abouts coffee or meal without being asked)

Why <u>True</u> Champions

(Not fear or paranoia) HUMBLENESS / SWAGGER (Not pride)

<u>Here's what you're probably thinking:</u>

"What's the writer's plan here? Why would he put together a section with two seemingly opposite topics? Humbleness? Swagger? Isn't that just pride with extra steps? Didn't he say pride was bad?"

<u>My definitions:</u>

<u>Humbleness</u> – the ability to admit faults/failure, or admit you don't know everything; adept at adhering to constructive criticism to become greater

<u>Swagger</u> – the feeling of knowing you can perform greatly in a situation; knowing exactly who you are and having confidence in yourself; to have respect for your capabilities in the understanding you intentionally honed your gifts

Both of these words have a special place in my heart, because I've been in both extremes at many points in my life.

<u>Yet, I can say with confidence:</u>

The quicker you know how to work the balance of your humbleness/swagger spectrum, the better suited for success you will be for any situation, regardless of outcomes within the moment.
The reason this balance in mentality is great, is it serves to better understand the next steps to adapt in any, and all obstacles you might encounter for all roads of life.

Until the balance of the spectrum is understood. Both words in the parameters of life have the ability to give you the highest of highs, or the lowest of lows, and neither are beneficial, nor healthy for your overall mentality.

In order to break out of the deep end of either side of the spectrum, you will need the opposite pattern mentality that put you there in the first place.

Everyone <u>naturally</u> falls on their own point within the humbleness/swagger spectrum, based on the internal patterns developed within them from an early

114

age. And when I say internal patterns, I mean, when psychologists tell someone, "The reason why you do (blank), is due to the fact that when you were younger (blank) happened to you, which is why you do (blank)".

It is your preference/default impulse pattern that stems not only from a particular relatable situation or circumstance, but also leaks into other aspects of life. These impulse patterns derive from patterns you've seen and related to, are not necessarily directly correlated to the "T". So, your subconscious takes portions of patterns, then adjusts them to you own preferences, and applies them to different applications based on your mental pattern preference (sliding door of wisdom). But your ability to understand how to perform a pattern, depends on your confidence through repetition and growth of said pattern.

That known, as you know from the first chapter there are infinite, but finite choices within our minds containing certain percentages that narrow down the performance of any certain number of actions. Then as the follow through action occurs of said choice, it creates even more situations in which you will perform any certain number of patterns based on your intellect and understanding, in conjunction with the current mentality pattern you've decided to place yourself in.

Meaning, where you're at in your current head space determines how you will perceive the best course of action in the moment of the situation(s) you've related to, from previous patterns you've been exposed to. (Take a few steps back to wrap your head around this if you need to, because patience in understanding key.)

Due to the importance of your headspace, patterns of in the moment best course of action patterns, it is imperative to not let your emotions drive your actions. Rather, let a pattern of patient understanding in your emotion to honor, respect, and truly love yourself and others in the greatest way possible, by acknowledging everyone is human and makes mistakes.

Placing patterns into people is what companies are trying to accomplish with marketing of all kinds, and artificial intelligence in all applications. Marketing is easy to impose, manipulate, and figure out when in regard to people (Don't know why? Re-read the first chapter).

But you want to know why you could never really have true autonomous intelligence?
There is no computer fast enough to compete with impulse pattern of the human mind, or capable of comprehending why we as humans perform smaller percentage actions in certain situations.

When the cards are on the table, artificial intelligence will never have the ability to feel humbleness to take a step back. Nor will it ever have the swagger to listen to your gut and go for it. Artificial intelligence or computers do not have the capability to understand, and/or comprehend the reasoning behind a changing of pattern-allistic mentality, while using the "sliding door" of wisdom.

Now for a switching of gears within the spectrum towards life:

At every point of my life, I had been repeatedly told things on all sides of the spectrum. I was smart, I was dumb, I suffered from a variety of mental problems (as told by several teachers), I'd do this after college, I couldn't do this, and even questioned why I was born only to go through so many things that would've broken others many times over (as told by other people about my life). That being known, I did not let the voices stop me, because I understood the patterns of greatness I had and things I wanted to achieve.

Over the course of life, you hear an insane variety of opinions through varying filters, from all walks of life. So, you will either let those voices become insecurities, or an understanding of what the world needs.

That being understood, in my opinion, school, sports, and college or continued education in any way, are the best places to develop your balance of humbleness and swagger. So, I strongly suggest kids work hard to get into college or trade school, and work to get something <u>VIABLE</u>. Become involved in something that will benefit you in the real world. But know getting a degree is not necessary for life success, rather like my father always said, "A degree is like a magic potion. It'll get you into more places than if you didn't have it".

College is not for everyone but having the ability to humble yourself to strive for something greater, is not easy in any situation. So, if there is anything you've learned in this book, especially from my grandfather, is you do not necessarily need a college degree to succeed. But it does make your fallback options a lot less appealing than if you did not at least pick up a trade.

Having a college degree, picking up a trade, or having a higher education is the greatest back up plan anyone could ever have, because it creates a base to build off of or fall back on.

There is one slight problem after getting a degree or trade, that is directly influenced by the spectrum itself in how the individual sees the small goal they have achieved. Most people do not humble themselves in a way that makes them want to push to greater heights. Even those who get a masters or doctorates, do not seem humble themselves in a way that makes them want to be even greater in any other area of life.

In either case of degree or trade level, some people end up having this amazing gift, but do not build upon it because they think their journey is over, when in reality…it has only just begun. **Being content within your mentality is what causes frustration to build, so when stagnation is finally perceived, it feels as though a tsunami just hit your mind and life. So, to help mitigate the amount of water rushing towards you, evaluation through the humbleness/swagger spectrum of your talents, is key in making sure your mentality is one bent towards growth.**

You have had plenty of the appetizer, so now it's time to get to the main course of this section through a short example.

<u>A lesson in the swagger/humbleness spectrum:</u>

You might not believe it, but I wasn't the best college student. I remember one day walking into the head of the department professor's office trying to get assistance for what was to come next. He was my favorite teacher. He taught me so many things over the course of the 3 years I had been there and believed in how smart I really was, by constantly telling me while I served others in helping them study.

Walking into his office, I entered a young naïve kid, thinking I had prepared everything just right. Before even setting up the meeting I knew my GPA, but thought I understood the grading scale. I had heard rumors that when leaving the school there was a significant GPA boost when going into other major schools when getting accepted for master's programs, so I banked on that info helping me.

That being known, I never really cared about the other classes outside of my major and minor, because I never found them interesting. Most bored me to tears, because I wanted something that was going to challenge the patterns of thought that I worked through, concerning multitude of topics growing up. I didn't want to "waste my time" with things that were not going to benefit my major or at least intrigue me.

There was also another slight problem in college that didn't really appear in all of my past classes. My parents believed my ability to take standardized tests was high, due to my ability to handle pressure in conjunction with time management skills. High school and the ACT (even on pain medication after surgery) was a breeze.

In college, I aced all the quizzes and homework. But something stopped clicking in my mentality when it came to the pressure, I put on myself concerning tests. I panicked many, many times, and always second guessed my abilities. So much so, even in the classes I loved, I panicked, just not as deeply.

From my freshman to junior year, I struggled more than any point in my life with the pressure I put on myself in academics. Which was something new to me because I had never felt anything like it before. But once the ball started rolling of the second guessing, I couldn't seem to stop the cracking of my mental armor from my freshman to junior year. I could only barely slow it down.

All those years of achieving anything I set my mind to, by learning from myself/others and adjusting/adding to my pattern-allistic mentality so many times, unknowingly adding layer upon layer to my sliding door of wisdom, but I couldn't handle this pressure I put on myself like I knew I could. I seemingly couldn't recognize which simple mental light switch to turn on. For 3 years, things stopped flowing naturally.

Needless to say, in that meeting with the professor, my pride (furthest end of the swagger spectrum) in planning everything out, came back to break me when facing the teacher whom I dearly enjoyed being taught by. But I'm glad he broke the news that I wouldn't be able to achieve the path <u>I BELIEVED</u> I should be on, and I remember looking at him trying to hold back his tears of disbelief.

    This was the person who told me constantly if I could stop second guessing myself, then I would easily have a 4.0 GPA. As I read the emotions displayed on his face, they were ones that expressed extreme grief for me, because we both had battled together through so much already.

    I'll never forget trying to make him laugh the week of tests, because I found out he was having personal problems at home from being at the college so much to serve, and tutor students. So, I tried to serve him in the way he needed to be served in those moments, because I knew he truly cared. And I'll never know, but I think he knew what I was trying to do.

    I'll always remember the look on his face as he smiled holding back the tears while telling me everything was going to be ok. After both of us regained composure, he right then and there, led me down another option path that I thankfully setup as a backup plan years prior by taking certain key classes.

    After walking down this new path on a piece of paper, we were both in agreement on, I looked at it trying to figure out what happened with my plans. By this point in my life, I was so used to being spot on with anything, because I believed I had been brutally exposed to almost everything anyone could go through already.

    I left after thanking him, and I'll never forget the internal voices as I walked back to my room, "How could someone others went to for help in the same classes not make it to their level? I was one of the best students at the school from an intellect standpoint in any given realm. I was the only student in a decade my mentor (a prestigious man with more degrees than any one human should have) claimed to have something special and bragged about it to other professors. He was someone who correctly predicted many things that came to fruition for others, and he let me know I was even greater than previous people he had told that to. How did I of all people mess up?"

    In my head, I went on and on about the accolades I had achieved for hours. The statements I heard regarding how special I was, and all the nay-sayers I quieted over the years. Then I began to think about everything I had fought through in order to get to where I was. I was so <u>PRIDEFUL</u> as to take it all the way back to elementary school, being a part of chess club, and never losing a match in the three years of tournaments against kids who were older than me.

Then I took it all the way back to fighting the politics to get into the gifted and talented program, when my family couldn't donate to the school like so many of the other, "gifted and talented", students. I remembered receiving the test back basically saying I did better than everyone in every subject except one.

From there, I remembered how I turned every stressful situation into something that no one else could see. All of this <u>PRIDE (on the very far end of swagger)</u> led to one conclusion in my mind. "I was the best without needing much help. How could this happen to me?"

I dismissed all whom I had given the ability to help me along the way.

After the voices of pride were over. The voices began saying how I would never be good enough, and how I was a complete failure. So, I began replaying all of the times I fell flat on my face, and the times people told me I would fail in the end. Then I began to believe that I wasn't good enough, and I never would be. From there, the voices began to mock the things I had accomplished. I began to think it was all luck, or by chance, all I had achieved.

I began to tell myself I did not deserve high praise from anyone. I was a nothing, a no one, and that's all I would ever be.

I began to think I couldn't do anything myself, and I became extremely dependent on others for help in some areas of my life that I didn't used to need help in. I became <u>too</u> humble for my own good and related the patterns of my past of failure to paint a mentality of paranoia/fear.

At the time, when I did do something correct, people would ask if I could help them again like I used to before. But with a smile on my face, I told them I couldn't help, and made up some terrible excuse. When in reality, I didn't want to, because in my head I told myself I wasn't good enough, **even when my gifts were obviously still there**.

The deepest parts of the spectrum are paranoia into fear (Humbleness), and pride (Swagger).

*Everyone can find themselves within a certain range on the spectrum, due to their pattern-allistic mentality. So, it is important to first understand the relationship of patterns from the past to the present, in order to access the full spectrum itself within your own mentality. The best way to start on the **baby steps** of understanding is by saying out loud both sides using your past events (patterns). Then you can go in and work on correcting the symptoms of pride, paranoia, and fear (insecurity) with precision.*

Continued from the example:

Thinking about it now, I could come up with A LOT of excuses as to what happened in college. But I needed to have that fall from grace, because I had been on my highest horse for so long through sports and academics, by surpassing my limits, and passing many educational cheaters. Yet, that is the result of not comprehending the spectrum of humbleness/swagger, the highest of highs, or the lowest of lows. I put myself on a pedestal so high because I thought it was all me. I couldn't see the ground, and wow it hurt when my future had been shattered right in front of me. (You've felt that too, haven't you? We all have, and if you say you haven't then you're stuck in pride.)

Shortly after my fall, it seemed to only get worse during that next summer. But this next trial is what pulled me out of the pit I was in and became the rebuilding of the pattern foundation for more future success than I could ever imagine.

About a month after having my dreams shattered, my father came down with a life-threatening illness the doctor had only seen once before, and that person died shortly after contraction (There was a high likelihood of being a quadriplegic, or at best, in a wheelchair.).

I know it might be weird to read that having your father and family go through so much pain, is what set another up for success. But the reason why it brought me out the pit I was quickly spiraling into, was due to the fact, it took me back to my roots. It took me back to a time before achievements, and all the things' people said I could do or would never be.

When my father contracted the disease and went into the hospital, I had to drop my internship for the summer, and take over his business. My mother had to take a leave of absence from work to help the nurses, and doctors take care of him during the day. As for my sister, I wanted her to stay there in the hospital room just in case things turned for the worst, because she was so young and needed all the time she could possibly get.

So, as a 21-year-old I had to be the provider of my father, mother, and sister. I had to work out of a van that had no A/C in the Texas heat for 9 hours a day, and needed to use what I learned over the years about my father's business to implement my own way of doing things to increase profits to make ends meet. And all while providing, I had to make time to go see him and wanted to spend time training for the upcoming basketball season.

If I was lucky, I woke up every morning after 6 hours of sleep and always hoping my father was still alive. I wasn't getting paid for all this work or time either. The only money I spent was on the one meal I would eat all day, because bills were coming up. So, I had to make do with what resources I had.

During this time, I was forced to stretch my mind in a way that most young people never have to, while under a pressure that no young person should ever have to go through. But ultimately, the stress and gravity I put on myself, became a catalyst of what I would eventually become, because it reset my humbleness/swagger spectrum.

Throughout this situation, I had to throw the pent-up pride from the previous decade away and replace it with humbleness through effort. Because the more effort and time I spent in the situation; the more I realized I could still handle immense pressure. So, my fear/paranoia from my great mental failure months before, was slowly stripped away as the knowledge I could do something of great importance came rushing back in.

My father did not have the most glamorous or easiest business to run either. But had I not gone through my greatest fall to date, there is no telling what I would've done in that situation. And through it, I re-discovered with an even greater understanding, what very few have ever found again.

I regained, increased, and found a greater version of myself in the balance of swaggered humbleness.

I knew what I wanted to become, but now I knew I could do it without getting too high or low within any circumstance. I learned how to control the spectrum.

At the start of my senior year in college, I walked into every room with a swagger that I once again knew what I could achieve. But this time, I better understood I wasn't the best, and I couldn't control everything. I wasn't even close to being the greatness people said I could achieve…yet…

When I returned, my friends noticed a change in my attitude and how I presented myself the rest of the time we were in college.

Here is what I think about when that time runs through my mind:

My greatest achievement was I failed so spectacularly. I went from subconsciously thinking I was a special person in the room, because of what I had already achieved. To thinking…
…MY OLD MENTALITY OF THE HUMBLENESS/SWAGGER SPECTRUM WAS NOT GOING TO HOLD ME BACK ANY LONGER. I WAS GOING TO BE SPECIAL BECAUSE OF WHAT I HAD NOT YET ACHEIVED.

End of example

- "Swagger/humbleness balance" – means to have the ability to know what you're currently capable of, but you understand you must become greater to reach the heights of where you want to go

- "…GOING TO BE SPECIAL BECAUSE OF WHAT I HAD NOT YET ACHIEVED." – you know exactly what you have gone through and may have done things not many people have. But you have not reached your potential yet.

We as individuals must understand we are not "God's gift to the earth". Yet, we are aware, and confident in our current abilities through the understanding of what we've overcome and have *yet to personally accomplish. This understanding is what it means to be balanced in the humbleness/swagger spectrum.*

The balance of having this humbleness and swagger can help you in any situation in life. Having the mindset of not being afraid to do something, but knowing you still have growth is what makes success in life happen.

Remember where you came from, but always look ahead to where you want to go.

If you're constantly looking at the past, then you'll never move on into the future. But if you're always looking ahead to the future; then you'll lose sight of your present patterns built from the past, to discover your potentially great future.

I know you might be thinking, "Wow, that's pretty deep!", and might be running memories about your past, rethinking everything you've been through. So, in your mind you could be saying, "Have I changed, or do I need to?"…"What was my childhood like?"…"What is my potential?"…"Have I reached it? How do I get there?".

<u>Let me stop you there</u>

1. Those questions are a good thing. This book was made to challenge your mentality and to raise the level at which you currently think.

2. Relax…if you dive too deep into this you'll go into a mental back and forth that can last for weeks (trust me from experience).

After reading this book, those questions are a detox you will need to comprehend over the course of a few weeks' minimum, by writing down what you are or are not good at (talents). Then write down the problems in life you've been through, and I also suggest you research what your base personality type is.

For example, I am an INFJ. (I'll leave you to research exactly what that means.) Through this type, I <u>understand</u> the good parts of my personality, but I <u>RESEARCHED</u> all the negative. Then I worked hard to better round myself out as a person. Do I still drop the ball with some of my subconscious negatives? Yes, but have understood in how I've been able to grow through what I struggled in? 100% yes!!

Now, for those who did not immediately go through those questions go ahead and take the time to do so. If you believe you don't need to think about those questions, then you could suffer from the same problem I did…

…You have waayy too much pride.

There is a huge difference between pride and swagger. Swagger is the ability to have your head up high through anything and everything. It also means you have a certain "strut" about yourself in knowing what you bring to any table. So, you take pride in how you look, you take pride in the things you do, but you know not to let pride completely control your life. That is why it is called, "Swagger".

If <u>you</u> have way too much **pride**, <u>you</u> see no need to care about what <u>you</u> do. <u>You</u> do not care what <u>you</u> look like. <u>You</u> don't care what people think about <u>you</u>, and <u>you</u> are going to do your own thing because, "I'm gonna do me!!".

<u>To that, I have few things to say:</u>

<u>YOU</u> MAKE AN EXCUSE FOR EVERYTHING. <u>YOU</u> HAVE NEVER BEEN SHOWN TRUE LOVE, AND <u>YOU</u> DO NOT KNOW WHAT IT MEANS TO TRULY LOVE YOURSELF OR OTHERS.
<u>YOU HAVE A LAZINESS OF THE MIND AND SPIRIT, FROM THE ROOT OF PRIDE.</u>

If you do not like me calling you those things, then good!! Prove me wrong, write down things you aren't good at. Really take a deep dive into yourself, and learn what it means to be humble, then take it to heart by adding it to your pattern-allistic mentality.

Did you really achieve your highest potential? No? Then write down what it takes to get there, and over the next couple of days or weeks, research what it takes to reach your end goal. Over the course of that time of researching, create a road map of steps in what it takes to get to your goal.

It doesn't matter how small the map is. The fact that you now have a visual path to get there is huge! Because after you complete this road map, you will have just stretched your mind in a way that will help you forever if you allow it to.

Having too much pride in oneself can be detrimental to success. People with too much pride will set goals that are unachievable in their current pattern ability-mentality.

(Make sure you adhere to these words of wisdom.) Your parents and people will say, "follow your dreams". And I'm not telling you to give up on your dream(s), but here is what I say:

NO MERIT IS UNATTAINABLE WITH HARD WORK. BUT GIVEN CERTAIN CIRCUMSTANCES, YOU MIGHT BE FORCED TO ADAPT INTO THE GOAL YOU WANT TO ACHIEVE.

For example:

Growing up I loved music and thought I could sing the songs I wrote. But there was one huge problem…I couldn't keep a tune in a metal bucket if I wanted!!! (LOL) Do I still write music? Of course!! But I've humbled, then adapted myself, to know the songs will more than likely be sung by someone else if I do get that opportunity in music.

As you just read, being prideful can hurt you big time if you don't humble yourself. But being strictly too humble can hurt you too, by lacking confidence in any area of life.

So, I surmise, someone being too humble (living on the deepest end of paranoia and fear) is the hardest to break, because pride causes its own fall thus leading back to humbleness. Yet, being too humble, means you look down on yourself in any way, even when others notice you have a gift.

Everyone can be great at something and there is potential talent in every person. But cultivating that talent is what can determine how successful in life someone will be. So, if you lack the swagger necessary to determine what you're good at, follow these steps in order:

1. Get out a pencil and paper

2. Write down these questions then answer them:

    a. What 2 hobbies do I currently have?

    b. What 3 things that pertain to making extra money do I think are interesting (what am I good at)?

        i. Write down 2 patterns to get better for both a & b

3. Look yourself in the mirror in the bathroom point at yourself and say:

    a. I'll never be anything. Everything I have achieved to this point is due to luck.

4. Walk out of the bathroom, turn the lights off, then walk right back in, say this with a smile on your face, and point at the mirror while doing it:

    a. "WATCH ME RISE! I'LL PROVE TO YOU I CAN DO IT! YOU WILL NO LONGER KEEP ME DOWN!"

This is very important because you are your own worst critic.

You can choose to listen to anyone, but you have to live with yourself. That's why you need to do the above mirror exercise.

<u>Why True Champions</u>

<u>Swagger/Humbleness:</u>

    This is without a doubt one of the longest sections of the chapter, because it is at the root of everything anyone can do or be. So, I believe a balance in the mindset you gain within this section, is absolutely key in life, as it feeds into all of the other sections and all of the others pour into it. (Because this spectrum deals with your emotions.)

<u>In order to help me remember to maintain a balance, I always have this on my mind:</u>

    There is a tale of a person who was the strongest in the country due to a certain aspect of their look. They were told that as long as they did not change this physical part of themselves, they would continue to get through any situation, and conquer any circumstance they came up against. Given the nature of their ability, this person was warned that they should not tell anyone of this special physical aspect, as it would surely mean their demise. In fact, the person was specifically warned about one person they were confiding in, as that person had ties to the evil country that was looking to enslave this special person's people while living in evil patterns.

    This special person though thought nothing of the warnings in whom they confided in, yet continued stay humble enough to not change what made them so special. But in pride this person decided to share what made them so strong to the one they had been warned about.

    After the prideful telling of the secret. When the special person was the most vulnerable and had fallen asleep, did the person this special person was warned about, changed what made them so special. The one the special person had confided in betrayed them and let the people who wanted to overcome the special person know that the conquering power had been taken away. The roadblock in the evil people's way had now been removed. And before the special person could realize it, they had lost of their abilities and the evil nation had already infiltrated the land to take the now normal person away, back to their palace to make a mockery of them and the One who gave this person their abilities.

    The special person was then placed between the main pillars of the evil palace after having their eyes gouged out, was tortured, spit on, and made a spectacle of. Furthermore, not only did the evil people mock this person for the situation, and what caused the loss of the ability to be special. But the evil people mocked the One who gave the now normal person their capability to be special.

Battered, beaten, and humbled by the fall of pride this unique person once had. The former special person began to ask the One who gave them their ability to give it back one last time, so they could defeat those who mocked Him. The One ultimately granted the request and gave the ability back one last time, and the special person who was placed between the main pillars of the palace began to push with all their might to bring the building down.

At first, this once special person was mocked by the evil doers for making such an attempt. But quickly shut them up when they noticed the building began to shake, and eventually the weight bearing pillars had been destroyed. Leaving those who once mocked the special person under the rubble of the collapsed palace. In this special person's most dire need after being humbled, they performed their most conquering act.

<u>In no way am I say to go out of your way to harm those who mock you, because that is not the honorable thing to do. Nor is it the main premise of this story, but never be afraid to respectfully/honorably stand up for yourself.</u>
The point I'm trying to make, is the special person was warned to not tell anyone about the nature of their gift and was also warned about who they were spending time with. But they refused to listen, and it led to a great fall into humbleness, back into swagger for honor.

We as individuals have limitless potential, but tend to have too much pride, ultimately thinking we don't need assistance. Yet, some are too humble thinking that they are not good enough and lack the swagger to move forward in their goals to take that next step.

Like the special person (conqueror) from the story. You can grovel in self-pity (being too humble) chained to pillars that are this life and listen to the voices who mock you saying you aren't good enough. Or you can be considered the best at what you do, only to one day reach a level of pride that causes you to fall from the pedestal you were once on, to be chained to pillars in your mind.

Either way, you're chained to pillars representing a stagnate life. Both pathways without the balance lead to the same place of being beaten, battered, broken, tortured, and mocked in one way or another. That's life. So, you can choose to stand in stagnation in all of those bad things, or you can have a different patter-allistic mentality; one that adapts in every situation for the greater to discover the next steps.

As you learn to gain control of the humbleness/swagger spectrum you will find yourself slowly causing the pillars of life holding you down to shake. But unlike the person (conqueror) from the story, you will live <u>when</u> the building (the weight of the life you built) could come crashing down. Don't get me wrong, harnessing this spectrum does not mean nothing bad will ever happen, but you will be more prepared in your own pattern-allistic mentality <u>when</u> life does happen.

<u>*This spectrum (as you could probably tell) deals with the emotions of the heart, mind, and soul.*</u>

BABY STEPS ARE KEY

YOU SHOULD HAVE ALREADY BEEN FILLING OUT WHAT YOU NEED WHILE READING THE SECTION (IF NOT, WRITE THEM DOWN BELOW). THEN GO AND LIVE IT. LIFE ISN'T EASY, BUT GIVING UP IN THE MIDDLE OF SOMETHING HARD WILL HAUNT YOU FOR THE REST OF YOUR LIFE BECAUSE OF NOT ADAPTING TO WHAT COULD'VE BEEN

I WANT THE ABSOLUTE BEST FOR YOU. GET RID OF THAT PRIDE AND BEING TOO HUMBLE!! EMBRACE A MORE DETERMINED MINDSET, KNOWING YOU CAN GROW IN ANY SITUATION IF YOU'LL ALLOW IT!!!!!

Control the emotions of the spectrum.

_____

RESPECT/INTEGRITY THROUGH HONOR/RIGHTEOUSNESS

My definition of <u>Respect</u> – the ability to understand that everyone is human, we all have great qualities, things we are not good at, and varying opinions. But will show one another honor regardless of if they agree or not, and admire those who consistently have performed great deeds out of integrity and <u>true love</u> for someone else

<blockquote><u>Honor</u> – adhere to what lies on the pathway of integrity to serve others how you would like to be served</blockquote>

<u>Integrity</u> – the quality of being honest and having strong moral principles in a way that is righteous

<blockquote><u>Righteous(ness)</u> - quality of being morally right or justifiable</blockquote>

I believe these definitions need to apply even more given today's world of technology.

<u>If you are ever in one of my business or coaching meetings, happen to be at a conference where I am speaking, and are doing the following, be prepared to be called out:</u>

- Obviously/blatantly on your phone for an extended period of time

- Talking louder than a whisper, attempting to have a conversation with someone near you while I am trying to help you be greater

- Constantly interrupting me when I speak, interjecting nothing productive into the conversation

- Feel the need to make a scene because you don't like the opinion I bring to the table

If there is one thing I cannot stand, it's when a lack of respect is being shown. Those who show no respect lack integrity, honor, and righteousness within themselves. If someone is trying to help you, don't perform any of the list above if you can help it. Because in the end, you will gain more respect for yourself, and whom you are respecting by showing them what you would want them to do for you.

<u>For example:</u>

If you're at a conference, and someone on stage believes the earth is round, and you believe the earth is flat; don't stand up yelling to make a scene. Instead, after the speaker finishes what they have to say, simply stand up, leave, and think to yourself, "Wow!! They really think that?".

Free speech is a liberty that applies to all speech on any side of the spectrum, and plays an important role in maintaining the overall liberty of freedom by allowing for criticism.

If you feel so inclined (which you should after reading this book), go home, do your own unbiased research, and come up with your own conclusions based on <u>non-biased or manipulated facts</u>. Then, if there is a Q&A at the next conference this person who believes what you think it crazy is at, have a civil, and educated conversation.

<u>A few more examples I cannot stand are found in the church and schools:</u>

- You would not believe how many people in a congregation sit there on their phones, while the pastor who just spent all week researching to help them out is preaching

- Then there's the fact that many kids nowadays sit in class, trying to hide the fact they are on their phones, when the teacher is doing their best to help them learn

The kids in school wonder why they receive bad grades, and the people in the congregation wonder why they struggle in some aspects of life. Then <u>when</u>

later in life happens, most of those people blame the teacher or someone who tried to help, for not doing their job correctly.

But was the person trying to help totally to blame?
Did you constantly respect them in a way that exuded the respect you would want to be shown?

There is an old saying I used to hear, "There is no such thing as a bad student, only a bad teacher." But that statement is only partially true. I've had absolutely horrible teachers, but one thing that doesn't help the situation is being an equally horrible student.

After a certain age of cognitive ability, it's on the individual to decide when those sayings stop being completely true. I've been a bad student more times than I want to admit, with teachers on all sides of the spectrum of horrible to great. But one thing everyone should work on, is righteously-respectable-integrity that honors in every situation.

Then there is the aspect of people not feeling respected at work.

Well, are you doing anything to warrant more respect or more responsibility?
Respect is not taken, it's earned through consistently living with integrity filled greatness, and shows respect to others.

Even when someone does not show respect back, eventually it will be shown. And if you show respectable integrity to some, but still show disrespect to others; what are people more likely to remember about you? The respect you projected, or the disrespect you have shown.

What are you more likely to remember? Someone who cut you off in traffic without using any kind of turn signal, or someone who slowed down to let you into their lane.

I discovered the below using my sliding door of wisdom, using simple patterns from basic scientific academic and engineering knowledge, to translate the interworking's of the mind:

*We all tend to remember the perceived bad things/obstacles that happen, because anger/stress/anxiety is caused by a fight or flight response in our brain that releases adrenaline. Adrenaline then causes a rise in blood pressure. Which causes the brain to function faster due to an increase in oxygen to the brain. Meaning, our **pattern** impulse of memories become more imprint-able, thus more memorable and relatively easy to access. But due to the increase in in activity, the part of our brain that relates patterns is being pushed harder than most individuals can determine. Which is why as the pattern is built in our brains from the memory, our brain tends to fill in the gaps of what happened. Meaning, when angry or stressed, the memory does not line up to the actual event unless your quick breathing from your adrenaline is under control.*

<u>How to break this pattern</u>:

Most people quick to anger or anxiety more than likely have a portion of the brain that causes anger to function faster, and process mental patterns quicker than most. So, one way to focus the mental pattern is to learn to breath or focus understanding. One way to learn to control this function of patterns in conjunction with adrenaline, is to work out or develop a patience tool to get better at. Working out forces breathing to be controlled while adrenaline is released. A type of honorable/respectable patience tool is to setup a timer, and when the timer goes off you can partake in the respectable/honorable thing you want. In both patterns for growth someone can become greater for the benefit of their overall life.
<u>*Example of a patience tool*</u>*: A timer is an obstacle that creates stress or anxiety in the mind for increased adrenaline, then brain activity. So this pattern of understanding focus in the mind for patience through the obstacle, goes straight to the "sliding door" of wisdom for many aspects of life.*

I understand sometimes we tend to project emotion based on the situation or what we are around. Then I also understand, some people, "don't know any better". And for them I pray they meet someone whom they respect, that shows them how to correctly show respect/integrity to another, regardless of the situation.

Yet, even without someone to look up to, there is no reason not to display respect/integrity of how you would like it to be shown to you, regardless of emotional investment. The unfortunate thing is, sometimes people decide not to show respect/integrity even if they had someone display to them how to correctly perform the action unto another person. (In regard to that aspect, please see the story about the girl from the broken home again.)

Respect/Integrity:

I decided to keep this section short and to the point, mainly due to the fact it can be very closely related to showing honor/true love. Yet, there is no excuse for someone not to show respectable integrity to another person. Everyone respects someone else in some way, and those who listen or follow people who describe respect/integrity as someone else agreeing with every opinion you have, is a liar unto their own lives.

<u>I have always kept this story in mind, even when someone makes the excuse it was the environment they grew up in:</u>

There was once a nation that went through a coo to overthrow the royal family. The palace was taken, and those who opposed the royal family had won. The winning side decided to make a public spectacle of the family, beheading the king, queen, and anyone associated with them. The only person and member of the royal family spared, was the prince, who was a baby at the time.

Instead of performing the same act upon the royal baby; to further make a spectacle of the royal family, the winning side devised a plan to make an example of the young prince, so the royal blood line would forever be deemed tainted. The plan they came up with was to give him to the most vile, disrespectful person in the city in the hopes it would corrupt the prince. Thus, they gave the baby to a prostitute that broke families a part when given the chance, stole, and slandered others at every opportunity.

Even before the prince came of age to cognitively understand, he was told everyday how much he didn't matter by his "caretaker". When he did cognitively understand, he was told everyday how his parents were publicly shamed and beheaded for who they were. Furthermore, every day the "caretaker" lived the example of how not to act.

Yet still the young prince would continue to show respect and integrity towards the vile person and those around him. He did all the chores the "caretaker" intentionally created for him to do, and as the young prince walked down the streets, the vile person incited mockery by others becoming a spectacle for everyone to partake in. But he ignored it and continued to respect/honor everyone.

One day, the corrupt government that was put into place eventually heard rumors of the young prince not wanting to follow or obey the disrespectful acts of the vile person. Thus, not becoming what was displayed every day. So, they talked to the "caretaker" of the prince, asking what was going on and why would he not adhere to the environment he was in? But the "caretaker" had no reasonable response, other than she was doing her best, and eventually the young prince would succumb.

After this encounter, the vile "caretaker" became even more determined to get the boy to change. Which led to more terrible things done to the child on behalf of this terrible venture. Yet, still the young prince would not crack, and ultimately become the embodiment of what everyone else saw him as.

One day in the market, the "caretaker" told the young prince to steal an apple, but the boy refused. Finally fed up, the "caretaker" made a scene yelling at the young prince pleading for him to steal and began to beat him, causing the people around to take notice of the situation.

Suddenly, in a frantic cry, the "caretaker" said, "Why won't you steal the apple?! Why do you not listen when I tell you to do these things?! Why will you not adhere to what I'm trying to show you?!"

The young boy with tears in his eyes from being beaten, mustered up all the courage he had, raised his head in confidence, and calmly said, **"It's because…I was meant to be a king…"**.

Anyone can claim to be a "king" or "queen". But the level of respect, integrity, honor, and righteousness you show, determines how much respect you truly deserve and if you befit the title you claim to have.

<u>For today's constantly offended world:</u>

<u>**The best way to not be offended by anything, is to show respect/integrity to everyone. That being said, you can't gain respect/integrity from others if you do not first apply them to yourself.**</u>

Chapter 2 Conclusion

I know you just learned a lot about patterns you do and don't practice. But this process isn't done yet. You're merely just learning about your potential. I want the very best for you. If you use what is in this chapter, heed the stories I presented, and work to apply greatness patterns using the **baby steps**; I believe you can grow in ways you've never dreamed of.

That being known, just because you have the ability to read a book doesn't mean life is going to be easy once you implement these new patterns into your mentality. At first it might seem hard as you will break habits, and you might even have to slowly phase people you thought wanted the best for you out of your life.

Then you will have certain people who say, just living life is hard, but here's a little-known fact…it's really not. If you fight through the struggle and learn to use the details, to adapt, persist using determination, have discipline through accountability, show love through honor, have the right balance of humbleness/swagger, and respect/honor everyone (including yourself) you'll reach great heights.

Comprehending all those things, knowing how they work in conjunction, and understanding which ones you might need to grow in, is what can make life hard.

Having the knowledge of what it takes to be greater is amazing, but you need to cultivate your latent talent. It will not take a week, a month, or 4 months. Heck, maybe not even a year depending on how hard you work. So never stop growing.

As for some of you. Barely winning should not be a reason to stop cultivating your latent talent, because winning is something that you learn to consistently do over time, through a consistent pattern-allistic mentality for growth.

These upcoming chapters are filled with even more wisdom that I believe will elevate your thinking even higher, as they reveal more about you and this world.

<u>REMEMBER WHERE YOU CAME FROM, BUT ALWAYS LOOK AHEAD TO WHERE YOU WANT TO GO!!</u>
<u>*Equanimity is achievable while using a growth mindset, but it starts with baby steps first!!*</u>

You cannot pave a highway to subconsciously do something, without first putting in the effort to attain the knowledge of your pattern-allistic mentality in your mind, heart, and spirit to lay the foundation, or change the patterns needed for whole body growth.

**In an ever-changing world, I challenge you to look up that word above. I did not know about it until right before this book went into print. Yet, after hearing the definition, it describes the same verbiage my grandfather used in a letter to me he wrote 40 years ago that I found after I finished typing this book. So naturally, I put things on hold until I found a way to fit the word in.

The word, <u>equanimity</u>, is exactly how the top-level works for a certain pattern-allsitic process practiced by anyone from that previous section. It pours into all the sections, and all the others in turn, pour back into it.

Do you remember what section that was? (Here's a hint: H/S, the deep ends of each side are fear or paranoia/pride.)**

BABY STEPS ARE KEY

No one is perfect. All of us have failed or are weak in one, or all the sections in chapter two. I know I personally have not reached my potential and believe I can still be better in all of them.

What sections do you believe you need improvement in?

You can do anything you set your mind to. I believe in your ability to achieve greater things. How do you plan on growing after you read this book? What will be small patterns that turn into strides?

Why **True** Champions

Part 2

What to expect on/in…

-…your path to greatness.

-…the world along your path to greatness.

…and why/how to be greater in all pattern aspects.

CHAPTER 3: Respect the Failure

<u>You see it in the gym, school, jobs, and anywhere in life……FAILURE</u>

- People lift weights to <u>failure</u>.

- Students do their best to learn from what they <u>fail</u> at within a certain subject.

- Coaches and teachers at all levels do their best (or should) to push players and students, to the points at which some will <u>fail</u>, then point out said failures in the hopes of making that person greater while working with them.

- On the job, if someone does not have success and <u>fails</u>; wisdom must be given to attempt correction.

Failure is something that happens to everyone. After the first draft and editing this book, I failed MANY times over in the grammar portion alone. I'm also humble enough to admit I failed more times than I can count in life, because I'm not perfect and I respect the fact that no one is.

That being known, learning from failure is definitely an acquired taste, because no one wants to fail. Let alone admit they did, but once you understand how you failed; you just figured out how to grow, and potentially become greater than you were before you failed. So, a direct outcome of those who learn to apply knowledge from failure will grow in wisdom. Which is why most people regard the elderly as being wise, because they have had more chances to fail and learn from it.

Now, does being elderly and wise always correlate? No. There are plenty of people of all ages who might think they are wise, but did not learn to respect failure, and thus keep doing things that caused them to fail in the first place (see definition of insanity).

The sad part is, some if not a good portion of people, are too prideful to humble themselves in the circumstance(s) they or someone else, failed or succeeded in, to gain wisdom.

Can I wholeheartedly say there are situations in which people are set up, or they set themselves for failure in? Yes. But even in those situations, those people did not have the wherewithal to realize it was a failing situation, because they had not yet acquired the wisdom or understanding necessary. So, these next sections will lend a helping hand into SOME of the various ways failure can happen.

You understand me by now. I'm might step on some of your toes, but I come from a place of true friendship, and true love.

I want the very best for you in a society that consistently tells you, you are always right, and there is no reason to think otherwise. When in fact, we all have problems. So instead of lashing out at others for what they do not think…

…why not show through respect, reflective history, and your individual great life, the reasoning why change should occur. Respect is not taken; it's earned through the reflective light of the heart you show to the world.

RELATIONSHIPS
Romantic

Let's start with the divorce rate. (I know I'm diving right towards the root of many problems in households today.)

Nowadays, stats show there is a 50% chance of a married couple getting divorced. Thus, depending on who you ask, that person will tell you whether or not it is a good idea to seek marriage.

But if you ask those people who say those things, what happened in their previous relationships, they'll more than likely go into some deep long story explaining the reason why THEY have those opinions (pattern-allistic mentality). Yet, if you ever had the opportunity to ask the other party their portion of the story, they will probably say it was the other person that caused the relationship to fall apart.

So, at the end of the day, after hearing both sides, each party might blame the other, and neither will more than likely ever admit any kind of ownership in the chain of events that led up to the break. Thus, disregarding shared the blame that occurs.

Then there are those relationships that fall apart in which someone decides to have a pity party for themselves (myself included). They blame themselves for everything that happened and would do anything to get someone back. Without the realization that everything happens for a reason, and the situation is an opportunity to grow your whole body (mentally & physically).

Neither in either scenario had the ability to respect the failure and grow from the situation yet. And even after recovery, those people add patterns into their mentality that could be detrimental to their overall growth in all relationships in the future.

Respecting failure means, you take an in depth look as to why you failed. Now, is it hard to do after getting out of a romantic relationship? <u>OF COURSE</u>!!

No one wants to be at fault when looking back as to why their relationship went south. But the truth of the matter is, even in relationships that went bad, there are pattern mindsets and events, that led up to the final split.

A failure to learn to respect failure is hard to understand afterwards. Which makes those same parties subject to the same failure over and over again, due to a lack of gaining wisdom within the situation. (see the definition of insanity)

There is always some percentage of blame that occurs for both parties. No relationship that has ever ended can 100% be one sides fault, and in any form of relationship you cannot expect perfection all the time from someone who is like you…<u>human</u>.

When in a true loving relationship, both parties should/will work together to become greater in a way that honors the other first. From there, there will need to be a deeper understanding of pattern-allistic mentality. In the form of understanding patterns of each other, that may or may not need to change, for sake of benefiting the two parties into becoming one, that is more conducive for a deeper overall relationship.

Take for instance, when I was in college. (I did not yet attain the wisdom I have after the situation.) I knew the person had cheated on multiple people in the 2 years they had been in school. But I like all the others, thought I could be the one to change that pattern. Yet, one day I was surprised when I caught said person in another person's room the morning after a party. (PEOPLE DO HAVE THE ABILITY TO CHANGE FROM BAD TO GOOD, BUT IT REQUIRES A CHANGE OF PATTERNS IN THEIR LIFE FIRST).

Was what happened in any way my fault?
On the surface, no.

…But did I share the blame for what happened?
Yes. There were points in the relationship where we both could've been better.

...At the time did I think I failed in any way?
No, but the truth is, I failed myself.
I had to learn to respect my failure in order to grow from it.

Do I regret going through with the relationship?
No, I needed that experience in failure to help me grow in ways I had no idea I needed growth in.

Too many people nowadays try to save people through romantic relationships pre-marriage. Then by the time they realize they settled for someone, most of the time it's too late. In their mentality they've already put up with that individual for so long, they feel a sort of obligation to that person, and ultimately get married.

I'm not saying it's not possible for someone to change via a relationship. But it is extremely difficult to navigate, and most of the time the relationship will never be a healthy one.

The only way to see significant lasting change in a romantic relationship is through a mutual decision of pattern-allistic mentality shift of one, or both parties. In conjunction with the mindset through commitment, that even if one party decides to display consistent greatness through true love (see my definition in chapter 2) regardless of if their significant other's patterns change immediately. <u>You both will work to become greater for the sake of the other</u> (Fight through tough times).
<u>***Either way, time must be allowed and intentionally committed to build for each other.***</u>

When it comes to the complexity of mentality in all forms of romantic relationships (not just married ones), it requires both parties to come to an understanding of what must be done, in order to define a solution, so each party can work on the execution of the greatness plan.
<u>If no understanding is defined and no effort through action is put into a relationship in any capacity, it is doomed to fail.</u>

<u>If your relationship ends abruptly here is what not to do:</u>

Do not go out and look for some person to have a one-night fling with. (I CANNOT STRESS THAT ENOUGH.) You will not learn how to properly respect or heal from failure by doing that.

The only thing it will do is give you a false confidence in yourself. Then one day a few weeks later you'll wake up, the person you miss will still heavily be on your mind, and you might end up blaming yourself for everything that happened (if you already haven't).

<u>Here's why:</u>

You didn't allow yourself a healthy amount of time to reflect on situations or circumstances to discern what happened, and where you both failed.

I don't care what your friends say. Having a fling does nothing for you. All it does is confirm you seek validation from someone else, instead of learning to have validation from understanding how you see yourself. Thus, ultimately are not mentally ready for a next level relationship.

<u>Now for those in all walks of life within the realm of romantic relationships</u>

<u>For currently single people:</u>

True love for another is not, never displaying emotion. But instead, knowing when or when not to apply emotion in an honorable/respectable way, in accordance to truly righteous actions.

It's okay and healthy to want to love, but you are not meant to be someone's crutch. One thing everyone needs to learn is on the sprint up the mountain called, Life. You will find that person who will truly love you as you truly love yourself. So do not give up on the world just because others tell you to do so.

Do not seek others validation, but instead grow to become something greater in <u>EVERY</u> aspect of <u>YOUR</u> life and concede periods of time for a <u>short</u> mental break to allow the whole body to grow.

Focus and level up yourself to prove in your mind you are worthy of your own time, before deciding to be destined for someone else's. <u>Understand that no one is perfect, and that includes yourself.</u>

<u>Here is something I want you to look up when you get the chance, and meditate on it to discover what it means to you (remember putting in effort shows you want to make something happen, and it starts with **baby steps**)</u>:

<u>1st Corinthians 13:4-8</u>

<u>If you are not married but dating (still for single people):</u>

True love for another is not, never displaying emotion, but instead knowing when or when not to apply emotion in an honorable/respectable way, in accordance to truly righteous actions.

We as individuals take our single-minded pattern-allistic mentality for an individual, then try to translate it to spending the rest of your life together.

We set ourselves up for failure, by thinking someone's life should revolve around our own. So, in order to combat the problem, the worldly opinion has created the thinking we should live together while dating; without understanding <u>what</u> subconscious mentality is being formed regarding that decision. (c'mon, you already read it)

In living together while dating, both parties pre-commit to someone they <u>know</u> they can put up with, without knowing whether or not the other truly loves themselves, let alone are ready to truly love someone else.

<u>…That being known, you know what someone who truly loves you will do?</u>
Someone who truly loves you, will show it by pursuing you without having to constantly be told, or reminded to do so. They will also not put themselves in promiscuous situations that could compromise the compliments you (should) tell them they are.

WARNING!! AWKWARD TOPIC

Do you think that having casual sex has no effect on you? Think again, "living my best life" and casual sex for either gender, hurts your ability to connect with someone, and numbs the ability to sense a true connection with another person.

Imagine trying to talk to the best guy or girl you've ever met in your life. You can see yourself with that person, so both of you start talking, then dating, and things get serious. One day, one of your old casual flings sees you and tries to flirt like old times. But you ignore the advance without addressing it and continue to converse with them after your current significant other takes notice. What do you think is going through the person you are dating's mind?

Let's play a game of real life called, "I wonder what they're thinking?". Is it:

A. "I trust him/her fully"

B. "What is going on here?!"

C. "Is he/she cheating on me?"

D. "He/she would never cheat on me."

E. "He/she would never do anything like that to me……..would he/she?"

The correct answer is…ALL OF THOSE THINGS AND MOOOORE!!! ☺

So, without you realizing it, your past just put stress on your present, and could seriously just affected your future. That being known, it is natural, and in some ways healthy for your significant other to be a little jealous of an interaction like this. But these situations require clarification. You simply can't say, "She's/He's only a friend." If there were relations in the past, it needs to be addressed.

This is one way to show you truly care for the other person you are choosing to do life with.

It might be awkward at first, but when in a dating romantic relationship, you can't be secretive or selfish, with these types of things. Because everything will eventually come into the light as you learn to appreciate the quirks each of you have. Now this doesn't mean address it all at once overwhelming said other person. But when situations do arise the communication needs to be clear, and boundaries of some degree need to be talked about.

Understand that no is perfect and that includes yourself. Yet, the amount of respect you show for yourself, is a mirror reflection the respect for you're capable of showing someone else. So, if you're looking for a significant other, then it starts with the respect and true love you practice in the patterns of your life.

Communication is key!!

<u>If you are married (still for dating or single people):</u>

I know, I know…every marriage is <u>perfect</u>. (heavy, heavy sarcasm LOL)

True love for another is not, never displaying emotion, but instead knowing when or when not to apply emotion in an honorable/respectable way, in accordance to truly righteous actions.

But one thing I don't understand, is why people <u>make</u> marriage so hard. It is simply two people doing life, and all you have to do is spend time together. So here is where I believe the problem lies though….

…we take our single-minded pattern-allistic mentality for an individual, then try to translate it to spending the rest of your life together. But fail to understand what it means to overlap those two pattern-allistic mentalities and intertwine them.

Wait…that first sentence seems familiar? Ahhh, because it is just as applicable in marriage as in dating. So now that you are married, the next level up is intentionally celebrating each other!! Encourage greatness and validate it in yourself first, before encouraging or expecting your spouse to follow suit.

Are you married? "<u>Yes</u>". So why did you stop taking each other on dates and celebrating each other as if you stopped dating?

*Terrible excuse number 1: "**Kids**." Hmmm…understandable from a time standpoint. But why did you let kids keep you from doing the simple things like a movie night together, set aside a day a week, or every two weeks for a date night (if you can find someone to trust to watch the kid(s))?*

*Terrible excuse number 2: "**Job schedule**." Weird, while dating, I'm quite sure each of you found a way to spend time with each other regardless of time schedule.*

*Terrible excuse number 3: "**Money**." This was never a marriage problem, because it started in each or one of your own pattern-allistic mentalities, prior to marriage. Now it's time to be responsible adults. Sit down with a pen and paper, then talk through the questions: Where every dollar is going, and why? Does it make real world sense to spend money on those certain things?*

I understand the 5 love languages and you should too. Although I am no expert in love language, I understand every human is different in how they operate. So I highly encourage you to show effort by studying sources, and talk to each other, so you can incorporate it in your intertwined pattern-allistic mentality for an even deeper and fuller relationship.

Allow time to get away from the real world and do the simple things together. Put down your phone(s), stop judging yourself by what you don't have, and instead, sit-down conversing with love complimenting what you do have.

One more thing for married people (still for dating or single people):

If you were/are in a relationship you need to be aware of what I call, "The Hidden Pattern".

It is something most couples are not aware of, because it happens so abruptly. Everything is going great, then one day a fight ensues over a small change in your individual pattern driven daily lives.

Nothingness doesn't change how you mentally perceive life with someone, unless there was a sudden interruption of patterns. So, you need to sit down and talk about a possible "hidden pattern", discussing ways with your spouse that can be beneficial to the new pattern that should be set in place.

We are very pattern driven beings to the core, and once you perceive a good pattern, we as individuals do not want to stray too far off said pattern we know. But in order to grow in a relationship as life happens, you must always be prepared to talk about anything and everything, with your spouse for the betterment of each other. Otherwise, things will begin to gradually get worse until one day the boiling point is hit. And from there, who knows what can happen.

Do not be afraid to step up and be the first to talk to your spouse about the perceived areas of stagnation that lead to frustration, before the boiling point is reached, because ignoring frustration only leads to the mentally worse beyond.
Understand that no one is perfect and that includes yourself, so do not be afraid to respectfully <u>apologize first</u>.

<u>**Women**</u>**,** *truly love yourselves and your husband. This world (especially in America) is now constantly trying to prove men are insignificant. Which has caused the great patterns of chivalry and respect of men to women, to slowly disappear. Truly listen to his patterns to understand how to best love and make his life a little easier, without requiring anything in return all the time.*

<u>**Men**</u>**,** *truly love yourselves and your wife. Compliment and shower her with gifts, because God created women to compliment what men are not good at. He who finds a good wife, means you have found favor on your life. Truly listen to her patterns to understand how to best love and make her life a little easier, without requiring anything in return all the time.*

Truly loving yourself and your spouse when in a romantic relationship to work together to become something greater, is quickly approaching an extinct art, because of the belief that there is no need for growth patterns as an individual or couple.

<u>Communication is key!!</u>

Ohhh yaaaaaa!!! I don't have to be in the room to know you could be feeling the pressure after that section. Wisdom can be gained in several ways. You can choose the easy way by listening (reading in this case) to someone who has been there, done that, or take your chances with the hard way. I just hope and pray it doesn't affect your future too much if you decide to not adhere.

I WANT you to respect the failure I had to go through and seen others fight through, by gaining wisdom using the details to apply to your own pattern-allistic mentality.

So here is something this world will tell you that is only partially true, and is something some of you need to get through your head right now:

Anytime someone says a relationship is 50/50. <u>*Stop taking it at face value.*</u>
DO YOU REALLY EXPECT TO SUCCEED WHEN YOU YOURSELF ARE ALREADY GOING IN WITH THE MENTALITY OF DOING ANYTHING AT 50%?

Don't get me wrong. I know those who say 50/50 (hopefully) mean, "Be yourself 100% of the time, but the other person should put effort into the relationship too." But once again, the problem is most people hear that saying of 50/50 and abuse it.

People don't bring their best because they heard the face value of 50/50 and put it into their pattern-allistic mentality. Which leads to having some relationships be 100/50, so the other becomes a parasite to their significant other. Thus, bringing down the average of what could be great, to 75%.

That being known, there are some relationships you need to continue to go 100% through truly loving/honoring in the best way possible such as your parents, siblings, wife, husband, kids, family, close friends, and those in your inner circle. Other than those people, you aren't obligated to anyone. But you are obligated to continue to truly love/honor yourself while continuing to respect everyone, no matter if they hurt you or not. Being petty or holding onto jealousy only hurts yourself in the end.

Do not let the best parts of yourself go, but instead workout what needs help to become greater by…

…understanding that no is perfect, and that includes yourself. So, when in a romantic relationship, never be afraid to apologize first with respect to one another.

<u>*Communication is key!!*</u>

Non-romantic Relationships

Do you think having casual sex has no effect on you? Think again. "Living my best life", and casual sex for either gender, hurts your ability to connect with someone, and numbs the ability to sense a true connection with another person. (Ahhh yes. This saves me from more typing because it still applies. The good ole, "I don't have feelings for this person, but we did use to…", situation.)

Let's take an in depth look at who you are really hanging around. What are your friends like? How do you all mainly spend your time together?
Whether you want to believe it or not, you are a combination of the people you spend the most time with (because patterns build on patterns). So, it's important to evaluate from time to time, if the people around you truly want the best for you.

Take myself for example. I was not initially raised in the best of neighborhoods. So, as I grew up, I developed relationships with various people I shouldn't have been hanging around. I did not do anything too nefarious. But when I was in other environments, the people around me could tell the type of person I was projecting, based on the collective personalities I spent the most time around, because I subconsciously added portions of their pattern-allistic mentality.

Thankfully, I never really grew too attached to people who did sketchy things. And one aspect that definitely contributed to me not becoming too involved with sketchy at best people in school, were the many sports I played (extra-curricular activities are perfect for mitigating an idle mind).

One such "friend" in high school had been involved with so many DUI's there were warrants out for their arrest even as an underage individual. Many times, this person offered to drive me places. But had we been pulled over, I could've easily been guilty by association or lumped into a problem I did not want to find myself in (Yes, that is a thing. So once again, be wise about who you hang around).

Later I found out, said "friend" (whom I had given many chances) was doing things that would land them in the penitentiary and asked if one of my other friends if they could help. Thankfully, they said no, but from that point on,

I decided it was best not to be around that person in any capacity, other than texting them to see how they were doing as to be someone they go could go to for advice.

I did not leave this person completely in the dark, because of the connection we did have growing up together. But I did have to make the tough decision that was best in the moment, knowing some people are not meant to be in your future.

Understand that no is perfect, and that includes yourself.

Communication is key!!

I just gave you one of many examples from my life everyone agrees is obvious, but you wouldn't believe how many people would still hang around someone like that (Are you?). If I had been caught with that person and possibly had something on my record, it could've ruined my chances at potentially having the greatest life I could achieve.

My point is, even if it's going out drinking and partying all the time to, "Live my best life!!", there are always repercussions that can more than likely hinder the future you, <u>when</u> life happens.

Do you think partying could have no effect on you?
Set aside <u>when</u> life happens. See how much money you spend in one night and translate that into one year.

I'm not saying to not relax occasionally, but there are ways to have fun without getting drunk. So, you need to constantly evaluate yourself and the people you hang around, to determine if everyone around you is on a resemblance of a path to become something greater in all aspects of life, in conjunction with how they treat other people.

Potentially having bad friends or bad people in your life is a given. But not recognizing someone or a group of individuals are not beneficial to your

future, is a lack of respecting the failure that will lead to future heartache when life happens.

THIS DOES NOT MEAN TO DROP PEOPLE LIKE ROCKS AT A SMALL SIGN OF TROULBE. INSTEAD, TAKE HEED OF CERTAIN PATTERNS, AND HOW YOU ACT AROUND THEM. THEN, STAY TRUE TO YOURSELF IN A WAY THAT WILL HONOR, TRULY LOVE, AND RESPECT YOURSELF IN LOOKING TO BECOME GREATER THAN WHAT YOU CURRENTLY ARE.

Understand that no is perfect, and that includes yourself.

Communication is key!!

This world has made it the norm to see honorable kindness is as weakness and turned it into an action of imposing on another. Meaning, people who would show honorable kindness stopped, because they know the world will look down upon them in a certain manner. As a result, people have begun to believe in the statement of, "What is the point of being this way?". Which has led to individuals becoming a society that would rather hurt, than be hurt.

Let's break this by learning to individually, constantly, be honorably great, regardless of what the world thinks.

*A **true woman** will consistently respect herself to not be a "walk around" (constant casual sex, or validate themselves through attention of others), show compassion, kindness, respect others, do what she can to help others around her, respect for herself in the light she puts herself in, and leads herself/others in honorable ways.*

*A **true man** will consistently respect himself to not be a "walk around" (constant casual sex, or validate themselves through attention of others), show mercy, kindness, respect others, be a leader unto himself, respect for himself in the light he puts himself in, and do what he can to help/lead others around him in honorable ways.*

<u>This past year(s) in quarantine proved one major thing to the world (2019-2021):</u>

<u>Everyone was shown how close or disconnected we are, with the people we do life with.</u>

Individuals were pushed to their boiling points either with, too much time spent with specific people in one area or the craving of wanting to do life with others in some way. That being known, either boiling point taught everyone a balance of relationships, are a necessary in life, and if taken away, we will adapt to have relationship (example: virtual meetings, virtual face to face contact, etc.).

Without relationship in some way, we as a relationship driven species will become very restless, because we cannot function properly without them.

*The problem this need presents in the relationship between the subconscious in an individual, and manipulators on all levels in **<u>any</u>** type of relationship, is now made apparent in the world of patterns (pointing out blatant hypocrisists). As this <u>taking away of relationship</u> can be used as a **manipulation** tactic in order to get a person, group, or nation of individuals <u>to perform in certain ways</u>.*

Do this sound familiar?

<u>One last thing that needs to be addressed:</u>

Do you think you're honoring/truly loving yourself by constantly hurting people you care about? If you abuse them constantly, whether verbally or physically, all you are doing is embarrassing and displaying an insecurity in yourself, and this needs to be addressed.

For those of you that are going through this situation. Do not give up on this person but seek help where needed, as it all starts with showing true love/honor to them, by sitting down and having an adult conversation about what is going on.

<u>For men:</u>

- Women/people in general do not wake up and decide to hurt you.

- No woman acts like a B**** unless provoked. (If they do have a certain vibe like this towards people and is someone you hang around constantly. A respectable/integrity/honorable/truly loving sit-down talk needs to happen.)

- Laying hands on a woman is not manly at all. All you've done is prove how much of a child you are (And if it were up to me, a group of respectful men should beat you for crossing a line that should never be crossed in everyday life.)

- Be a man, not a boy, and then act like it. Take charge of your greatness patterns, have respect for your body, and take pride in being presentable.

- How do you expect to be treated with respect by a woman if you cannot even treat yourself with respect?

- Constantly putting someone down will never lead to anything great, and only shows your own insecurities. Do not live in the past of what someone says or does to you.

- Learn how to do things that show true love to yourself, then show it through self-virtue as it will be translated into your other types of relationships.

- Stringing out potential romantic relationships like a carrot on a stick does not show honor to yourself or others.

- Emotionally cheating on someone is the first step in giving up on yourself and your relationship.

- Other individuals have their own pattern-allistic mentality and opinions. Now granted, some are completely wrong for overall pattern growth, but that doesn't mean completely ignore the fact that everyone should be subject to a disrespectful showing of your opinion. (Allow for human inadequacy.)

For women:

- Men/people do not wake up and decide to hurt you.

- Be a woman, not a girl, and then act like it. Take charge of your greatness patterns, have respect for body, and don't expose yourself to everyone (no respect for yourself). You're showing why you shouldn't attract a great man.

- Learn how to do things that show true love to yourself, then show it through self-virtue. It will be translated into your other relationships.

- Constantly putting someone down will never lead to anything great, and only shows your own insecurities. Do not live in the past of what someone says or does to you.

- Stop with the belief that men are impeding on your power (especially in America). This is just another tactic the world uses to control you.

    o Chivalry is disappearing due to a range of factors, but that doesn't mean it's non-existent. Yet, you must allow men to be chivalrous through recognition and be complimentary when it happens.

- Stop believing into the hypocrisy the exposing yourself to many people is powerful. This is the opposite of what self-empowerment is and by doing so, you turn yourself into an object, not a person.

- Do not hit men, otherwise the statement I put in the men's column can become harder to control.

- Emotionally cheating on someone is the first step in giving up on yourself and your relationship.

- Stringing out potential romantic relationships like a carrot on a stick does not show honor to yourself or others.

- No man acts like an A**hole unless provoked. (If they do have a certain vibe like this towards people and is someone you hang around constantly. A respectable/integrity/honorable/truly loving sit-down talk needs to happen.)

- Other individuals have their own pattern-allistic mentality, and opinions. Now granted some are completely wrong for overall pattern growth, but that doesn't mean completely ignore the fact that everyone should be subject to a disrespectful showing of your opinion. (Allow for human inadequacy)

Hardly anyone wakes up and decides, "Today I'm going to hurt someone". You are using a past experience pattern to apply to your current self, and ultimately project it on others. The <u>time</u> of life has moved on, and it's <u>time</u> for you to as well.

Understand that no one is perfect, and that includes yourself.

<u>*Stagnation leads to frustration, and the mentally beyond…*</u>
<u>*…but do not fret!! Fulfilling and validating happiness, is not something anyone else can provide. So, you must first validate it in yourself to see all of the joy life can bring!!*</u>

Why <u>True</u> Champions

BABY STEPS ARE KEY

I want you do to something very few people have ever done. (If you've done this and have already implemented it, might as well do it again for the pattern!!)

I want you to write down ways that both you and someone you were/are in relationship with have failed. Did both of you work it out? Did you/the other person really change their heart and ways? What life patterns work for you?

What are you looking for in a romantic partner? What do you look for in a friend? (Is it a yes person?)

What are you currently doing to show yourself that you deserve the person above? (Checkout the definitions of the individual, Fruits of the Spirit, to see if you truly deserve such a person. Your fruits and their fruits, are the best way to tell if you, yourself are or if you are dealing with, a man or an old boy, a woman or an old girl (maturity or lack thereof).)

If married, write down one normal/everyday pattern your spouse currently does for you, that you appreciate about them. Then, have them write down one everyday pattern about you; they appreciate you for.

If married, you both need to get together and ask what are some everyday patterns you can do for one another to greater love each other? (Write them below)

Why you should be afraid to fail

Now relax, I know what you might be thinking:

"How is he going to title a section like that when he tells us to respect failure, and in the previous sections wants us to push our self to become greater even though we might fail?"

Here is why I want you to be afraid of failure:

In the right healthy balance, inner fear is the greatest fuel for your spirit when preparing or placing new applications into your life, to become something greater.

Inner fear has become one of my greatest tools in achieving corporate success, success within my businesses, patterns for success within my mentality, and success with relationships in general. It has also lent a hand in academics, home life, everyday life, and everywhere in between.

So what is inner fear?

Inner fear is the pit in your stomach you feel when you aren't sure what is going to happen next after you know life might not go as planned. This "pit" that is driven by inner fear, directly corelates to how scared you are of the <u>unknown</u>. The fear of failure or lack thereof, may cause some individuals to: not spend time preparing, have a healthy mentality towards preparation thus finding a balance, or spend way too much time preparing resulting from paranoia. (Reread the section on chapter 2 humbleness/swagger and come back to pair it with this section if needed)

That being **known**, there are many unknowns in life, and everyone is a combination of these two types of people in every aspect of their pattern-allistic mentality:

Some fear the unknown ***success*** *they could achieve, so they find ways to not to* ***fail*** *into their success, thus driving down their life potential.*

Some fear they will ***fail*** *when not knowing all that can go wrong, and so they never take the step forward into the* ***success*** *they could achieve.*

Fear of the unknown is to be human, but it can hurt all aspects of your pattern-allistic mentality if you let it control you. So why let it drive you down? Why not use it as fuel to take that step forward?

<u>Do not take on the mentality of either person above who sees the unknown failure outweigh potential *success*. Because even if you do fail, failure sets you up to gain WISDOM for even more future *SUCCESS* if you will allow it.</u>

Nothing great is ever achieved in what you 100% for sure know what can happen.

If you learn to harness the feeling of failure and flip the script to make it a part of yourself as a type of motivational fuel tank; not only will you help yourself spiritually, but you will also be more-free mentally when challenges/mountains arise. Because they will seem like mere hills, and you're taking action to conquer them.

<u>I do not know what your fear is, but I can help you better prepare yourself mentally for the unknown:</u>

Never forget!! With anything that is honorable, righteous, and truly meant for you, an understanding of the situation must arise in yourself first. The question is……will you raise your greatness level to go above?

<u>Step 1</u>: Apply the chapter 1 and 2 sections to your life.

<u>Step 2</u>: (because you've already done step 1) Close your eyes and think about your future. Look at in a sense of success, and what you <u>will</u> accomplish.

<u>Step 3</u>: Next, think about the future in a dark sense. Think about it in terms of situations that can hinder your ability to accomplish what you want to achieve (no matter how small), and how they may affect your life.

Step 4: Put everything into perspective of the plan you have on a piece of paper. So, you have the greatest successes you can create on one side, then you have the failures on the other.

Step 5: Now think about what you must do to mentally prepare yourself for what will stand in your way. Create avenues and pivot points to get back on track or adapt. Then visualize yourself performing these pivots, and avenues even if all the pieces (people are not there yet).

Step 6: With your eyes closed, put everything together. Think about the good, the bad, and the points of adaptation. Then write down the good things that can come from the plan on paper, say it out loud back to yourself, and hang where you can see it daily.

Step 7: Mentally process using pivots, and avenues for how you can turn the failures into success on your walk of life.

Congratulations!!! After doing this, you just stretched your mind in such a way that you can eventually do it subconsciously or in the moment, if you practice enough!!! Step 8 is to take the next step forward into the now semi-known unknown!!

This process has the potential to be crazy effective if you allow it. In fact, I've been able to come up with an insane amount of business, and life growth plans using this method. And as any businessperson or life winner should definitely say:

Building a business or life of growth, is not easy. There are so many things that can go wrong, and it's impossible to plan for them all.

Which is true, you can't plan for everything. But using the method I showed you, has the potential to create a pattern of ascertaining roadblocks in any situation. In turn, it will give you the experience to subconsciously grow your ability to adapt to any situation quicker if you execute the plan within some resemblance of the pathway for success properly. But you must first discern what can be the most successful route first.

To make the above pattern more effective, you need to expand your pattern-allistic mentality to take more possible routes of choice from the infinite and add them to your finite choice pattern. The result being, your pattern-allistic mentality leveling up the patterns of thought in your mind, for all aspects you <u>choose</u> to be greater in.

The idea behind this method came from when a good family friend described how to create a pathway for success of a simple business plan. But I applied my own growth pattern to help speed up the subconscious mind to be used for all patterns, and applicable for almost any aspect of life.

<u>For example:</u>

I would go into a store (preferably a coffee shop) and close my eyes. Then open them, and the first thing that I saw I would plan on how I would make the object myself. For instance, take a wooden chair. How do you take a piece of wood, and turn it into a beautiful chair (growth)?

<u>Immediate needs for this successful pattern</u>

- What type of wood? Why that specific wood? Where are you going to get the wood?

- What machines or tools will you need?

- Will you be the only one making it? Are you going to hire someone?

- What kind of blueprint are you going to work from?

- How long does it take to make one chair?

- What kind of wood glue are you going to use? How are you going to keep the chair held together?

- What grade(s) of sandpaper will you be using?

- What skills do you have now? What do you need to learn?

- What platform will you use to sell what you make? How do you plan to distribute them?

- Are you going to use marketing to gain customers? What customers will you target?

- What money platform are you going to use to sell the chair? What are your price points?

- Who are you going to use to keep up with your finances? Will you do it? Do you need an accountant?

    - Taxes need to be handled

- What are you going to call your business? Will it be a LLC, Inc., etc? How do you claim your business under the state? What forms are needed? What classification does it fall under?

- Do you need permits? If so, which ones?

- What tax forms do you need? What is taxed in your business? What's expensed?

I believe I hit all of it, but I've never actually made and sold a wooden chair (unknown). So, I'm quite sure I missed something. Yet, if there is failure anywhere along the route and a question I can't answer. I know that all difficult questions are made of really simple unbiased questions, that come together to point to answer what was once difficult to obtain.

You should not fear the unknown, because the unknown will eventually become known, as you learn to optimize life's difficult questions, into

smaller/easier questions that point the arrow in the direction of the once difficult to find answer.

<u>Hint</u>: the arrow may not be pointing to something you want to know. But you can either live in ignorance of what must be done for personal growth, or come to an understanding within yourself, as something you must righteously/honorably grow through.

It is said that Einstein always asked questions, but he sought to answer those questions. In being afraid to fail, you will learn to ask questions and seek the answers. Then once you learn to use this practice of correctly discerning the correct questions that need answering for yourself, I believe you will notice a change in the way you perceive everything.

You will gain more confidence in not fearing the failure of the unknown, and instead, will use the fear of failure to drive you to take that step into the known-unknown as you begin to grow yourself as a whole (mentally and physically).

The most amazing part is you can apply this knowledge to any aspect in life too!! Not just business. Everything you do, imagine, and even life itself, has easy questions that can be answered that come from a hard broad question. Here's what this pattern can help you discover:

Knowledge and wisdom you want. School, relationship, or lack thereof guidance. Family problems (ex: What's causing this problem? How can we fix this?), starting a business, or other worldly problems. They all have some form of answer from an understanding that derives from righteous/honorable growth patterns.
The method I showed you can be applied everywhere, because it is a pattern that you can add to your "sliding door" of wisdom!!!

Where you get your guidance to answer questions is just as important as the answer itself. Because a biased question skews itself into a biased result. So you must first find the correct wording of the question to better understand the greatest answer.

Do the people around you truly have your best interest in mind? (Maybe?) Does media of any kind have non-biased answers to the questions you have? (Let's be honest. Not really) So it is on you to stop listening to the world's opinion, and instead adhere to wisdom of history, wisdom of those who truly love you, and then formulate it all to find the correct questions that direct the arrow, pointing to the once difficult answer.

This pattern-allistic mentality way of thinking has many benefits to your personal life, and as you get better at using it, you will become more adept in many (not all) roadblocks. Thus, increasing the ability/availability to move your "sliding door" of wisdom along the bar of potential life aspects.

<u>DO NOT FOCUS</u> ON USING THE METHOD I GAVE YOU IN THE EXAMPLE <u>ALL OF THE TIME AT FIRST,</u> BECAUSE USING IT IN GREAT AMOUNTS HAS THE CHANCE TO CREATE A VERY ANXIOUS WAY OF THINKING IF NOT CONTROLLED. ONLY PERFORM IT ONCE OR TWICE A MONTH TO START OFF WITH, THEN EXECUTE ON YOUR PLAN. AFTER ABOUT A YEAR YOU SHOULD BE ABLE TO PERFORM THE METHOD WITH EASE IN YOUR SUBCONSCIOUS ON COMMAND, IF <u>CONSISTENT TRAINING</u> IS PERFORMED. <u>ESPECIALLY AFTER YOU SEE RESULTS FOR A TRULY RIGHTEOUS CAUSE WITHIN YOURSELF TO BETTER SERVE YOU. THEN YOU CAN WORK ON BEST SERVING OTHERS HONORABLE AND RESPECTABLY.</u>

WHEN YOU GET TO CHAPTER 7, IT DESCRIBES A <u>GRAVITY</u> THAT CAN HAPPEN BY USING IT TOO FREQUENTLY AT FIRST. REMEMBER, THE BEAUTIFUL CITY OF ROME WASN'T BUILT IN A DAY

BABY STEPS ARE KEY

Come up with an inner fear(s) you have (everyone has one). Write it down, then write down easy questions that can be answered attributing to overcoming this fear (small pattern solutions).

Why you are going to fail in life

NEVER JUDGE A BOOK BY ITS COVER, or in this case. Never judge a section within a book by its title. What matters are the words between the covers, and the details within the facts you discover. (I'll leave you to find the hidden meaning behind the previous sentence. If you've stretched your mind as far as I know you have, then you should be able to come up with something rather quickly. Hint: Maybe something to do with wisdom?)

Now back to the roots of this section.

Failure is going to happen. I've failed so many times in my life, and in every aspect too. But what sets me a part now, is my ability to humbly admit it, and know how to learn from everything. Failing is just a part of life. It can hit you at the highest points and can attempt to knock you down even deeper than you thought you could go. That being known…

…IT'S NOT THE FAILURE THAT WILL DEFINE WHO YOU ARE. IT'S THE TYPE OF PERSON THAT COMES OUT ON THE OTHER SIDE. ARE YOU GOING TO GROW OR GO LOW?

If you let failure have a foothold in your life without doing something to adapt to break the spiral, failure will stay around, and you will see failure everywhere in your life. Which makes the failure mindset very hard to break out of. Unless you choose to adhere to someone who truly loves you, or something pattern-allistically changes within you that reignites the flame, so you individually choose to break it.

Perceived (tangibly real in our individual minds) stagnation leads to frustration, and the personal problematic beyond.

The main reason why we fail:

We are naturally prideful beings, and out of that pride we tend to want to present to those around us, we have power in some way. So, what do we do? We try to do things alone to show we don't need help, and it's not until we reach a point in our minds of dire need will we possibly choose to ask for it. Meaning, as long as we individually live in that pride of do things ourselves; believing we can wing certain aspects to get the desired results (expectations), we individually are doomed to fail.

Two heads are better than one, and more are even greater than that.
This is another reason why I believe playing <u>team</u> sports in some capacity is key for future success in life.
Team sports force you to learn you can't do something greater alone, you are not always the best at what you do, you are not going to always be involved in something successful, so you must stay consistent in greatness patterns to see change, and you are not the smartest person in any given place.

Not even the greatest sports superstars, scientists, or people of all time, could accomplish great feats without learning they were not the best at everything at any point over the course of their life. <u>They CHOSE to push themselves in all patterns into the beyond with the help of others.</u>

There are many things over the years I've had to admit I'm not, and will never be specialized in. But that doesn't mean there aren't people out there who can join me on my journey or help me learn.

In all walks of life, there are experts in every field to some capacity. So when trying to reach a level you want, you must first seek the knowledge patterns, or work ethic of someone in that realm. While remembering that not every pattern translates over into greatness for your personal pattern-allistically individual life. Also, it is important to remember the voice of blatant hypocrisy. As even in good intentions, this voice has the potential to skew your perception of the world around you.

With that warning and the knowledge of knowing you can't do it alone, here is more reassurance…

…keep this in mind:

When you watch or listen to any real-world successful person worth anything in life, they should/will be the first to say they couldn't have made it where they were without (person's/people name(s)).

It is extremely improbable, if not impossible, for someone to become successful in any field solely by themselves. I'll go as far to say, that the reassurance an individual is doing a great job or that they are on track, is given to them in the form of a compliment or criticism, of how to be greater from someone who specializes in a field the individual seeks to become greater in.

The compliment or truly loving criticism from an expert, should give the greatest confidence boost we individually potentially can feel, to go even further. Because it should provide a subtle fuel to the flame within. Furthermore, this "boost" has the potential to carry an individual to the next level, where they will inevitably look to receive another "boost" in some way (it is human to seek a boost in some way, so do not be afraid to respectfully/ honorably boost someone else first) to climb even higher.

No matter how small the action(s) we are involved in, or how often someone says they do not care what other people think. We all like to be told we are doing a great job. That being known, this is life, so obviously there is another side to every coin.

While we have those, who will tell us we are doing a great job. It's the negative opinions that tend to cling to us the deepest. Those negative opinions (whether factually true or not) stay in our minds and linger. The problem is, even when the opinion has finally left our mind, we tend to let it subconsciously control us, because WE as individuals have decided to keep the claws in our metaphorical skin.

For example: being told we can't do something, then taking that pattern to heart, and letting it control more patterns of life. **But how many times do people give words that should carry no weight, all the weight in the world? Answer: too many**

This clinging can lead the individual to eventually blame others or their internal self for the insecurities, and perceived pitfalls in what they can accomplish. So, to combat this, we as individuals have a tendency to adopt the notion, we are all justified in how we think (PRIDE). Which leads to a false justification of the way we are in any given headspace, or are perfectly fine, with being perfectly fine (comfortable).

This PRIDEFUL way of thinking stems from the fact that from a very early age we are told constantly there is nothing wrong with us the individual, and the world is the one with the problem. So those mindset inherited individuals, tend to develop a problem with constructive criticism regardless of who tells them. This mental PRIDE is the leading producer of problems with truly integrity/respectable leadership, because prideful individuals believe they should always be leading.

We are all mentally capable of achieving great feats. But we all need help or advice from someone to get to where we want to go, because (most importantly)... WE ARE ALL MADE PERFECTLY-IMPERFECT.

Regardless of the manner in which wisdom is gained, only you can decide to want to learn from the experience/criticism itself. Because listening to advice/gaining wisdom through experience, might not always be what we want to hear. <u>Nor is it always</u> represented by a situation we wanted to grow through. Yet, either will cause a pattern-allistic mentality change, that will be ingrained in our minds for any period of time, so we as individuals must learn to mentally be capable of accepting greatness patterns, in order to achieve lasting growth.

While some may hear wisdom filled constructive criticism, in a truly loving manner (advice) of how to be greater; a sense of pride might take hold, and some will say they can do it on their own without the advice, regardless of if they think it should be put into practice or not. Those types of people were the ones who thought it wasn't necessary to go to tutoring, ask someone for help, or even like to be told they are doing a task wrong. In fact, these types of people have a tendency to talk back to everyone who tries to provide constructive criticism/advice and have problems with authority.

That being known, everyone goes through this phase, as it is a part of human nature, and some stay in it longer than others. Which is mainly due to their parent's or parents of choice, not addressing the emotionality of mentality (H/S spectrum).

These types of individuals also tend to group together to mitigate or put down constructive criticism, out of fear that someone they consider a friend within the group, will begin down a pathway to become something greater. All in the hopes to keep the statement, "misery loves company", true. Thus, these groups will say constructive criticism is "infringing" upon them all.

This way of thinking towards constructive criticism, (growth through experiential wisdom) contradicts individuals who are truly great and mostly live outside of the hypocrisy in this world. Those who want to be great, are willing to live and learn under a righteous authority.

As a result, when the time is right (depending how much effort has been exerted to be greater) that person has the potential to step into patterns of authority to help others gain wisdom, and know what it takes to be real world great/ successful. Meaning, once pattern-allistic mentality for growth in life is established, an individual has the ability to spread the knowledge that it does not take millions in the bank, or an extreme number of social media following (others validation) to be considered a great or successful real-world person.

Words from one of the wisest people I've ever known. Words that I want to tell you in person but obviously I can't:

No matter what happens, I want the very best for you. Life goes on, and you will transcend your hearts desires......IF YOU will allow yourself to not let insecurities you have no control over hold you back, thus not allowing them to ultimately control your mentality.

By not adhering to constructive criticism, and honor/integrity led authority now, you are proving why you should not lead others, when the time comes.

BABY STEPS ARE KEY

What places do you believe you have failed in life?

What pattern mentality did you learn from it?

How can you work to be better, and transcend your previous self?

Why you shouldn't "care" what others think if you fail, and mentalities between the lines

As you learned, failure is going to happen. But what will others around you say/do if you fail? Heck, sometimes even before you fail, people are going to tell you, you can't do something. I've been told many times that I would amount to nothing. One time was told by a "good friend" of mine, how successful I wasn't going to be. Yet, if you ask anyone around me currently, they will say I'm doing pretty good for myself.

Voices and outside opinions are always going to be within ear shot, and they might even come from someone you truly love/honor. But do you know when a voice is a good one? Do you know when to listen or turn a deaf ear to it?

Everyone has had someone they've told dreams to in wondering what someone else thinks about said dream, only to have that someone present some form of doubt as to why the dream will fail.

After being presented with such a response; there are two pattern mindsets that person who heard those words will take on from adhering to doubt, and three pattern mindsets formed from adhering to criticism.

Before I move forward, I need to clarify these:

Critic – someone who gives an opinion through a voice of reason to provide an explanation as to why you MAY OR MAY NOT fail, but also can point out ways where you MAY OR MAY NOT succeed. **CAN ALSO BE YOURSELF IN YOUR OWN MIND/WORDS**

Doubter – someone who gives reasons why you WILL fail WITHOUT presenting honorable ways to succeed. These types of individuals have more than likely had bad experiences in the previous venture you are about to attempt, or do not want to see you rise above them in any number of ways. **CAN ALSO BE YOURSELF IN YOUR OWN MIND/WORDS**

Mindset's pattern-allistically developed from a **doubt** background (**Mostly recognized in the mentality of the economic poor, to lower middle class. But not always 100% discovered unless done through intention of patterns**):

Albatross – a mindset that develops after someone (or even themselves) point out a failure in the previous venture(s). Thus, leading to doubt in everything performed, which leads to a lack of self-confidence, and need for validation of others for a confidence FIX. This mindset will also learn to develop excuses as to why they cannot grow to greater heights and will always have a figurative weight in their mind that keeps them down. The result is this type of mindset tends to lean on others to lift the mental weight they hold, without doing anything to become stronger themselves. Most if not all albatross-based individuals will take differing opinions and constructive criticism, in an extremely negative light.

There is hope to reverse these types of mindsets through <u>baby step</u> patterns!!
But first they must GET USED TO THE FIGURATIVE WEIGHT:

They must apply the Owl and the Lion criticism mindsets mentioned below.

This transformation of the pattern-allistic <u>mindset</u> does require a significant cost of time. As it can only be changed by the individual themselves consistently building on their own pattern-allistic <u>mentality</u> through growth. Meaning, the individual uproots what was once programmed into themselves over time, coming to the realization, they do not want to constantly rely on others for validation and to hold up said person's figurative weight. (Roughly translated into learning how to stand, then walk, and ultimately sprint with their weight, as it is no longer a burden. Instead, the "weight" is now a reason to keep growing.)

Phoenix – one of, if not the strongest mindset someone can obtain. That being said, it is also the hardest mindset to <u>CORRECTLY</u> achieve, because it is the hardest to control and can easily turn into an Albatross, or Mustang if CONSTANT growth in some way is not maintained. A Phoenix will stop becoming a phoenix when they do not see themselves as a benefit to society/environment, or until they do not see themselves as having the ability to achieve great things any longer, because the doubt in their mind will have taken over. The Phoenix uses the doubt that is placed on them as fuel for the fire to continually shed its former self, while <u>APPLYING THE</u>

KNOWLEDGE/WISDOM it previously had or gained, from others to their next greater level achieved.

The Phoenix mindset is the rarest, as it does not put a limiter on what it wants/can achieve, because they constantly reflect on history and wisdom. Thus, creating a mastery of carrying the massive figurative weight of the Albatross. Naturally, their beautiful flames will gather a steady stream of people and experts which can help grow a paired Lion mindset with ease. So once correctly achieved, the only thing stopping a Phoenix's growth, are the constant influences of cumulative mentality from those they hang around, and time.

<u>There is one problem the Phoenix mindset has:</u>

If a Phoenix grows too much, too fast, and all without learning how to acquire/engage with someone of a higher healthy Owl mindset to help tame the flames produced, it will become an unstoppable force for the worst. Thus, leading to the possibility of burning everything around it, destroying the society/group it lives in, the friendships, or perhaps the people around it to try to continue becoming greater.

<u>Mindsets formed from a criticism-based background (**Mostly** recognized in the mindsets of those the middle economic class and beyond, but not always 100% discovered, unless done through intention of patterns):</u>

Mustang – though the mustang is a beautiful creature, they are known for their sprinting. These mindsets are developed after achieving minimal steps towards any one goal. Then allows pride to take over after achieving a small task. This type of mindset is the most prominent today, because no one likes to be criticized. So, they will run in herds like the actual mustang of the plains, to potentially put down criticism.

<u>Criticism background for growth</u>

It is not until the Mustang becomes tame; does it realize the small tasks they achieve are simply the bare **minimum**, before they work to achieve anything of great importance. This type of person will continuously roam with the herd believing it is significant, until someone sees/decides their raw potential is worth the strenuous effort of taming it. If the Mustang mindset learns to carry the figurative weight of the Albatross and has a greater healthy Owl mindset involved in their life, the Mustang has a great chance of becoming a Lion.

Owl – known for their wisdom. The Owl mindset learns from criticism to become great listeners and wisdom appliers. Which makes it the hardest mindset to mentally overcome when being infringed upon by another individual. They take criticism and set themselves up for future success, using the knowledge they've gathered to swiftly strike. Thus, eliminating barriers with little to no problem if they so choose.

<u>Criticism background for growth</u>

The drawback of the Owl mindset is they are so knowledgeable within themselves (unless done through intention of a lion or phoenix mindset), they will not achieve the ability to lead. Which is mainly due to the fact, they don't know how to put their intellect/wisdom into verbal words. So, most Owl mindsets will lack the ability or choose to not feel the weight of the Albatross, in order to learn how to gain strength to fly higher than their natural abilities will take them.

While this mindset might the hardest to break, it is also the hardest to alter, and achieve massive growth in, because relationship with others is the turbo charger to the engine of growth. But one way to help change this mindset for one of growth is to in-act a portion of the Mustang mindset, because it means temporarily joining a herd, so the person learns how to form a relationship with others more easily, while exposing them to the possibility of developing the Lion mindset. (I chose Owl because as animals, they are associated with the most wisdom/intellect of when to strike, are very territorial, and more solitary by nature in the wild.)

Lion – the Lions are leaders. They adhere to criticism using it as wisdom to reach greater levels, understand the weight of the Albatross, and how to walk then sprint with the mental weight at an early age (they cannot carry it as well as the Phoenix who soars with said weight). A Lion mindset also has the gift to naturally enable the Albatross ability of leaning on others to help left the figurative weight, so the pack as a whole can climb to greater heights. Meaning, the Lion mindset leads by example first, as a way to convince others to lead themselves.

Criticism background for growth

There are different levels of Lions/leaders, just as every pack has a hierarchy. Each individual Lion mindset indulges on the testing of their current strength against each other. Of these mindsets, the Lion becomes stronger at a faster rate. But like every lion in a pack, it can become old, essentially waiting until another younger, stronger lion reaches a level to challenge it. That being said, the Lion is the only one who can gather more people in its pack by the masses based on how much it has achieved, the charisma, and likability. The Lion (already knowing how to sprint from the closely related mindset of the mustang) will always find itself around others. So, if paired with an Owl, or develops an Owl mindset; the Lion will rise to the top ranks of any pack it finds itself in.

Everyone can potentially achieve great things. Some may stumble upon it, and others will work for it. These individual mindsets do not have 100% complete control within any one person, but instead, all share a percentage in a certain aspect of life within said individual.

For example:

Someone can be 40% Phoenix, 20% Mustang, 10% Owl, 10% Lion, and 20% Albatross when it comes to sports. While for academics, it can be less or more, balancing out any one of the mindsets. These percentages of mindsets do vary within everyone. But as you look back at your past and write down events, you'll be able to see what percentage takes precedence in each aspect of life currently, or in the past. The result being, you can see growth or decrease through life patterns, and learn how to grow to greater heights from a mindset point of view.

The pattern-allistic mentality of an individual greatly depends on the primary mindset that holds the highest percentage in any one aspect of life. So the sum total of all aspects percentage wise, is the mindset at which someone views life within their pattern-allistic mentality.

Now that you have the knowledge of the various mindsets someone can develop, I'm quite sure you've already begun to wonder what your dominant mindset is. Hopefully I'm about to rock your world, because once again, you need to evaluate your friends, and those who you believe truly love/honor you and are wanting you to become greater.

<u>Here are some things to consider when listening to the voices of critics and doubters:</u>

- How successful was this person in this aspect in the past? Are they blaming everyone/thing but themselves?

- How has this person helped you in the past? Did they offer HONORABLE/TRULY LOVING advice?

- Is this person well respected by the people around them? Who were they recommended by?

- Does this person come from a place of reason, and willingness to help when they can, even when it seems difficult to say?

These are all questions you need answered before you should decide to listen to what a critic or doubter has to say. Evaluate the people around you (Think back to the non-romantic relationship section). Are your, "ride or die friends", truly, <u>ride or die</u>? Or have you just known someone longer than any other person to formulate the definition of what you consider a true friend?

It doesn't even have to be your "friends", you can receive "advice" from anyone, because everyone has an opinion.
But the biggest the lie we can tell ourselves is either, <u>no one</u> or <u>everyone</u> has our best interests in mind. That is why it is imperative to understand the definition of true love.

Unfortunately, this lie is portrayed through figurative tsunamis in our everyday life. We let media of all kinds, from all sides, and the people around us, control how we think and portray how life should be.

In a world where anyone can tell us we as a person will fail or are failing; we as individuals need the knowledge to, <u>acknowledge/apply</u>, what they say, depending on ours and their evaluated lives. While keeping in mind everyone has the right to their opinion, and you or an individual shouldn't force someone to think the way they or you do. Instead, display integrity/respect-reason-filled facts unto yourself, through details of patterns that lead to a possible understanding that your mindset may or may not be for the betterment of greatness for yourself as a whole (physically and mentally).

***Answer the questions. I like having things become heavy and the pressure on, because diamonds are made under pressure. So, once you learn to regulate that pressure, I believe things will become soooo much easier.

You might have a sense of embarrassment while reading sections like these as you go through images of your own life. But you feeling that embarrassment means you've never thought about aspects like this in a raised level of thinking and are currently growing yourself in ways you couldn't imagine prior to this.

I want to challenge the way you think now, because I truly love/honor you even though I have or more than likely, will never meet you.

From me to you, writing this book is the best way to show true love/honor, and the accountability presented is to help you become greater. I want the very best for you, and I believe you can potentially achieve more greatness than even you currently know, if you apply the wisdom I am trying to impart on you.***

BABY STEPS ARE KEY

Use the page (or a bigger sheet of paper if needed) to write down situations from your past that caused pain, joy, learning, embarrassment, you felt energy, and compare/apply emotion you research. Then compare what you action(s)/patterns you performed during those situations to feel the way you did. From there you can create patterns extending into more aspects of life to determine why you might react to certain situations more than others (meditating on various comparable situations).

ONLY YOU CAN CHANGE YOURSELF TO BECOME GREATER, BUT IT REQUIRES DISCIPLINE/SELF-DISCIPLINE/ACCOUNTABILITY THROUGH CONSISTENCY.

Why you shouldn't be afraid to fail

It's pretty straight forward. You shouldn't be afraid to fail, because you apply gained knowledge/wisdom from what caused you to fail the first time. So the next round, you should inherently do better. But if you don't (see the definition of insanity), then you need to evaluate your ability to recognize patterns, because you lack the capability to gain wisdom or easily cave under slight pressure to go back to what you previously did.

Don't focus on failing, but instead use the details of a failure to gain wisdom and become greater.

ANYONE can pick themselves up off the dirt. But not EVERYONE knows how or wants to dust themselves off.

What happens when you dust yourself off? Do you get all off the dirt off? No, but that's the hidden beauty of this analogy. Once you dust yourself off, you've brushed off everything extra that could continue to weigh you down.

The dusting off represents your ability to recognize, then move on from the failure. Are there particles left showing what happened? Yes, but those particles and stains represent how you've changed, and learned from what caused you to fall in the first place.

There are A LOT of people out there I know who don't want to dust themselves off, and it is very much a major problem in the world today. In fact, some people will take on the dust of someone else just to show they can, without knowing how to properly help mentally.

People who do not dust themselves off will begin to accumulate dust, dirt, and grime until it begins to weigh them down. Then when they realize just how much they cannot move due to the weight; these same people will ask for help from someone else in cleaning off the accumulated grime, but others can only do so much. Because the fact of the matter is, only the individual can dust themselves off better than anyone else can.

<u>For instance:</u>

    I knew of someone who had a relatively big business. They were successful, young, and cocky. Said person did not believe that anything could harm them, and it wasn't until a business deal with the wrong person gone haywire, did they fall, and they fell HARD.

    Before the fall, this person was so prideful, out of their own arrogance they did not follow the proper steps of signing a contract with the person they were doing business with. After the work was completed, the young person was paid, and the person who received the work put out a good word to the people around them about the job well done.

    That being known, a few weeks later, this person who told others to use the young person for work felt like they deserved some kind of compensation. (Even though this is not how the business world works. Then every coffee shop I go to, I **feel** I would deserve money when I tell others to go there. See how dumb that sounds?).

    Yet, simply advising someone to use another for business does not warrant compensation without a business sales contract in place. So naturally, the young person who did the work refused to provide money for the recommendations, and ultimately the person performing recommendations let bygones be bygones…or so the young person thought.

    There was one little problem. Without a contract signed for the previous job, the young person could be sued and taken to court for wrongful work. Now I know this doesn't sound fair, but there was no paper trial to back the young person up whom performed the job, and unfortunately the person they had angered was very powerful in the community.

    After a lengthy court battle, a slandering of the young person's name, and doing the wrong course of action of moving away from the area, hoping to avoid the warrants for their arrest for not paying. The young person's past arrogance finally caught up with them and they were ultimately sent to jail.

    Thankfully though, while in jail the young person decided then and there, to come back even stronger. They decided they didn't want the dust, dirt, and grime to keep them down any longer leading to a growth in wisdom/intellect.

    Today, the once young person now has an even more profitable business, but that jail sentence and show of pride will be on their record for a long time.

Which is the reason they are now more cautious, and mindful of the people they do deals with and work with/for.

Today, this person would rather take time to dot the "I's", cross the "T's". And discover an aligned understanding before engaging in any work, to protect them self and now their family. In the end, after picking themselves up and gaining knowledge of failure in a pattern, they are not afraid to go through failure, because in the end, failure provides a means to adapt to become greater in the end.

Jail is not a reason to be confidently arrogant, because those who say jail is street credit resulting in greatness, do not want to become any kind of winner in life. Jail was put into place to cause a reflection of previous patterns to instill correction onto a greater path, but it is up to the individual to consistently follow that pattern towards something greater.

A family example of someone who keeps the dust, dirt, and grime on them would be the opposite of the granddaughter with the former alcoholic grandfather and the bad parents. They would continually blame the environment they grew up in and seek validation in others for confidence.
<u>What dust, dirt, and grime are you holding on to?</u>

BABY STEPS ARE KEY

Write below what situation(s) made you fall in the dirt and answer the questions to go with that situation(s).

Do you know how to pick yourself up, and wipe the dust off?

In what healthy patterns do you do that?

Do you put yourself in a negative light leaving the dust and dirt on?

Do you dust yourself off in healthy ways and grow (ex: working out, meditating, writing in a journal, etc)? Why not start with **baby steps** today?

The Mountain **made** of mountains

We all are born at different points on this hypothetical mountain, and only we as individuals can choose to climb higher or not. **No one** *can take that decision from you, but yourself.*

For some people, they throw in the towel on the way up and stay where they are losing all momentum they had built to that point. Once someone loses that momentum, it might become hard to gain a growth mentality unless intentionally recovered through improved patterns. If not recovered, they will more than likely begin to isolate themselves with others who lost momentum at the same juncture. As time goes on, there will be a group of people who think the same way, encouraging each other that they cannot reach the next highest point, due to an outside force.

Perceived stagnation leads to frustration, and the beyond to more negative mental patterns.

Real *Life* on the *Mountain*

When an individual sees someone else at the next highest point, or even a few levels above, it is natural to wonder how said person climbed so high. So, when they get back within the group they built in their current location, there are those who hear of the higher point, then work/learn how to reach the next level and beyond; through hard work, opportunity, and by applying themselves.

Then there are those that unfortunately, want to achieve the next level without adding greatness patterns within their own pattern-allistic mentality to climb the mountain to reach that next point. Thus, they never put in effort of understanding to potentially navigate the rocks or pave their own path. Which will likely potentially lead to these people envying the next level, and as a result, never learn to respect failure or overcome their inner fear of the unknown. Furthermore, they will live and become content in a failure mindset, as they will begin to see it everywhere within various aspects of their own life.

Those within the group that were left behind at the point below, will continue to maintain the opinion there is no way to get up to the next level. This is where the forming groups who pattern-allistically think the same way, and slowly see no progress in any other aspects of their individual life, stay. Which results in creating more stagnation, leading to frustration, and the mentally negative beyond. This negative mentality only breeds more failure within themselves and the group.

People who live in a failure mindset will blame certain aspects of the point they are at and give into the emotions that feed the failure; all while looking at the bumpy incline leading to the next level. Resulting in them becoming so fixated on the failure they perceive; they will say they are in some sort of unique situation ignoring/blinding themselves to those around them who choose to be greater and climb higher.

Excuses will continue to flood in and these people living in a failure mindset, will begin to pinpoint certain qualities of someone else at a higher point on the mountain, saying those factors must have been the reason why they reached a higher point, and these factors are keeping them down. When in fact, there are many types of people that were in the exact same spot as the person living in failure, who've climbed the mountain to the/a higher point than the failure mindset individual with excuses of keeping them down.

Take your blinders off. We all struggle in some way, and once you take them off, you will see a multitude of people who are climbing out of similar situations you consider yourself in.

Now here is where things can get twisted, causing many problems in the world today out of the need to feel the ability to "care" for those around us:

In feeling pity for those who did not want to put in the effort to reach the next level or add the needed mental growth patterns. People higher up will listen to the cries and excuses, as to why the mountain is hard to climb. So, some will then offer to provide a route, or try influence others to build a time-tested-failed elevator, in order for those at the bottom to "climb" higher (The elevator that has been built, and used in the past always does the opposite, keeping/taking people down). From there, those who have embodied a failure mindset will cry even louder, as they expected to not have to put in any effort whatsoever to climb higher.

So out of trying to get others to sacrifice through a false sense of "care". The ones who provided the advice and are trying to convince others to build this failed "elevator" up the mountain, will throw away consistency, only to end up living in hypocrisy.

These people on a higher point will listen to the cries/excuses, then in an attempt to "care" will assimilate the same certain qualities to those on their same higher plane. Thus, blaming everyone else who fits the CURRENT EXCUSE for those stuck below. When the truth is, those below do not even want to simply walk through the **mirage mirror facing** them, to take the first **baby steps** to climb higher.

The sad part is, in the end, those at this higher plain will use the ones below to further their climb, then claim they "care" about what's right. But they threw their consistency out and put it in a locked drawer, as they will live in a life full of hypocrisy and ignore the true meaning of the patterns instilled. Thus, forgetting what it means to climb the ***Mountain*** of ***LIFE*** that is made from aspect-based mountains.

So, in the end, you have people with a failure mindset becoming influenced by others whom live in hypocrisy, in order to maintain a false sense of "care" through fake empathy.

Stop making excuses that you related back to life through your own pattern-allistic mentality as to why you aren't somewhere higher. Life is inherently unfair, and full of failures. Failures you've brought on yourself, and failures brought on you by other people failing to be the greatest version of themselves.

But once you decide to climb the mountain, don't stop for long periods of time. For when you stop for long, it means you've become content in your current wisdom in that aspect of your life, and being content in wisdom is what breeds excuses and stops growth. So, continue to grow in anything and everything. Take what I've said so far to heart. Develop the growth mindset, adding it to your pattern-allistic mentality I am guiding you through, and I believe you could potentially become something greater than you could ever imagine.

Keep your eyes up, constantly working towards greater things in every aspect of life.

There are always going to be growing pains. But unlike the ones you experience while physically growing up. The **Mountain** *of* <u>**LIFE**</u> *is nothing but a series of mountains that lead to another potential peak. They are simply stacked one on-top of the other, with various resting points representing levels of greatness we all subconsciously want to achieve. Yet, can only achieve through intentionality of greater patterns put into place,* **<u>once a goal is defined</u>**.

Once again, life is inherently unfair. We are all human, and we can only control what we do and where we as individuals end up on the <u>*Mountain*</u> that is <u>*Life*</u>. The problem in our pattern-allistic mentality we have developed since children, has become so flawed, that some don't even know their path to achieve greater things is blocked by their own transparent image staring back at them.

The ability this entire chapter gives you, is one that truly opens your eyes to yourself, how you potentially see the world, and how the individuals around you probably see it through their own eyes.

<u>*Find the greatness in everyone. Take no offense to anyone because the world is made up of humans and give thanks for LIFE experiences on the MOUNTAIN. As it provides wisdom to reach higher points if you'll truly listen, then apply greater patterns.*</u>

CHAPTER 4: Why the world doesn't like True Champions

Here is what's wrong with the world today as a whole:

Everyone is their-own individual. No two people's pattern-allistic mentality will ever be the exact same.

There is always a difference of opinion, or some way someone sees the world compared to anyone else. Yet, how you potentially see the world is directly influentially dependent on where you used to or currently reside, on the **Mountain** of **Life**. So, as you climb and discover more details about the known-unknown wisdom you are slowly gaining, you might maintain some opinions, and others may change.

*But one thing remains the same for every person with a healthy growth mindset, "I have to keep climbing. I'm not perfect, no one is, and I never will be. But I can become greater than I was the day before if I stay consistent in my **baby steps** and raise my bar of mentality through currently applicable patterns."*

People who know what it means to want to grow know that excuses get you no-where and blaming others or outside forces, will not cause things to change in your personal life. You'll never gain the alignments or relationships you need to help climb mountains; if your mind is constantly running through patterns that keep you down, instead of adapting to develop ones that incubate greatness.

Patterns of crying about why life isn't fair, will only cause you to look like a fool in the process and is not what it means to honor yourself. Instead, it will cause you to become something you were not intended to become…a whiner that is steeped in failure.

Those who know what it means to grow, know the hard work, obstacles, bumps, bruises, cuts, and failures they had to grow through to get to where they are today. So, these types of growth minded people hate to listen to excuses, because they understand anyone can accomplish great things. But they know people must be willing to go through the growing pains.

People who make excuses, want things handed to them. Because these people never receive the handout they desperately want; they will begin to resent others around them, when they don't feel like they are being heard.

Everyone has an opinion, but other than, "I want or give me.", what is the reasoning as to why you should be heard? Is it viable, or are you trying to grasp for straws in order to believe you've done everything you can to grow yourself?

True greatness lies in the control of mind, body, and spirit. People who have a true greatness mindset aren't fazed by an obstacle; they see mountains as a way to grow, gather more wisdom, and potentially have others around them who have the same thought process towards the reality of a growth life.

Through this hard work, these people will become more aware of the excuses people make. But instead of indulging on them, the excuses are like hearing nails on a chalk board. So, a growth mindset person will distance themselves from those who don't want to at least attempt to grow and will not be afraid to tell the world how life truly is, when given the opportunity.

That being known, let's take a step back to look at today's society. Most people would rather listen to a screen with someone talking about non-sense that does nothing to benefit true growth, than plan out how to achieve the things they want to get accomplished, when life is at hand. **We have fallen into the world of, "If someone else stands for something and someone doesn't like it, we should all feel offended because that is what it means to "care"." Which in turn, has created a society that would rather listen to people who tell beautiful lies and ignore the ugly/hard factual truth.**
The real, non-biased truth will set you free. But if you conform to the ways of this world, you will become lost in a sea of normalcy and resentment.

Once you teach yourself to not take beautiful lies to heart, your family and even people around you, will take notice. Through that awareness, you will have some people encourage you, some will help you, some will want your help, and others will condemn you for even thinking about changing yourself for the potential greatness within.

Family might become less encouraged to be there for you. Resulting from a spiteful, envious spirit, jealous of your success thinking it should be theirs. Or they might always want something from you.

Friends who never truly loved you, will turn on you, relishing when you fail, and enjoy watching you struggle as you fight for greatness.

People will bring challenges, hoping to put you in a corner, wishing you cave under the pressure, and completely forgo the patterns you will have or want to form.

All of this known, it is not all darkness and judgement. There will be many joyous moments in your life as you taste true success. As a result of effort through patterns of a potentially great life, you will eventually find yourself around people that are victorious in many realms of life. Which is why it is imperative to celebrate the victories of others. As you celebrate their victories and hold them accountable to their potential greatness, they will in turn possibly do the same for you.

If you lack true friends, you will meet many people through natural encounters of growth. They will share many of the same values, and it will not be uncommon to gain a true friend for life.

Through this pattern, life will not seem as hard, because you know what it means to hold yourself accountable to the potential greatness within. The group around you, will become accustomed to the gravity of your greatness and learn to sprint with theirs in all aspects of life.

The standard of your pattern-allistic mentality within you will rise, and as that standard becomes higher, so will the things around you in life become greater.

For example:

I didn't have much growing up as compared to others around me. But as I started assimilating all the sections in chapter 2 and growing my "sliding door" to fit more aspects of life, I noticed something rather peculiar. Everywhere I went (after some time had passed to show consistency of patterns) I always found my way into rooms of people who were considered extremely successful, or in leadership, whether I was internally a part of the organization/group or not.

In fact, there was one time I wasn't even trying to be in a room full of greatness seeking individuals and leaders. I just was lost for about 10-15 minutes (LOL). I was trying to figure out where I should be in the building. It just so happened that someone I knew was there, and they led me to the room they believed I should be in.

It was very much like when I was little. All while growing up in school/sports and even in corporate America (while I was doing my own thing in leading myself), I was not afraid to encourage, present places of growth, or ideas through patterns that could potentially lead to something greater.

In that greatness through growth patterns within myself. I was placed in leadership of groups or areas. And I noticed from a young age, the situations of talking to someone in command of a region, conversing over ideas or next steps with them, without even seeking the opportunity to do so most, if not all the time. Most of the time they were simply presented to me in a way much like when I was lost.

But it wasn't until I began to intentionally think about the reasoning around 3 years ago, (eventually led to the day I started writing this book) did I know how to share the wisdom of this pattern:

It was my ability to not only have swagger/ humbleness, but the pattern-allistic mentality to continually practice self-discipline in everything I did, to others. From the way I spoke, to living out greatness through the actions I performed when honoring others, to the amount of intellect I sought to connect, and the level of greatness I cared for in how I performed combined; that led to this uniquely achievable ability.

Self-discipline is contagious, and when practiced consistently is like a magnet for attracting other well self-disciplined people. But what you do with these alignments, combined with your gifts and greatness, is the key to how successful you CAN be.

Every successful person who has ever served others in life, would in some way say, self-discipline/self-accountability, is one of, if not the most deciding factor in how they made it to where they wanted to go.

Yet, I chose to learn the combination from a variety of various viewpoints. I chose to serve/saw my father work since I was very young, even when I did not want to. I chose to learn from repercussions to my actions and follow through. I chose to be an example in sports, showing/vocalizing others how to get the greatest results, and chose to adhere/witness daily what happened when certain patterns were not practiced.

However much success you want to have or how great you can be, depends on your ability to find yourself on speaking terms with other greatness minded people. So how do you find yourself in those rooms?

Well, it depends on how you answer the questions…
…how do you lead yourself using your pattern-allistic mentality to become great(er)? What greatness patterns can you add, to start the **baby steps** of becoming something greater?

<u>If you can't think of anything, start small, ask yourself, then answer this question instead:</u>

Do you do anything on top of simply going about your day, to practice greatness unto yourself growing your mind, body, or soul? EX: read a book (mind), workout (body), give/serve others, even if it's small (soul)

<u>What is the other constant besides consistent greatness in yourself, in the equation for success?</u>

<u>RELATIONSHIPS</u>, *so* **communication** *is vital.*

<u>Case in point:</u>

My father would converse with everyone and anyone, no matter of job title or life standing in a very human, down to earth, and playful manner. So, me being me, recognizing the pattern and how much fun they had, I quickly followed suit.

When we would walk into a company together, everyone (if they had the ability to) would come by and start a conversation with us. Though most of the time these were not the greatest of life choice people, my father treated them with as much respect as he would an executive, and honor them in a giving way.

As for when they talked with me, they helped me develop availability and provide reassurance of the need for chapter 2 patterns.

I'll never forget at the old age of 10, executives and workers alike, would go out of their way to talk with me to ask how everything was and sometimes, even ask business questions or have a business conversation. It's funny to think about now, but they would do it so often, sometimes my dad would get agitated because I was talking to all of these people, when I should've been helping him.

Yet, it was the conversations I wasn't a part of, through simple observation or was told about, that had the biggest impact on me building the mentality I have today. And helped develop the wisdom of patterns to push a business to a higher level, no matter their current standing in the world.

When executives or managers would have conversations with employees, (whether in a manner of verbal discipline or simple interaction) I would observe the words they used, the tone of their voice, and if possible, body gestures. In doing this, I luckily, subconsciously added patterns of managers and executives into my pattern-allistic mentality. Resulting in developing the verbiage to go along with the communication skills of a great or not so great leader, from a very young age, and slowly applied it all to my sliding door of wisdom.

<u>People under-estimate the ability to shut-up and listen to people speak. Being quiet, yet filling yourself with information, is a lost art of great communication.</u>

While quiet, you are gaining more information to use in order to develop your own pattern-allistic mentality. Which, in conjunction with using your "sliding door" of wisdom to formulate and gain more possible answers, you can find an arrow that is a combination of all the proposed information. Thus, meeting everyone's mentality for a longer lasting solution in the end, and all you had to do was what?

<u>**Know when to shut-up and listen.**</u>

The pattern of knowing when to do what you've got to do:

One day, as a kid helping my father, I saw something I had never seen before.

We were in one of the hottest warehouses in the state (before the time giant fans were installed), on what seemed like the hottest day of the summer, when my father and I "joyfully" walked into the sauna (LOL).

As both my father and I worked on the dock, we heard a door burst open that led to the upstairs offices. It was a VP of the company in a suit with a determined look on his face.

Naturally, I thought to myself, "Oh someone's about to get it." But he took off his jacket, hung it on a pole, grabbed a clip board, and hopped on a forklift. Which led me to think, "What a terrible way for someone to go out of this world." (LOL).

But, to my surprise, he started doing "normal" work and I became even more confused. By the time my father and I completed what we had to do, the VP of a well over a 1000 employee-national-company was sweating profusely through his expensive button up and continued to work after we left. I remember climbing into my dad's truck not understanding how to feel about what I just witnessed.

The next day, when my father and I entered the warehouse, the VP was standing on the dock when he turned around to greet us with a smile. Naturally curious about what happened the day before, my father and I asked him why he did what he did, or what happened. With a smile on his face, the VP said,

"Everything is ok. We were just short staffed and extremely busy, with more customers on the way. So instead of asking someone else, thinning out the crew, I decided to do it myself. Plus, it was kind of fun to be back on a lift. It reminded me of old times..."

What the heck??!? What kind of VP of a big company says something like that?!?!

From speaking with him at previous moments, I knew he was a great leader and had a special way about connecting with all people. But this was next level self-discipline/accountability, because he could've assigned anyone one else to do what he did. Yet, he put into practice the pattern of doing what you have to do without needing to be told, as he had no reason not to tell someone else to do it. But showed the rest of the workforce an example of, true leadership.

Today, the company has more than tripled in size, and been able to pay for bigger and better buildings ***in cash***, without the need to finance (workable capital...just wait until my business book comes out). Not only that, but the company has also since gone global, and made it on the Forbes list of worldly businesses.

The sad part about today is, that type of person in general is a dying breed, and most managers I've met from my generation might be smart (considered the smartest generation). Yet, they are what my grandfather coined, "Educated fools". Which basically means, they are book smart, yet still have little to no understanding of how the real-world works. Nor, do they know how to treat people in order to become great leaders to accomplish great feats.

Then again, regardless of title, we all need to put into practice the type of leadership displayed above, in going above and beyond, regardless of where you are currently at in the workforce. Because it is truly the only way to become greater and achieve more in that aspect of life. (Baby steps are key)

In becoming the best in "whatever" position you are in, it will show not only yourself you can take on more weight, but it will display to the people around you, you are worthy of being followed to greater heights. Even if it is not currently being appreciated, someone will recognize your patterns of greatness, and give you the opportunity to climb higher. But you must learn a consistent pattern of effort in patience when desiring leadership, because you need more than just a "do what I've got to do" mindset, due to the fact communication skills are a major key in leading people around you.

There is no need to worry about achieving greatness if you have a pattern-allistic mentality of constantly and consistently, doing things great.

My knowledge of history and the formation of America, contributes to what made America so great in the first place. This dying breed of the type of person that leads others, represented through leading themselves by example, is exactly what made America the greatest liberty/freedom given country on the planet ever. So when a country is seemingly feeling uneasy, attacked, or pushed over, it this type of person or the lack of mindset not being passed down, that leads to weakness of a conducive great mind.

Write down ways you can become greater in communication of all types and grow patterns of what it means to lead yourself. Example: non-biased growth videos/books/academics (mind), serving/giving to others (soul), putting in more effort (body).

<u>Here is what's wrong with America and countries who try to mimic her greatness today:</u>

Social media and technology are the greatest things to happen to the world today, because they have the ability to bring us all individually closer together. But they are also the worst thing to happen to the world as we know it.

Here are some statistics and explanations in which you need to use your head, in order to connect some personal/national dots. Then I will go into a few of the pros and cons of the most powerful, worst, but most beneficial tools on this planet today. From there, you can possibly use patterns to <u>connect every dot at once</u> (The highest level of your pattern-allistic mentality. Even if you fail, the discovery will provide insight into how to access this realm within yourself.).

All the info below is the provided by:
https://ourworldindata.org/rise-of-social-media
<u>Down the rabbit hole we go!!</u>

Remember, there is a reason behind everything in this book. Even down to the specific layout I have chosen. Though sometimes it may seem like I'm trying to adjust your viewpoint of life, it is actually you having a conversation in your subconscious of a needed change in certain aspects within your own pattern mentality for growth, from past experiences, but will you listen?

With this mentality brings the knowledge and understanding, that worldly opinion may or may not agree with you, because…

…**although people want the <u>truth</u>; the <u>fact</u> of the matter is, people who feel offended, would rather their "truth" be the correct one in the end.**
<u>There is no such thing as coincidence when presented by a group of closely relatable facts.</u>
Everything has a reason, and everyone has a purpose. The smallest rumors or biggest conspiracies have to start somewhere with multiple people's opinion. Which means (most of the time), there is always some level of truth behind it.

So, deciphering the real truth, means to decipher hypocrisy and the untwisting of the narrative of the biased "truth", which is a part of the other side of the coin of wisdom. Otherwise called, Deceit.

The graph below shows how many people have logged into their social media accounts within the last 30 days. It is pretty astounding just how much social media has grown over the last 20 or so years isn't it? Social media is a big part of everyone's individual life, isn't it? But is this <u>truly connecting</u> with people, or are we trying to be lazy attempting to navigate putting effort into relationships? In short, no, it's not the true way to connect with people, and though it is a type of relationship, it only brings snapshots of real life.

So why do we let media control us?

.....because it is exactly that......easy to check/do. Don't think so? Check your phone for certain apps and take a look around you in a group of people...the lazy, easy access is everywhere.

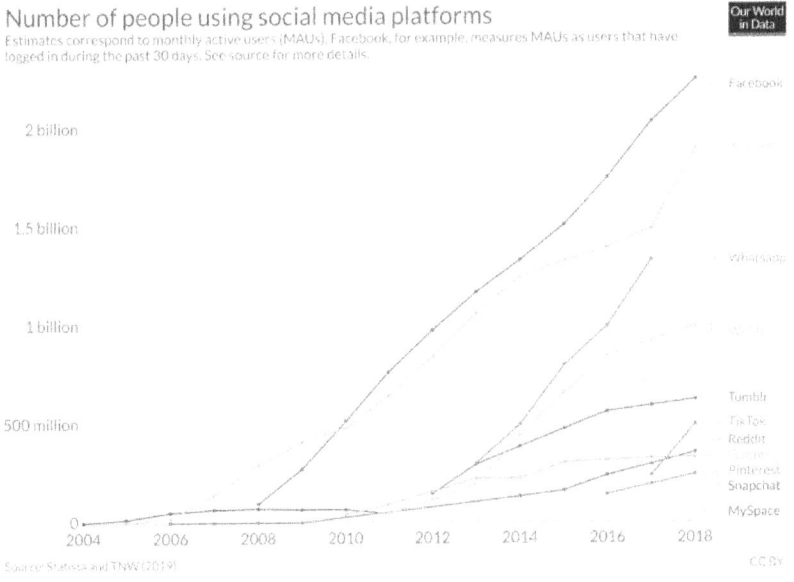

This graph provides stats from the platforms, and age groups who use them. Remember what I said about the most adaptable generation, and how what helps play a role in becoming something greater? (Effort and not constantly worrying about what someone else has in life.)

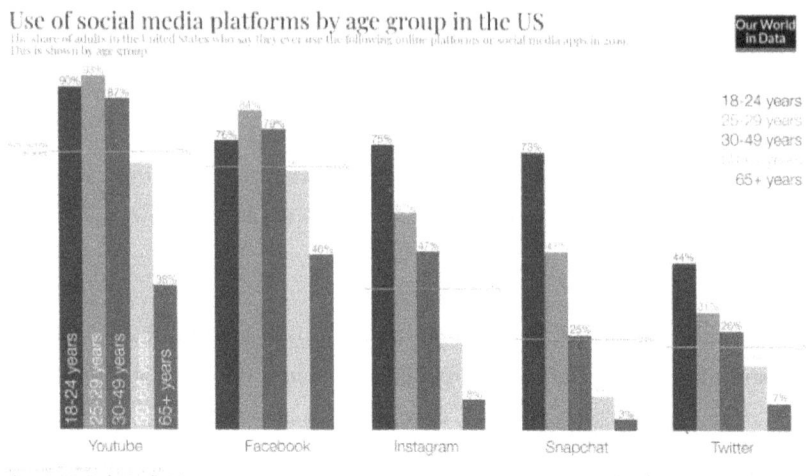

Remember from earlier in the chapter how I talked about the way people would rather listen to a screen, rather than plan for greatness?
This is a direct arrow pointing towards why the 1% have what they have.

<u>For example:</u>

You see commercials for normal cars but will rarely see anything for the most high-end ones. Hmmmm…weird….so you have to be told constantly this is the best way (fast food, <u>medicine</u>, etc), rather than putting in the effort to find the best way (healthier food, stay in shape, etc).

The same works for the news and statistics as well, which is crazy. That is why a "sliding door" of wisdom that easily moves across the bar on top into other aspects of life is necessary, because you can ascertain many connections at once for the truly beneficial patterns of your life.

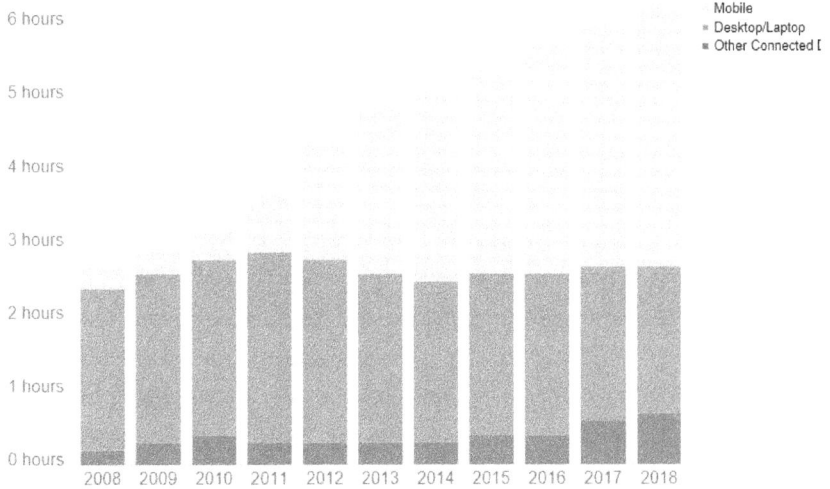

<u>Here is where things can get heavy, and dots start to be connected of what happens when people would rather listen to a screen, than derive or apply plans of effort.</u> (www.statista.com/statistics/18747)

Deaths by suicide per 100,000 resident population in the United States from 1950 to 2018, by gender

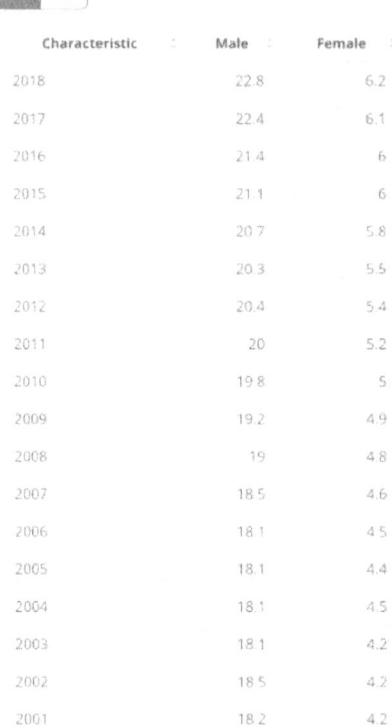

Characteristic	Male	Female
2018	22.8	6.2
2017	22.4	6.1
2016	21.4	6
2015	21.1	6
2014	20.7	5.8
2013	20.3	5.5
2012	20.4	5.4
2011	20	5.2
2010	19.8	5
2009	19.2	4.9
2008	19	4.8
2007	18.5	4.6
2006	18.1	4.5
2005	18.1	4.4
2004	18.1	4.5
2003	18.1	4.2
2002	18.5	4.2
2001	18.2	4.2

Bonus for you to think about: What happens when you constantly, inadvertently, or intentionally tell someone they are insignificant or not as good as someone else (social media, news)? Thus, giving off the notion someone will only succeed if (blank) happens, creating immense pressure on another that wasn't meant to be there. Which results in **mentally affirming** someone won't be good enough otherwise; all while constantly helping the opposite, and telling them they are doing great no matter what? (Dot: Maybe mental health problems. You should probably stop looking at 30 second clips of someone's not real life.)**

Are you starting to connect the dots? No? Don't worry, I help inhibit some connections for you in the conclusion, but I want you to at least try right now. These numbers and graphs may just be sheer coincidence, but how many coincidences need to be put together before the opinion gathers so much close, relatable, and factual truth to the argument, it becomes inevitably a factual trend (group of patterns)? (www.statista.com/statistics/25232)

Percentage of U.S. youths with a major depressive episode in the past year from 2004 to 2019, by gender

Characteristic	Male	Female
2019	8.8%	23%
2018	7.7%	21.5%
2017	6.8%	20%
2016	6.4%	19.4%
2015	5.8%	19.5%
2014	5.7%	17.3%
2013	5.3%	16.2%
2012	4.7%	13.7%
2011	4.5%	12.1%
2010	4.4%	11.9%
2009	4.7%	11.7%
2008	4.3%	12.5%
2007	4.6%	11.9%
2006	4.2%	11.8%
2005	4.5%	13.3%
2004	5%	13.1%

<u>Bonus for you to think about</u>: American Psychological Association study (www.apa.org/monitor/feb05/jealousy) : links females to being more emotionally jealous, which is due to the chemical reaction that occurs before birth (stop trying to say there aren't genders given upon birth when science actually confirms it). Jealousy is a dangerous topic. And what happens when you have access to things like social media where you constantly see backstabbing, what others have, friend's enjoying life without you, and perceive the world is after you, so you need to constantly be told you're empowered (thus becoming addicted to being told you're awesome)? All of those lead to states of **mental problems** in various ways. That being known, females are more likely to admit depression and seek help, as opposed to males. Also, females do not perform as lethal ways of taking their life as males, but females are also catered more to talk about what they are going through in today's world. Males tend to bottle things up, and are told emotions are bad. But when the tipping point hits, males choose those more lethal ways to end their life. Either way, suicide is bad and we all need to be better at putting the stupid phone down, turn the screen off, and connect with people who want to be greater.**

Conclusion:

Perceived stagnation; leads to frustration and mentally worse beyond.

As you can see, in every graph that talks about progression of time, the numbers went up. The number of users, hours spent, depression, and suicide rates all have growing trends across the same timeline as growth of media/technology occurred.

Here is what is possible when you are self-disciplined in building small patterns of greatness, leading to creating pathways out of stagnation towards more greatness, and do not constantly feed yourself with what the world and offended people show you:

When you get something done that you perceive as beneficial, it releases a chemical in your brain called, Dopamine. Dopamine, is directly associated with (Dopamine is released when you expect to receive a reward after completing a task.):

- Pleasure
- Learning
- Memory
- Motor system function
- Mood
- Pain processing
- Sleep
- Stress

Do you see what happens when you get things meant for growth done?

Now you don't have to always get tasks done in order to be considered a good person or lead a good life. But in terms of your overall health, the ability to achieve levels of greatness, patterns of self-discipline, recognition of avoiding stagnation, and life growth productivity, are crucial. That known, there are cheap ways to get an influx of dopamine into your bloodstream that we all have become accustomed to. But in the end, those things will only hurt more than they help (example: social media, watching tv, alcohol, coffee, shopping, a participation trophy, etc. How do you truly grow from these? You don't...). Which is why it's important to balance these patterns in the best way possible.

By the science:

A perfect example of natural dopamine level raising is going outside. Vitamin D can be produced when the Sun's ultraviolet B rays hit cholesterol found in our skin, which plays an integral role in the production of Dopamine. But make sure to be cautious of how much of the sun you get, because too much of a good thing, CAN be bad. So, make sure to be mindful of how much sun you get, due to the detrimental effects that can occur.

Cons of social media/technology:

- Heavily influenced patterns of looking to other people as validation

- Made it easier to destroy other's lives (deserved or not)

- Easy manipulation tactics through marketing

    o This is why you see certain media posts talking about how someone else is bad if they don't think the way you do

- Finding the factual truth is harder than it should be

    o Everyone has their point of view of truth, but the facts of whether or not that truth is known to be beneficial are hidden, or skewed

- Some have a media way of life which ruins their ability to truly connect with people

- - Causes stagnation in the growth of what makes human beings what we are naturally hard wired to do…have community with one another

- Has made us lazy and un-driven to get things done. Leading to more depression, anxiety and other mental problems (By the science of Dopamine and getting things done)

Pros of social media/technology:

- Made it easier to achieve greatness through all of the information to be great there and at the ready for anyone

  - Physical health

  - Knowledge

- Made it easier to maintain relationships with one another

  - Example: In the past, if someone left the city you lived in, there was no way to connect with them

- Easier to connect with the proper people you need to in order to achieve greatness

  - You were not meant to do life alone. Even the most selfish people can determine where they have been helped in the past in some way

  - Business alignments or simply driving to locations

- Protected and/or saved people's lives (one example: defense industry)

Hmmmmm…so knowing today's world of offense, people crying on certain points of the *Mountain* of *Life* which leads having others tell them things will change (reward through "care"), and the patterns people or media use to influence you to think they will help be the change. Do you think we have all become addicted to the feeling of getting a reward, and crave to be told we are doing the right thing (Dopamine influx pattern)? (100% Yes)

This section roughly translates into, stop truly believing everything you consume of the world's opinion, truly has your best interest in mind. Stop trying to live out greatness behind a screen, or what someone tells you is great to do or have. Instead, put forth non-hypocritical patterns of greatness, that provide a lasting change in your life for the potentially greater (chapter 7).

BABY STEPS ARE KEY

How much time do you spend on social media or spend using technology?

Do you think it is, affecting/can affect, you? How?

Write down a certain amount of time you can spend doing something else, instead of being on your phone or watching a screen (it doesn't have to be super long). (Example: Read a book – 15 minutes, working out – 30 minutes, etc)

__Why the world does not like a *greatness* pattern mindset__

Everyone has an opinion. Schools, mainstream media, social media, your car mechanic, and if it could talk, even your dog or cat might have an opinion of you. Life seems to be all about opinions nowadays. In those opinions, labels are given by someone else or our self. So, we as individuals tend to throw out facts to form labeled opinions that fit the norm for what we see in all forms of media, or the group of people around us.

But as you develop your personal growth mindset, you will learn to stand up for your opinions in a healthy, educated, and truly loving respectful manner. Yet, you must be willing to adhere to life based on the REAL FACTS.

THE INDIVIDUAL'S THAT MAKE UP THE WORLD, ARE SCARED TO KNOW THE UGLY TRUTHFUL FACTS. UNBIASED FACTS ARE COLD AND HARD; YET ARE NEEDED FOR TRUE GROWTH. PEOPLE TODAY FORGOT THE MEANING OF, PERSONAL EFFORT, THAT LEADS TO PERSONAL GROWTH. BUT TRUE GROWTH PATTERN PEOPLE WHO WANT TO INHIBIT LONG LASTING GROWTH PATTERNS, WILL NOT BE AFRAID TO TELL YOU.

We all need values to stand for in the end, because we need a concrete base (patten-allistic mentality) for our metaphorical life "house" to build off of. The problem is, most of us will not search for facts, but hope/pray someone else will do it for us. Which is hypocritical for growth patterns. And what we do not take into account is the conundrum; when we find those facts, is the individual might lack the ability to determine if that person who found them comes from a place of true love or not. Which leads to the matter of providing bias lies (beautiful lies) that seem "truthful" to give labels.

The result pattern of life being, some individuals neither know what it means to have consistent core values or recognize the base from which pattern-allistic mentality, to develop their own ideals of patterns to live off of. The result being, a pattern-allistic mentality of confusion in what the individual's heart, mind, and soul truly see or can accomplish, as they blindly give themselves labels.

<u>From the prologue:</u>

I've seen schools take out praying, among other things revolved around Christianity over the years. They've made patterns normal for kids to conform to this worldly opinion of **forcing** people to change. And without realizing it, we took out the backbone of this nation, "One nation under GOD…". Thus, leading to some having taken on the mindset pattern, of conforming that they would prefer to be, "correct", then adhere to truthful facts as to not to "offend" anyone. From this, it has created an alienation and in-adherence/ignorance of those who speak factual truth(s), not conforming to the world's opinion of that specific day.

Some have chosen to try and live in the past by blaming everyone but themselves, when that past no longer exists. Then some have tried to get rid of history completely; when it should be taught as a reminder of where we've come from and see patterns we should not go back to.

Since being in school and having seen my religion completely taken out of them to compensate for everyone else. It could be factual coincidence. But since the early 2000's, this new generation of individuals/time period for the country (America) has become a slave to ignoring truthful facts, loving beautiful lies, and/or not allowing <u>ALL</u> to have an opinion.

Which has created the average mentality to become one of a victim pattern mindset. Resulting in to how we would rather search for blame to find a reason to be mad or offended, than search for hypocrisies in our own life to discover in our self why we are not as great as we could be (ergo, victim patterns of the mind are lazy).

<u>*We are not led by true champions anymore, but instead are seemingly led by who is more "correct", whether unbiasedly factually truthful or not.*</u>

I believe this book will make you something different if you put in the effort of discovering your pattern-allistic mentality of greatness. So having this growth mentality will make you a unicorn, as most have forgotten what it means to truly lead yourself in greatness patterns.

Once you apply this "unicorn" standard, you will become a magnet for all types of people, and see doors open in ways you've never imagined.

Outside of the correct relationships/alignments around you, that effort, and greatness pattern mindset could possibly be despised by people of this world. That being said, it is not their fault. They just have a hard time understanding why, because they have become lost, no longer seeking something greater in themselves.

With the pattern-allistic mentality keys given to you imparted within this book, you will begin to move in confidence (faith), not succumb to fear patterns, and hold your ground in unbiased truth for greatness (But always remember to do it in ways that are respectful/ honorable.).

When others ask why you don't believe the same way they do, you will speak using the research, hard work, blood, sweat, and tears you have spent or seen spent, in becoming greater. With this pattern mentality you will have picked yourself up many times and dusted yourself off. You will also be able to have a sixth sense when an entity/ someone is selling something for their own benefit and beliefs, then determine if they truly care.

You will effectively treat everyone with a smile and a great attitude, even when it seems hard. Yet, will not be afraid to speak your mind to those who will listen as long as it comes from a place of educated reasoning and true care, from the heart of wanting the best for the person you are speaking with.

You will be capable of knowing how to best truly love someone, as you will then know a high degree of how to truly love yourself.

As you develop your pattern-allistic mentality of greatness, you will not be fazed within a circumstance of life, because you will slowly start to subconsciously understand the next steps within yourself to climb higher within a situation or circumstance.

I'm telling you, once you reach a pattern level/place of spiritual enlightenment and growth within yourself, the problems going on around you will seemingly become mere blips. As you will figure out **baby steps** in patterns to keep climbing higher on the *Mountain* of *Life*.

<u>This is something the world will not like, because misery likes company, and people can be rather jealous of greatness, and a mentality that is not easily broken.</u>

Life is not an easy journey, and people within your world might despise you for greatness. But I would rather prepare you mentally now, because there are many worldly sacrifices to becoming something greater, as you discover great patterns for your personal pattern-allistic mentality.

Have a humble swagger knowing you live by the moral standard that you're not better than someone else. But rather are confident in your abilities to ascertain what it takes to reach a higher level, and consistently put those greatness patterns into practice.

<u>Here's a story from my college days that might give away my true identity, but it needs to be said:</u>

College is a whole different beast all together. It is not so much it prepares you for what you want to do, but it tells the person hiring, that you have a knowledge of things others did not want the discipline to learn.

Other than that discipline certificate, I (and people in general) could've been taught how to perform any job with just a high school education. And I'm pretty sure anyone else with a job out of college in what they wanted to do, would say the same thing.

That being known, college, any form of higher education or a trade, are not for the mentally weak. But all of them should be something to strive for, because of the possible greatness patterns within individuals that can be discovered along the way.

College will eat you up and spit you out if you let it. Not only that, but college more than anywhere else on the planet, will push the opinion of conforming to this world, because you are surrounded by people your age from all walks of life.

Although everyone on the planet will agree, no one wants to be around you if you aren't kind/respectful. Some people (even adults) have the opinion of, if you aren't "kind" enough to agree with the complete opinion of what worldly kindness is, then you don't deserve a voice. Which is not truly loving/honorable/respectable in any way shape or form.

That known, professors and teachers alike, are taught that to reach sabbatical and not be black balled by the system; they need to stay out of the limelight with the student body in an argument of opinion. Which is fine at the end of the day. But this world needs factually correct opinions to help out everyone for educated arguments, to inhibit growth in the group as a whole.

Instead, professors who are once again taught to stay out of the limelight and be "kind", adhering to the world's opinion, are more inclined have someone read what I had to.

A book called, "<u>Rules for Radicals</u>", by Saul Alinsky. A political book created by a socialist in 1971 (Socialism has proven to never work only leading to pain and suffering **the failed elevator mentioned in the mountain section**. Think Nazi Germany, Russia under Stalin, Columbia under Castro, and China. The countries who <u>SILENCE</u> any varying opinion.).

This ingenious manipulatively written book tries to present a way of controlling the minority, to silence the majority (It doesn't take a rocket scientist to notice one particular side plays the narrative without presenting any unbiased facts, or numbers). If that book's ideals come to fruition, the only people that truly benefit from what the book teaches are the elites. Which is hypocritical in what the book uses to manipulate the minority by believing they can have all they desire if they put into power people who think this way. In that book and in socialism, there is no middle class.

Only the higher ups (for their image/life) and the poor who have no life, share the same opinions on paper, but both have that opinion out of fear.

<u>*Does this type of narrative control sound familiar?*</u>
"We want to help you, but the people who think this way (blank) are the ones keeping you from that…….so you should or should keep doing (blank). Because we are the only ones who can help or do something about it. In the meantime, keep silencing these types of opinionated people as to get them to change their mind, or have them suffer the consequences otherwise."

<u>Let's recap/think really quick about what we've learned so far:</u>

There are parents not wanting to lead their children because, "the child has their own opinions", no matter what the age is, who are/were taught by teachers (after the 2000's that teach not to be educationally confrontational) in schools telling students not to stand for anything out of fear of backlash from someone else with a varying politically "correct" opinion, and then led to being taught by college professors who don't want backlash by the politically "correct" either.

So, what happens when that crap show of a confused young-impressionable-individual goes into the real world or college, with people who are politically "correct" having the most power, and can cancel anyone who presents a differing opinion?

You get a weak generation of people who have the most mental health problems ever % wise. You have a media that plays the politically "correct" game, and finally, you have social media led by people who know what it means to gain attention (attention for them is more money, so they search for fault against mainly one side to gain views/eyeballs). You have people who group together to be afraid of being wrong, so they are ignorant to change, and in fact despise others who think differently.

All of that nonsense combined and the cherry on top, is the fact that individuals are constantly watching all media. They see people skew the narrative suggesting, "If you don't support, you do not care, and you don't deserve an opinion." Which is why a country is subject to having people who ignore the ugly hard facts, getting into power.

<u>**This makes for one giant and crappy, individual ice cream sundae that ruins the area in which they are active in, due to the patterns of self-failure they spread. Even then, those who do not buy the narrative, find struggle in those areas, because of those failure mentalities. Which is why people want to leave, and not be around those who follow the failure-pattern-producing and fake care mindsets. (Look at the American states stats for those who think like this. You will notice that in 2021 people and businesses especially, are moving out of California.)**</u>

https://www.forbes.com/sites/adammillsap/2021/08/27businesses-are-fleeing-california-along-with-its-residents-and-president-biden-should-pay-attention/?sh=7fff1d962327

Do you understand why I say the world will not like your growth mindset?
Not only is it hard to put in effort, but you are fighting the narrative/world now. You are going against the now natural views/grain of the world. But it can still be changed for greatness…one growth individual at a time.

People who want something but don't want to work for it, don't like to be truly loved. Then when you tell them how life really is, people will try to silence you.
DO NOT FRET THOUGH!!! I BELIEVE YOU CAN ACHIEVE MANY GREAT THINGS WITH THE MENTALITY YOU WILL GAIN FROM THIS BOOK, THROUGH EFFORT AND PRACTICE. SO MUCH SO, THAT NOT EVEN THIS WORLD CAN KEEP YOU DOWN!!!

<u>LOOK FOR THE BEST IN EVERYONE AND BE A TRULY LOVING EXAMPLE OF WHAT GREATNESS IS!!!</u>

Why the world will love your greatness pattern mindset

This section is short and sweet.

A multitude of reoccurring hypocrisies have kept the world in a state of confusion and depravity, thus leading to a yearning to witness true greatness.
Hypocrisy has created a state of frustration, because of the perceived stagnation in growth of those we see to have power over our lives.
This world wants to see someone who strives for the stars while giving and serving, without being steeped in hypocrisy at every turn, because true hypocrisy is what causes others watching, to lose hope. That being known, your personal hope should not reside in the world, because of the simple reason, we are all human. (Chapter 7)

*When you hear someone say they have given up hope that people can change. It is like that of a cockroach in a house. You see one and there could be up to a million. Which means, your house (the world) is infested with a lack of hope. So, **you** can be a type of hope the world needs to bear witness to.*
A majority the world has lost some sort of hope that people can produce true greatness beyond greatness, because the "great people" constantly on display, are consistently living in blatant hypocrisy of what true greatness patterns really are. Stay strong in greatness patterns and seek to avoid blatant hypocrisy.

We should all understand that we are all human and have all made mistakes. But when someone keeps proclaiming greatness for the sake of maintaining good graces with the public eye, they are not truly great. Those types of people just want to prove in their own mind they have done truly great deeds. When in reality, the difference of aspiring to be a truly great person and someone who does not, is through maintaining the mindset of being beneficial to others without a need for a picture or video, to prove it every time. They live in consistent patterns of greatness, but admit they are human too.
True Greatness does not pick up trash on the street, hold the door open when entering a store with a smile for all, and is respectful of everyone/themselves; only to make up for throwing two pieces of trash on the ground when no one is looking, or telling an individual they should disrespect others when someone does not hold the door open for them.

<u>All the above known, as you prove to yourself, and give/serve when opportunity arises to others while seeking nothing in return; the world will love your mindset.</u>

People around you will see how great you can truly potentially become, and by translation of bearing witness to the pattern; those around you will rise through you. And as a result, you in turn will rise in higher standing of the world. But you must consistently stay in true greatness, with the <u>understanding you are human</u>. So, <u>when</u> you do fall from time to time, take ownership, have accountability in yourself to dust yourself off, and put greater patterns into place.

Do not lower the standard you set for yourself day after day, <u>after</u> you fall. Instead, work to raise the greatness level pattern standard of your heart, and the determination of your mind even higher.

In order to achieve the true greatness of releasing the untapped potential, you will not be able to do it alone. So always seek to be with others that will hold you to a higher standard of greatness within yourself, that come from an understanding of the definition of, true love. Upon finding yourself constantly around these people, you will subconsciously learn to level yourself up to a higher standard within your own heart, mind, and soul, for the rest of the world to witness and rise to. No matter how *<u>minutus</u>* (Latin).

The truth of why a true growth mindset is starting to disappear

As you go through this journey, the "nails on a chalk board" (people's excuses) will become more prominent. It is not ENTIRELY the fault of the people around you. Rather, a shared blame of their parents, a society of victim mindsets, media, and teachers; all mixed with the circumstance(s)/situation(s) gone through within an individual life.

That being known, the most to blame of impartation for those involved today, are parents (or lack thereof). They either do not pay enough attention to their kids (this includes bad situations such as divorce or lack of parenting), they focus on becoming friends with their son or daughter, rather than intentionally leading them (remember what I said on page 41), or they push their kids too far/hard without true love, to not want to listen to instruction of discipline.

So as kids grow up, they are left with will either taking on the embodiment of shaky parental patterns, or the world's opinionated greatly flawed patterns ("what the world believes is correct").

Parents or parents of choice, have an obligation to intentionally lead those who look up to them (such as kids) to break bad patterns, help those kids of choice understand the consequences of actions, and allow areas of independent small failures to provide guidance to create foundations for pattern-allistic growth.

Yet, like I've said, we all have the ability to determine our pattern-allistic mentality. So, blaming your parents for what you've seen/did not see, hear/did not hear, or had/did not have, is an excuse. Because within those patterns, we all understand certain patterns are not conducive to reach greater heights (see chapter 2 girl whose family had major problems) *pg. 41*.

Sadly, some people never understand what it means to reject the bad habits (impulse patterns), so they go with the worst of the options; choosing to not learn from them. As time goes on, these types of people will take notice of the mindset you are trying to embody and might ridicule you for the greatness patterns you want to achieve. They will possibly ask why you talk that way, why you think like that, why you do some things instead of others, or why it seems like you don't care about what is going on in their life (mainly excuses).

That's why it's important to find a balance in your personal growth: relaxation (as to not get burned out), being around your true friends, and spending your time with growth pattern-oriented people.

One thing you will come to learn, is when you start to develop the patternallistic mentality for growth you want. At first, excuses will probably start flooding in as you will manifest many things in the way of putting into practice the patterns for growth, both physically and mentally. (Example of bad excuses: KIDS *the worst excuse when you should set the example for them*, friends, school, sports, working out, social media, games, RELATIONSHIPS, your past, your parents, possessions, etc).

There is no worst excuse, because they are all terrible, **all** *of them ooze laziness.*

Even working out and sports can be a form of excuses in lazy patterns for growth of the mind. For instance, you go home after a workout, then decide you're too tired to do anything else productive mentally. That is a form of laziness.

In some way, push your whole body (mental, and physical) to a higher standard of greatness patterns.

I'm so tired of hearing this statement:

"You are perfect the way you are!!!"
This is a straight up lie. We are all made perfectly-imperfect,

Meaning, you were born perfect the way you are, but it is on you to set and practice a standard of patterns that keep you climbing higher in your personal mountains. ***For this is what it means to truly love yourself.***

Our initial perfectly imperfect selves are like when you buy a brand-new car off the lot. It looks nice, sleek, and runs perfect. But as time goes on, maybe you neglect it. Sometimes you put the wrong fuel in the tank (for some of us constantly), you don't change the oil out when it says to, or ignore the check engine light, essentially not caring what is wrong (because you don't have time to worry about it). Heck, you might never get the tires changed, or even wash/clean the inside.

What do you think is going to happen to that once really nice car?
After time of neglect adds up, the car is going to look terrible, run terrible, you will end up hating the car, and people will not like even being associated with the car.

You see what I mean? Now obviously the quality and time spent on all of those things I previously mentioned will vary, but they are key to the OVERALL life of the car. The more attentive someone is to their own personal car and stops worrying about someone else's (unless they share the car: AKA marriage), the higher the value of the car will be at any point in the future. That is why it matters how you treat your car (yourself). Why neglect the car that can take you to higher points of greatness?

Neglecting great pattern standards in an aspect of your personal life will only hurt you more in the end, <u>when</u> the lights of life problems begin flashing on your dashboard.

Check this out:
HOW CAN YOU EXPECT A LOT OF NICE CARS IN A BIG GARAGE IN THE PHYSICAL REALM, IF YOU DON'T WANT TO TAKE CARE OF, OR HAVE A HIGH PATTERN STANDARD OF DISCIPLINE FOR YOUR MENTAL LIFE CARS (individual areas of life)?
THE HARSH REALITY OF OVERALL REAL-LIFE SUCCESS LEVEL, DEPENDS ON HOW HIGH THE AVERAGE PATTERN LEVEL IS OF YOUR MENTAL GARAGE.

Have respect for these metaphorical life cars and I believe great things will come your way. But I can't believe great things for you. You need to go out, stay consistent in greatness, and perform patterns yourself. Follow through with taking care of these, "cars", move in faith, and know you can always take greater care of them in some way, it just takes more understanding.

<u>Types of cars in your garage you already have when you're born:</u>

- Mind
- Body
- Soul/Spirit

<u>Type of cars you will accumulate over time (you must take care of the 3 above before you can properly take care of the ones accumulated over time as patterns attribute into the below):</u>

- Friendships/Relationships
- Marriage
- Business(es)
- Education
- Etc.

<u>Don't not just go with the flow of this world of being perfectly fine, with being perfectly fine. I tell you, stand, move in faith, and grow to heights you couldn't even fathom, as you honor yourself/others!!</u>

<u>For those who call themselves perfectionists and even those who aren't. Say these words out loud:</u>

"I try my best in everything!! I am not perfect, so I will not let my past control my future patterns of greatness."

<u>For those who believe they cannot achieve great things. Say these words out loud:</u>

"I was not put on this earth to give up. I know I can stand. So, if I can stand, I know I can walk forward no matter how slow it might seem at first. If I can move forward, then I can run forward. If I can run forward,

then I can gain momentum. If I can gain momentum, then eventually I can become unstoppable. If I can become unstoppable, then even when presented with a wall of life, I can eventually break through stronger on the other side. If can break through any wall life throws and end up stronger, then I can become unshatterable. But it all starts with simply taking the first step forward, no matter how small at first. If I can consistently perform patterns, and with more determination keep putting one foot in front of the other, I know I can achieve anything. I <u>can</u> become…unbreakable."

<u>For those who were not born with parents who did not respectfully discipline out of true love or have great people around them. Say this out loud:</u>

"I am going to show how great I can be, regardless of the environment I was placed in. I am going put forth consistently great patterns of effort through honorable standards. I will gain wisdom by not doing what is or was consistently being shown before me, that I know is not respectful. I am <u>going</u> to rise and am <u>going</u> to become something greater. I understand it starts with <u>baby steps</u>, but if I stay consistent, eventually I can unlock the potential greatness within."

What the worldly opinion tells you, you should have (WEAK)

If you listen to society and conform to this world when it is steeped in dishonor and a lack of integrity, you will have a weak mentally, until you are backed by a truly righteous/integrity pattern-based mindset.

Allowing a child to make huge life altering choices when they don't even know what they want off the kid's menu, is one of these examples.

Society says kids are people too (which is true), but if you look at the statistics of kids who end up making drastic life choices. They were born into a broken home, a home that was not healthy/void of leadership, or a home in where no honorable/respectable patterns of discipline were put into practice of right and wrong.

For instance, everyone has a certain percentage of masculine and femininity. Society will tell you if you seemingly have more of one or the other, then you should be the embodiment of that thing. Which is false.

That being known, I'm not saying you shouldn't truly love/honor/respect everyone, but people who whole heartedly listen to the ways of this world are conformists. And in many ways live hypocritical lifestyles, because they do not understand what it means to be mentally strong.

So where did this weak mentality originate from?

The household and lack of a healthy nuclear family is under attack by the worldly opinion. But there is no excuse to become the embodiment of hypocrisy, because we are all born with a choice in how great we can potentially become.

"We have the choice to do anything, and everything. But not all things are beneficial to do."
-Paul (reference of chapter 7 of this book)

People will say the in the moment life pattern decision was the best thing for them. But when the lifestyle pattern begins to take a toll on their mentality, slowly but surely, they will notice things are not as they should be. Which leads to perceived stagnation, frustration, and a multitude of goals not fulfilled in the mental beyond.

So, why condone the pattern choice in the first place if it will only end up hurting someone mentally in the end, or delay the greatness within from being potentially achieved?

Another thing society says, is you have the right to anything and everything, regardless of if you put forth effort. Such as you deserve to be somewhere, you deserve to be with this type of person, you deserve money, or deserve to have something someone else has.

No one deserves anything, and if we were given what we deserve based on our life, I'm quite sure it wouldn't be great for most, if not all of us.

We have all done something wrong at one point or another. So having a self-serving mindset is conforming to the world and makes us weaker mentally in the end.

<u>**RESPECT IS NEVER TAKEN; IT'S EARNED IN YOURSELF FIRST.**</u>

Why you should be educationally opinionated, in favor of honorable/integrity filled/respectable individual growth patterns (STRONG)

Having an educated opinion is formidable in itself, but not being able to have an educated argument is weakness at the highest level. If you do not allow for educated arguments, then neither person will grow mentally, know of the events that led to why they think that way, or learn to come to a middle ground in a respectable manner.

If you have to resort to pettiness or constant complaining, using your life hypocrisy to make sure you are heard, then maybe you should re-evaluate your ability to truly have respect for yourself.

Being educationally opinionated, in favor of honorable/integrity filled/respectable individual growth patterns means…you do your best to not condone truly hypocritical patterns that inhibit growth patterns through effort displayed by individuals.

Remember to always be respectful of people. But acknowledge a difference between respectfully standing up for yourself with conviction, and causing a scene that proves why your patterns should not be followed.

What it means to not truly listen (YOUR DEAF)

When you don't listen to other's educated opinions, you will never become a true leader. And if you have no values other than what someone else instilled in you, then you are nothing but a puppet/follower who wants to be liked by the world. You possibly stand for nothing your own mind can come up with, because you will constantly make sure the world around you is ok with the way you perceive life.

The key here is, <u>EDUCATED</u>, opinion. Like I've said, everyone has an opinion, but if you haven't done any research, then you are putting yourself at the mercy of the person you heard the mental pattern from. If they were biased or lied, then you are in turn a <u>lying follower</u>, aka:

Puppet.

DON'T BECOME A PUPPET TO THIS WORLD, BECAUSE IN THE END, IT WILL ONLY (AB)USE YOU.

<u>Inconsistency leads to a facade (LOSES CREDIBILITY):</u>

Being consistent in success (even small aspects) is the biggest sign of greatness. If you want to be known as great in any faucet, then hold yourself to a consistently great pattern standard within your own life.

<u>Take for instance this example that I'm going to piggyback from the real-world, regarding a specific sport, country, ethnicities, and athlete:</u>

If someone advocates for one thing that they believe needs to change, consistency in their pattern-allistic mentality is key. Otherwise, they are a liar and a hypocrite unto themselves for the "betterment of people".

<u>*Meaning, when opportunity arises to advocate for the same aspect (not associated with them) that could possibly hurt their popularity or wallet, what is the most consistently great thing to do?*</u>
You obviously stay constant throughout the entire ordeal or admit failure in your mentality. Else, your opinion will be thrown out by those who are considered experts in the matter (as it should). <u>If you do not stay consistent, then it shows that you don't really care about the matter, and you just wanted a certain perception about you.</u>

If you display patterns of the underlined, you are a hypo-crists unto yourself, and only care about what others think of you. You do not deserve to be regarded as an advocate for greatness in any respect, due to the realm of the hypocrisy ideal you live in. Your heart is in the right place, but your mental patterns of how to truly love/care for others are misguided.

<u>If you constantly see the worst in life through others, then you are living in a hypocritical pattern mindset that is just as bad as giving into the devil's chaotic wishes for your life.</u>

"If you stand for nothing (honorable and integrity filled while living in respect), then you will fall for everything (and live in hypocrisy of what greatness is). "
-Alexander Hamilton, mixed with my (Joshua Rose's) background of pattern recognition of what he meant as it pertains to people in America

Live in honorable/respectable integrity, and stand firm in it, without being overtly disrespectful to others. But that doesn't mean you simply become a puppet to this world.
Becoming a puppet to this world, is what it means to be truly deaf.

BABY STEPS ARE KEY

I want you to come up with or search for, then write down **4 CORE LIFE VALUES**. Afterwards, in a few sentences write your own opinion of the previous chapter below within the parameters of the definitions of those values, and why you chose them. (**If married**, have your spouse do the same thing.)

****Know you should not limit yourself to being great in 4 values, because to appreciate what others do through their greatness patterns should cause a healthy competition in yourself to keep rising in greatness as well.
That being known, I highly encourage you to have, <u>healthy competition</u>, as one of your values. The healthy competition value touches all other values because at the very core, life is healthy competition. The One mentioned in chapter 7 doesn't want you to be great in only 4, because the One wants the absolute greatest for you.****

If you and your spouse do not exactly share all 4-5 values, that is fine. You were created as two beings to become interwoven into one, upon marriage. Both of you have your own pattern-allistic mentality and differing strengths. But you both need to agree by talking through, and sharing at least two core values (I presented you one).

Chapter 5: Look to something Higher

It starts by serving yourself and others:

Whether you or I want to believe it or not, we both have achieved many great things already, but do not realize due to the understanding that there is something hidden deeper within our own expectations of what our potential greatness is. That greatness hidden deeper within is held behind the door of giving/ serving others. But in order to consistently live in that deeper greatness realm, you must constantly live in patterns that serve others, and in doing so, you will find more fulfillment in life itself. So, look to something higher as a way to keep your patterns more accountable, in order to maintain access to this hidden potential greatness.

Those who look to serve, instead of to be served, will eventually find themselves served by as many people they seek to serve. You will garner the attention of a leader, whether you are one or not. Your words and your patterns/actions will be recorded in the minds of everyone you touch. You will find yourself surrounded by people who want to share your values and strive to reach greater heights.

If you look at yourself as someone that should always be served, then you will not only be met with unmet expectations, but will surely parish a truly lonely individual, a liar unto yourself, and a fool.

That is not some famous Greek philosopher, influencer, or agency. That is a cold hard statement of real life that individuals choose to ignore, because it requires something more from them without anything necessarily being given in return.

Not everyone can automatically-completely fulfill the key to the potential hidden greatness door, to consistently have access to it. <u>Baby steps</u> must be taken in order to create a pattern of serving actions to develop within your subconscious impulse first, through constantly balanced intentionality.

As for me (not to toot my own horn), but the choice words/verbiage-patterns performed from a variety of people around me to describe my heart, has provided reassurance in my ability to access this hidden greatness within, that can only be fulfilled by serving/giving unto others.

That being known, they did not say those things because I asked for them too. But instead, told me out of the honesty of their heart long after I gave/served them to a degree of excellence without expecting anything in return.

Now that I think about it, I've heard words from the heart everywhere I've been, because of my ability to understand the pattens of how to best serve others. So, you must develop your pattern-allistic mentality behind serving/giving as well.

I've heard them my corporate job, church, from family, true friends, acquaintances, from partners of businesses I've helped start, and from strangers. (One day soon you will read about my approach to business, how to start your own, and <u>what the true heart behind business is</u>.) When you develop the ability to understand the patterns to serve others in any situation, the possibilities of growth in any aspect of life are limitless! But first, you must start with how to best pattern-allistically serve yourself in order to understand your endless potential possibilities.

How you best serve yourself, is by instilling or living in consistency of great patterns in life to become greater.

Now after reading that you might be thinking, "Geez...I wish I had endless possibilities..."
<u>**EVERYONE HAS HIDDEN POTENTIAL. BUT IT'S HOW AND WHERE WE DECIDE TO CULTIVATE POTENTIAL, THAT DETERMINES HOW GREAT ANY PAIR OF EYES WILL PERCEIVE YOUR LIFE TO BE.**</u>

    The point I'm making with those past paragraphs is, I don't close my eyes, and always think of how to best serve myself. After I developed patterns of consistency that grew from **baby steps** (aka: how to better serve yourself), I subconsciously/consciously understood how to best give/serve others.

    I think of things people/this world needs, and how best I can help them out. Whether that be doing my best to lead myself, lead others, help without always needing to be in charge, help navigate rough life waters, or simply encourage someone. I don't do these things to pat myself on the back or receive some kind of sticker to say I did it, and neither should you.

So, I <u>challenge you</u> to seek serving/giving to yourself in respectable/honorable ways, and then seek to serve/give others in greater ways, even when life makes doing those things "seem" hard.

<u>As for the world:</u>

    Naturally, after trying to be there for someone, and been down in the dumps knowing I could've been greater. I've been told many times that I can't help everyone. But upon deciding in myself to not give up on helping others, I began to wonder how many times the people who told me, have told others with a less determined heart. Ultimately, giving up on the people around them and in turn, told someone else to give up who could be going through a similar pattern situation concerning helping someone else.

    Through observation of the world, and what is constantly being portrayed unknowingly adding to our pattern-allistic mentality. I came to the conclusion; we are slowly becoming a society of "lost causes". We are more likely to leave a situation at the first sign of associated turbulence, and in conjunction; adherence of great integrity-based wisdom is slowly going out of the window, so people are less likely to give it to potentially benefit someone else.

Integrity-based wisdom is becoming lost, because we as a society would rather search the world for someone of like opinion or mindset, to fulfill our current need of acceptance. Instead of rising to the higher level of greatness in truth we so desperately crave. So as a result, we as a individuals live in a society (although we are not all angry at each other most of the time) that lacks understanding of what it means to look to something higher.

So how do we fix this conundrum our society is developing?
<u>**We learn to truly love ourselves and others, with the knowledge we are all made perfectly imperfect and can grow in anything through patterns of intentionality. Which results in the change of patterns in the subconscious. But we have to be willing to listen to integrity-based correction. Then understand how to best truly love ourselves, and let our hearts fulfill the need to serve others in an integrity-based honorable way.**</u>

<u>**No one is able to be their best 100% of the time, because we are all human.**</u>

Which translates to the fact, some people need time to learn to help themselves, because they will not allow anyone else to do it currently. So, you definitely can't save everyone. But that should not mean you should be afraid to try in a way that is honorable, respectable, and shows integrity to at least provide a mental pattern path of higher greatness within a situation or circumstance for someone else.

Because we have forgotten how to truly love ourselves and one another, we have become a society of whiny children. When we as individuals are told something, we don't like and are strongly emotionally connected to, individuals tend to throw a tantrum until someone comes along to tell us we are right, and they are on our side. Which results in making excuses to not look to something higher within yourselves (blind leading the blind).

As a group of individuals (especially in America), we tend to create our own problems leading to inadvertently creating a society of victims, through weakness abused manipulation, via many "good" people and businesses.

This need of validation of others, has resulted in society as a whole turning into sheep. As we potentially follow "shepherds" who are slow to say they led you to the ledge of a cliff but are quick to dismiss/condemn others who warn of the dangerous pathway as "wolves".

<u>Here are some questions we as individuals need to think about:</u>

- Why did that person or group tell you they'll let everyone else know your problems, only to do nothing feasible about it, nor presenting a pattern for you to be real life greater that is truly loving unto yourself?

- Did anything get better by using their advice, or what they told you to do?

- Did you do your best before you sought this "help"? Or did you lean on everyone else for validation?

The difference between those of us who are considered successful and those who are not (the victims), is simple. How successful you are in giving/serving others has a direct correlation in how much greatness you can potentially have, because we as humans are more inclined to follow those who will truly help, even when it is not convenient.

Successful people will rarely say how successful they are. But instead, show it through how they treat others in every walk of life, no matter if they agree with them or not, and should not condone patterns that will hurt someone's growth in the end.

<u>Perform the actions of what the Golden Rule talks about, especially when you don't expect to get anything in return (apart of serving yourself:</u>

"Do unto others, as you would have them do unto you."

I will never beg anyone to do anything, (and I for sure will not beg you to go to church), but Christ has played a bigger part in turning around more lives for the better, than any other religion, hotline, psychiatrist, political view, or company ever.

Did those lives get changed overnight?

No. Those people changed their lives through patterns of discipline, and continually living according to the Word for greater patterns.

Don't think I know what I'm talking about? Look at the places that despise the church, Christianity, and looking to something higher. Are they truly thriving through the growth of <u>everyone</u>?

Let's think about one country in particular (a world superpower today). A country that has silenced all other opinions that don't align with the government (something this world is slowly moving towards, and the country is not America…yet). People there do not have the liberty of free speech, every election is rigged, and anyone who offers a varying opinion are killed or "cancelled".

Those citizens do not truly like to live there and are not allowed to have an individual opinion whatsoever. That same country condemns church, and Christianity, so much so, if you are caught having service you could be put to death.

In these types of countries, the ones controlling how people think are the media and government. The media and a select group of individuals tell the people, "You <u>are</u> happy, because we have these rules from the government that tell you how to be happy." No one can have an opinion, because manipulation takes away the individual opportunistic right to transcend into greater things.

Do you see now what happens when you don't look to something higher as a nation? You end up getting taken advantage of, because it is in human nature for power to corrupt, when your mentality lives in constant hypocrisy of what greatness is.

Humans were given the power to fill the earth and take dominion (so do not live in fear). But we are naturally power-hungry beings, because we want as much of it as our individual conscience will allow us to have.

What is a country made up of though? <u>Individuals</u>. And the reason why America is considered the greatest country is due to the fact, it was formed of freedoms FOR THE PEOPLE, BY THE PEOPLE, and ultimately backed by the words, <u>ONE NATION UNDER GOD</u>.

What sets America apart from the rest of the world, is they have more liberties to take away. So, it irks me when people say they are not proud to be there. They have more collective individual honorable, integrity filled, and honorable liberties than ANYWHERE ELSE IN THE WORLD.

It might be a random coincidence (<u>even though there are no such things as coincidence when true facts/details are closely related</u>), but there is a reason why America became the greatest superpower ever.

Greatness starts with the <u>individual</u> CITIZEN looking to something higher than themselves, and not asking for a handout, or denying wisdom at every turn. God and individual liberties are/were the backbone of the American society that made it great. So, if you take away either one of the backbones, you'll end up taking out the other along with it and will eventually fall from greatness. The darkness in the world wants to take away the light that America provides, residing in the backbones of the nation.

<u>Here is the story of why I look to something higher, and the reasoning behind my heart of understanding the Biblical mindset (and clarification):</u>

My family and I were always involved in the church and served. But after a time, I became numb to it, because I never understood what it meant <u>TO TRULY SERVE MYSELF</u>. Ultimately, I knew what looking to something higher had to offer, but I was always careful not to try and make a concerted effort to form a type of relationship with those whom I often served with/for.

<u>Pattern dive from far past, but something</u> to <u>keep in mind for the main premise:</u>

As you know, my mother went through a tough time and brought it home (pattern I developed to become an example for people of what greatness is). Then my father had his own small business, but from a young age I noticed when things didn't go according to plan, he would become extremely frustrated. (Remember patterns from parent to kid.)

Now in no way was he a bad father, but he was so concerned with money, that it seemed to run his life. Which ultimately led to loud bickering from my parents about what they could/could not afford, and later an understanding in myself to not want to be controlled by money. I saw patterns of fear without understanding what the tool that money is and could potentially do.

That being known, I did not have the worst parents, but a kid asking your parents if they were going to get a divorce is not something that should be a topic to brought up at early age.

So as life went on, to avoid any type of confrontation, (a pattern that needed to be removed) I "<u>believed</u>" I did not need anyone else to be <u>individually</u> greater. Which caused me to fail many times over. But every time I did, I went crawling back to the church to get my "fix". Then I would slink back into patterns that (although was considered successful by most: great job, liked by many, lots of friends) were not beneficial for growth, and I became my own worst enemy at times, because of the lack of understanding of the pattern in my mentality.

<u>Pattern dive from the not-so-distant past, but something to keep in mind for the main premise because it is another pattern layer:</u>

After committing to tap into my potential. I became the greatest version of myself physically to date and reached a high level of greatness in the corporate world. But my mentality came crashing down, when my heart was broken by the girl I "<u>believed</u>" I was going marry.

I wasn't sure what happened. Everything was going great. We were both happy in each other and I was even told this by her, her family, and the people around us/her said they had never seen her so happy. But this is life, it can happen <u>when</u> you don't see it coming.

I'll never forget, one day I was laying on the ground after a workout, looking up at the ceiling of the house, and I began to think I wasn't good enough. Slowly, the feeling became overwhelming, my body felt heavy, and tears began to swell in my eyes.

As the thoughts of suicide began to dance in my head, I went through all the situations I had gone through, questioning if I'd ever be good enough in myself to be beneficial for anyone. Because this was the one time I couldn't close the gap in my head around the word, "why". Due to the lack of closure, and knowing I was the greatest version of myself to date.

Here is where this story is pertinent because it applies to my greatness patterns today. But I had to learn from my hidden patterns, in conjunction with my sliding door of wisdom, to understand how to be greater first.

It was ironic. I wanted to be there for people, but thought I had to become someone so self-sufficient; I didn't believe I needed anything, or anyone else. Yet, all that time I subconsciously wanted so badly to have someone in my life, that when someone I deeply wanted in my life left, I felt I shouldn't be around anymore. From there, the thought patterns began to bleed into another aspect of life where I didn't believe I could be of any benefit to the rest of the world, because I couldn't even get one person who said they wanted to stay by my side, to continue doing so (leadership is done through admiration/respect by others).

The times of everything I did up to that point to be there for various people I cared about, only to be let go time after time, and me seemingly picking up the pieces of my heart off the ground, with little to no help (it seemed like) began to replay in my head like a bad dream.

Here is the vision I had while lying there, that played on repeat for 20 minutes:

What played in my head was the mental image of a plate that started off perfect, then being dropped. Then me doing my best to pick up the pieces and putting them back together. Only to have the plate that was not whole anymore (because I couldn't find all the tiny pieces after) being dropped time and time again. Until so many pieces of the plate were missing, nothing could be held on it to give to others. In fact, it would definitely shatter in a matter of time if anything was placed on it.

After some time lying on the ground, I closed my eyes with what seemed like the full weight of the world, and <u>the feeling I would let it down</u>. The bad dream of the plate being repeatedly broken suddenly stopped, and my mind went blank. From there, looking into darkness, this massive weight was the only thing I could feel. I couldn't move my body. Then all of a sudden, with my eyes closed, I saw a distant light that was merely a dot and heard a voice say:

<u>*"Are you finally done lying on the ground? Even after saying you would FULLY tap into your greatness, you know you're holding back. I gave you many tremendous gifts, and know you prayed many times for the full weight of what anyone else or the world would feel, because you thought you could handle it. This is that weight. This is the weight of the world. Do you still think you can carry it alone, and still reach your full potential? Do you want to access your full potential or not? If so, all I ask is you simply reach your hand towards Me."*</u>

I had felt small portions of the weight before from previous life experiences, but I needed to feel the full brunt of it without the pattern of my own understanding to mentally comprehend how to push through it.

My body was still heavy, but all of a sudden, my right arm felt a little lighter. So, I slowly picked my arm up, and reached as far as my body would allow. With my eyes still closed staring at the tunnel of light, I grasped the hand reaching back, and picked myself off the ground.

    Even after doing this, life was not easy. I fought through many mental patterns and struggled for quite some time in many aspects of life. Yet, the only pattern that truly saved me and kept me on track, was my habit (impulse pattern) of crawling back to the church.

    Which drew me to the conclusion, that there is no greater mental match to overcome than something you have become numb to. And then try and have it become a bigger part of your life in the understanding, it is truly great. Thankfully for me, there was yet another shift of patterns in my mind through the vision.

I knew I was holding back, because I thought I was the main person holding the weight I placed on myself. But this time I knew I was not the only one holding the weight of the world on my shoulders.

I always knew where my abilities and gifts came from, and who granted me the mentality to rise above what others thought of me. But it wasn't until I freed myself of the feeling that I was always in complete control of my life no matter what did, did I understand the potential greatness I and anyone else could achieve.

I was tired of the life this world wanted me to have, and that told me I was great. I knew how to grow, but I lacked the most important key. <u>The key of looking to something higher (Chapter 7)</u>. Being a leader, someone who always grew to break their whole-body limits, and wanting to serve others were the best parts of me. But I was willing to throw it all away, because of what this world thought of me.

<u>So, I had to strip myself piece by piece over time of the tainted armor the world and my mind gave me, to grow to heights I had only dreamed of that God had planned for me, and is still guiding me to achieve.</u>

<u>This plate that I was putting back together myself over time had each missing piece filled with the more consistency of patterns I invoked from the biblical mindset.</u>

Today, I have multiple businesses, better friendships, gathered better overall people around me, and have seen a pattern mindset shift within my family.

The doors once locked behind the quad-lock (referenced later in the book) are now open, and I have no intention of just dipping a toe into my potential. I <u>WILL</u> become a world changer, letting my light that is a now a massive star, shine as bright as I know it <u>CAN</u> for all to see.

I want the absolute best for you, but you need to apply patterns of change through action. Don't just stand still in the Lord and Word. Do everything with a purpose and watch the change around you happen. Take heed the things I have done and said in this book, because they are not for my honor, rather for yours and ultimately the One on high I look to.

<u>Patterns corrected</u>: realization I can't better serve the world through myself alone to avoid conflict and lean on my own understanding of the why <u>when LIFE happens.</u>

<u>Wow, that last section got really deeeeep!!!! But I'm certain we have all gone through those types of feelings. Maybe not to the degree I have or under the same circumstances. But we've all felt like we couldn't get up, because the weight we carry called, our potential, can be too heavy.</u>

<u>But if I can learn to look to the One who wants the very best for me and was there to fill in the missing pieces of my plate, making it completely whole again, then you can too. Now making it so, where even when a crack appears from it falling down, I can take it back to the One who created it and it will be made new…and you can too. That is where your hope is in achieving greater heights. That is the greatest way you can serve yourself, to better serve others, through looking to something higher (Chapter 7).</u>

BABY STEPS ARE KEY

Even if you're still not a believer in the Biblical mindset, write down below what your mental plate looks like. (It's not perfect, is it?)

What patterns did you see in your parents or parents of choice that you are not aware of? Write down 2 good, and two bad patterns **bad you might be blind to as they are not always obvious**. (For me example, Good: display of fear of not having enough money. I discerned that money is a tool to make more money, so I learned of investing in myself and others through first looking/giving to something higher first. Bad: seeing strength in doing things alone to avoid conflict, when humans at the core want some kind of relationship with others.)

More ways of looking to something higher in yourself as proven by the patterns of the world

I am not sure if you've ever heard of something called a "Blue Zone". If not, don't worry, I didn't either until just recently. Literally, as I was going back through this book to see what additions I should make, and this topic was presented to me by someone whom I consider a great leader. I didn't dive too much into the topic, but I thought the idea was interesting. So, I created my own patterns behind the details, and made something worldly vague, more translatable to the real-world individual patterns. So, let's dive into the patterns behind the patterns!

Here is the definition:

➤ Regions of the world where people statistically live longer than average (https://www.bluezones.com/blue-zones-life/)

    o Categories that dive into what makes "Blue Zones" what they are

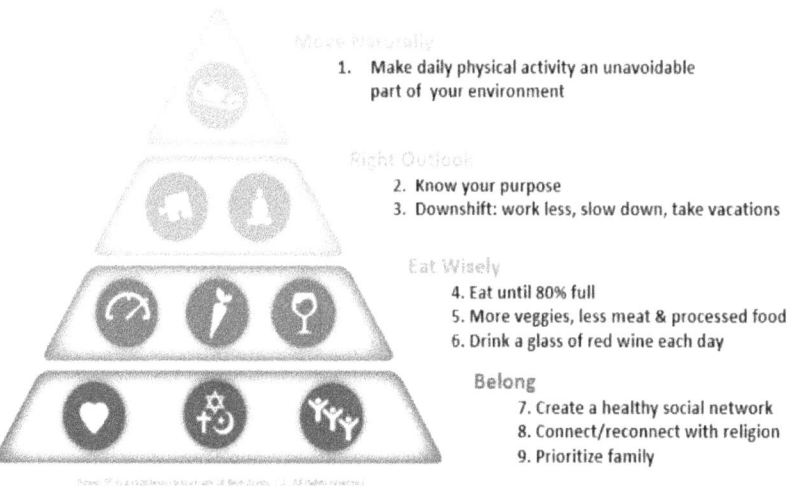

Move Naturally
1. Make daily physical activity an unavoidable part of your environment

Right Outlook
2. Know your purpose
3. Downshift: work less, slow down, take vacations

Eat Wisely
4. Eat until 80% full
5. More veggies, less meat & processed food
6. Drink a glass of red wine each day

Belong
7. Create a healthy social network
8. Connect/reconnect with religion
9. Prioritize family

All the numbers to the right of the pyramid represent patterns and co-occurrences people partake in, in these so called, "Blue Zones". But I say there are hidden messages and added layers within the patterns of the mind behind the message of these zones that aid in a successful life, because all of them derive from a grand pattern of the mind in everyone.

<u>All physical performed patterns do not necessarily lead to lives that can be seen as successful.</u> **Because just following simple steps will not grant you the ability to have the feeling of a successful person, due to us all having an individual pattern-allstic mentality, that is hidden in our heart, mind, and soul.**

Remember, everyone has the ability to potentially comprehend the greatness of their own life using their gifts and pattern-allistic mentality.

So fulfilled mentality success is not something that can be represented by a basic survey, or through simple observation. Rather, a combination of actions and mentality that must be practiced by everyone, based in their own pattern-allistic mentality that derives from a combination of their heart, mind, and soul.

Focused Obligation patterns (my term)

It takes a human-achievable amount of focus driven obligation to ascertain the patterns of numbers: 1, 3, 8, 9

Definitions (presented by, https://languages.oup.com/google-dictionary-en/):

Focus
Noun: the center of interest or activity, the state or quality of having or producing clear visual definition
Verb: adapt to the prevailing level of light and become able to see clearly, pay particular attention to

Obligation
An act or course of action to which a person is morally or legally bound, a duty or commitment

Focused Obligation (my definition)
an act you owe to yourself to truly live your greatest life according to Biblical values, and not according to the false pretenses of fake leaders in the world's opinion today

My opinion/wisdom and further elaboration:

All of those numbers are patterns you must have a focused obligation to as an individual, in order to potentially lead a greater life. These zones are known to be better places of living. But I fully believe the insight I provided in the earlier chapters of this book, serve as the mental blueprint, and cause thought pattern processes that are universal for anyone as an individual to achieve greatness.

Check this out:

(1) Physical activity is obviously the highest yielding on a physical personal level yet is the easiest way to create patterns for greatness that stem into everything else. That being known, don't just aim to do the bare minimum or else, life will give you the bare minimum in return. The bare minimum is boring and mundane. Which can lead to stagnation and ultimately to frustration. Create a plan for growth, setting up small **baby step** increases in what you do every 2-3 weeks when working out.

Doing this stimulates your sense of accomplishment. It also increases the natural amount of dopamine in your system, while decreasing the mental state of, "being down on yourself", or thinking, "the world is holding me back". This focused obligation is key, because it will not be easy at first. So, as you grow in this area of yourself, physical activity will become easier.

Patterns of the mind

The pattern-allistic mentality you are growing both physically and mentally, is self-discipline and determination of the spirit. When you work out, you put stress on the body for a certain amount of time, and should be determined to get better each time. Life is the same way. It will put stress on you for a certain amount of time. But <u>you</u> can <u>choose</u> to either put forth determined effort to get stronger, or determine you want to keep struggling with the same mental weight every time.

Getting greater incrementally with **baby steps** sets the mental pattern of not giving in under the pressure of life when things become hard to do, because you subconsciously realize there is no reason to give up when facing a ***Mountain*** of ***Life***.

Flashback to what I said about the military breaking old bad patterns of mentality. Well, in the most strenuous of military exams of becoming a navy seal. They have such a high dropout rate, because the weight of the journey will break you, if you think about it all at once. That being known, the gravity of any situation can be bone crushing.

Just as I used to tell myself when running up a steep 200 ft incline on the side of a water dam at a lake, with a 50lb weight vest as a kid, "I simply need to focus on each step, and over time this mini mountain will be conquered with ease." Eventually, the mini mountain was conquered many times for years. So much so, I paved a path (trail) of my patterns in greatness for others to want to follow on the mini mountain itself.

(3) <u>Knowing how or when to put forth work/effort in a job occupation or daily life</u> is a dangerous one, because we are pattern driven beings. So, we tend to become consumed and take on the embodiment of what we set our focused obligation to (Don't believe me? See the graphs again on social media or think of people consumed by an addiction, where the addiction to a non-living thing runs the patterns of a supercomputer *individual*).

Most people take this number to the extremes on both sides of the spectrum. Especially if the individual has more or are told they have more of any aspect compared to the rest of their current world. Which can include money, talent, intellect, possessions, success, family leadership, etc. Including the vice versa of any of life's good or bad.

All of those aspects and their vice versa, play huge roles in knowing when you the <u>individual</u> puts forth work/choice-effort, or <u>chooses</u> to not to put forth work/choice-effort in any task/choice-area of life.

You <u>choose</u> to make anything hard by <u>simply</u> putting too much effort into thinking, thus making it hard in your own mind. Which results in potentially making anything stressful for you or the people around you. You can <u>possibly</u> make anything easy by knowing precisely where to put forth effort. But first you have to answer the correctly worded question(s) in order to discover the hidden arrow pointing to the life pattern/answer you are seeking.

When it comes to knowing when to apply work/effort and how to learn to be more stress free, I learned a thing or two about the mentality of greatness. I learned the end goal of benefitting life/lives in greatness when I first entered the work force at the ripe old age of 8, that have only been reaffirmed in the real world today.

In the corporate world, I've been told several things of what it means to want to move up in that realm. Granted, I understand there are those jobs such as being a surgeon, lawyer, accountant, teacher, researcher, hourly workers, or having your own business that might require more than a 40-hour work week…

…but the <u>IDIOCY</u> of building a mental pattern of <u>CONSISTENTLY</u> working more than a 40-hour work week to, "get things done for the benefit of the company", has always baffled me.

<u>For those in the workforce, I'm going to let you in on a little secret I described in chapter 1 that has been reiterated over and over again to me, by those who I know to be successful in the business world:</u>

Unless they pay overtime immediately after 40 hours, <u>do your best</u> to never consistently give your employer more than 40 hours of your time. Because you are giving away your money, life, and precious time that could be spent on other things. If you consistently need more than 40 hours to finish your work to a high degree, then you need to rethink your efficiency pattern mentality to get tasks done. If you're producing at a high level, giving more time on top, and you see no movement up within that realm after a respectable time (3-5 years). Then you need to re-evaluate your current value within the company you're in with a manager or mentor.

What happens when you prove to become more efficient in the time allotted? You show you know what you're doing, while displaying to those around you, you can be a leader, and that your value is irreplaceable.

The reason companies work people to the bone, is due to the fact, employees do not realize that they should get work done at a high degree, with efficiency; in conjunction with knowing that their life should not revolve around their job.

An employer who understands their employees have/need lives too, is one who knows how to get the best from their employees and will only have greater success in the end.

<u>(9)</u> Family....

...(Recall chapter 1: Intro to Patterns) We all develop our own simple pattern-allistic mentality as a kid from parent's or parents of choice, and the world around us. The problem is, the world has affected everyone in the decision to choose when to be their own leader. Which has resulted in skewing the patterns of how to truly love someone. And the sad part is, this mentality has begun to leak into the parental/family pattern mindset.

Prioritizing family means to do life with them in an honorable manner. Even when it does not always seem convenient.

Family and family of choice, who know the definition of the true love displayed in this book, need to spend time together. Go do things without always needing a phone in your hands, because it will create a pattern basis for what a real-world connection truly is and can offer a glimpse into real-world relationship patterns for greatness/success.

Be the person to first to initiate conversation. The topic does not need to be some super hard take on life either. So, practice with baby steps, because it will help build the subconscious pattern feeling of true connection, with the realization everyone is their own person, and we were not meant to do life alone.

If you want to have a greater relationship with your kid or kid of choice, a simple text or phone call, even once a week, shows you are there for them. The same goes for if those who want to have a great relationship with your parents or parents of choice. Call or send them a text, telling them you love and appreciate them.

No matter how great or broken a relationship seems to be, be the person who will step up, and make a connection first. ***Baby steps*** *are key for great relationships of all kinds. If a family relationship is broken, do not be afraid if no response occurs immediately. Always try to initiate a conversation, because it will show you are willing to admit you're not perfect, but still think of the other in a truly loving way.*

Combination of (1), (3), (9)

If you can learn to stand with the stress you're currently under on your shoulders, you can walk with it, and then run. Which leads to other types of stress on the same level no longer becoming a factor, unless you choose for them to be.

The best way for me to combine all of these numbers leading to (8), is through questions I asked my group of friends in college:

Would you rather be born poor, but have the ability to overcome any obstacle, breaking any ceiling you see above you based on the deeper drive you naturally receive of wanting more than just a poor mundane life? Or be

born into a rich family, inherently not understanding that deeper drive from the lifestyle of what it means to pick yourself up from the bottom, ultimately not comprehending how to fully unlock the hidden greatness within yourself, so you only have 25% of the natural drive ability that breaks any of the same ceilings as the person born into a poor family?

<u>Question made easy</u>: Mental drive ability to break any ceiling. Either:
Born rich = potentially 25% max of the mental gift
Born poor = potentially 100% access to the mental gift

Most if not all my friends inherently said they would rather be born rich, so they could have the desires of their heart. When I asked why, they said they personally would never just only have access to 25% of the same ceiling breaking ability. Yet, they did not take into account the hidden mental pattern message behind the question.

<u>So I ask you:</u>

With the knowledge of what's more likely to lead to stagnation, then frustration, and beyond. **Someone who has the patterns to overcome anything. Or someone who only understands what it means to have 25% of the greatness patterns in what they could be. What do you choose?**

<u>Down a rabbit hole we go!!</u>

<u>Don't worry, I know what you're probably thinking, "Why only 25%?". The answer is simple:</u>

The greatest teacher is life itself. So intentionality of patterns aside, who do you think experiences more real life stress from an earlier age? The inherently well off, or the inherently poor?

Children of the inherently wealthy do not understand how to unlock the ability to create the patterns of greatness as well as the children of the lesser off. <u>Unless those born with more wealth fully grasp all aspects of what those beginning patterns of focused obligation to greatness are.</u> *The inherently wealthy <u>have to be shown</u> real life. While the inherently poor <u>are forced</u> to see the full weight of real life from an early age.*

That being said, the state of people today (2021), is <u>**MOSTLY**</u> due to the lack of leadership in parental practices (Family/9…awkward). Then schools, media, and a lack of true leadership in the person them-self follow a close second, third, and fourth.

<u>To address the problem of why only the wealthy, seem to succeed:</u>

It doesn't necessarily matter how much money you're born with, because at the end of the day, only you can choose to be greater than what life inherently expects from you.

Everyone can be great, but the reason why it seems most wealthy kids (past lower-middle class in America) succeed, is due to them picking up on certain patterns from the family members who were able to give the next generation what was created yesterday. What's crazy, is that wealth does not tend to multiply without the proper intentionality of teaching the next in line the drive of the poor to break ceilings.

"One person pretends to be rich, yet has nothing; another pretends to be poor, yet has great wealth."
-Proverbs 13:7

Which is why sometimes the exceedingly wealthy who had to work for everything, decide to give their next in line very little in comparison to what they achieved. This creates a drive of greatness patterns to break ceilings, because they want their children to create a legacy more impactful than their own or their grandparents. (Here's a book that helped me understand this concept as a poorer kid, because it displayed patterns of greatness **for anyone** to achieve: "*The Ultimate Gift*", by: Jim Stovall)

All that being said, you don't need to be born inherently wealthy, or have multiple things going for you in various ways/circumstances to succeed in life. It doesn't matter what age, color, economic basis, or problematic family you come from (we all come from imperfect families). You will grow

to unimaginable heights if you properly apply greatness patterns into your life.

<u>My response to my friends about being born poor or born wealthy:</u>

I confidently chose the ability to be poor but break through any ceiling. But, I am a little biased, because I was born poor, I understood the hidden pattern behind the main question, and discovered/was taught the ability to break any ceiling as I grew up with this pattern of understanding:

I know who I am down to the reasoning of how and why I act in certain situations, because I have worked hard to hone my mentality, patterns, and abilities in understanding. Even then, I know I can always be better, and I'm going to serve as many people as I can along the way, because I can't achieve a great successful life by myself.

Out of the rabbit hole!!

<u>**(8)** Whether you recognize it or not, this book was made on the backbone of Biblical principles (the light)</u>

The Bible clearly states the opposite of what this world thinks, or even among what some Christians think about prosperity. If you look at the passages correctly, God wants you to prosper and gives you the blueprint of how to do it. <u>All He asks is when prosperity comes, do not become consumed by the possessions of this world, as they are only temporary, and remember where the prosperity comes from.</u>

"From the dust we came, and to the dust we shall return." God has a plan and will for everyone. But those who have developed His patterns will come to change the world, and no certain amount of money is needed to be born with. Only the pattern-allistic mentality He wants you to instill in yourself is needed for greatness and prosperity to occur.

We are not all born economically equal, but all have the same opportunity to change our pattern-allistic mentality for the benefit of our individual world towards greatness.

You know what else is crazy? In Saul Alinsky's book: "<u>Rules for Radicals</u>", (a book about socialism and changing mindsets of people to get in power). He explicitly talks about manipulating the minority and poor with media, because they are the easiest to control through a lie of "benefiting" them. Yet, when you look at the patterns they instill, they do nothing but drive a bigger wedge between the wealthy and lower class (There is where the true devil lies in the details).

<u>Correlate the true devil in that detail above with this:</u>

A good portion of the people used to change the world in Biblical days didn't come from inherently wealthy families. God needed a change in the world's mindset into one of overall growth, so He chose carefully. He knew the poor already had the patterns needed to change the world into a mindset of growth. As they had already developed the most faith in Him from a young age, because they came from a faith-based background needed for provision.

So, He chose fisherman and shepherds to move the needle to ultimately take back His creation to give us all a better chance of prosperity, to glorify and be with Him in the end.

God used the seemingly, inherently, non-influential from both good and horrible backgrounds of the poor, to literally change this world and become its greatest leaders. Because He knew they would not use tactics normal to the world. But instead, use patterns developed through faith. All anyone needs to do is learn to figure out the wisdom behind the details of their entire life, to then instill patterns of greatness for success.

Faith + Belief + Understanding = Success

<u>Now for the flip side of the religious coin (the dark):</u>

The Devil doesn't want this world changed towards one of a growth mindset. For he knows chaos, stagnation, and uncertainty is what drives evil acts.

The poor driven growth mindset users and/or the seemingly non-influential, can't change the world for beneficial purposes if they are being manipulated by those who do not know how to truly love (as seen in the previous chapters). So, in the end, there is no beneficial change to individuals in the world themselves. Which creates a downward cycle of all mental patterns, unless broken by something just as powerfully devoted.

STORY TIME: I WAS MEANT TO BE A KING!!

(And you were meant to be a King or Queen as well!!)

One example of not born inherently wealthy or had everything going for him was, King David (arguable the greatest king of Israel *B.C.*).

David was a shepherd boy who God chose to lead His nation and was called a man after God's own heart, by God himself (even in after not being as great as he could've been in certain situations). But when it came time for the anointing of the new king, not even David's own dad thought he was able or worthy of meeting the disciple, to possibly be anointed. David's father invited all of his other sons physically capable but left David (the youngest) in the field with the herd.

Yet, even when David's own father did not recognize his potential, God saw the small boy who had nothing in terms of physical stature or wealth, as having the greatest potential in leading His nation. David, the one not even deemed worthy enough by his own father, had God's anointing and the focused obligation, to achieve all-time greatness.

No one's parents, nor other people are perfect, because they are human too. But each of us individually comprehends or has seen patterns of greatness. So, it is on us to choose to be greater in ourselves. (Remember what I told my own mother in chapter 1?)

If someone can realize the potential greatness within themselves, they too can succeed in great ways, once the necessary patterns within their own pattern-allistic mentality have been developed.
In the understanding of your greatness and what your talents/gifts are, is where you'll find your purpose.

Numbers of Diligence

The reason I say these numbers and not all of them require diligence, is due to the fact anyone can stumble upon them: 2, 4, 5, 6

6 - I understand the health benefits, but do not personally agree with it as being necessary for what should be called a reason for a living a longer life. In my opinion, it is actually the pattern wine represents.

<u>Diligence</u> – careful and persistent work or effort

<u>My opinion/wisdom and further elaboration:</u>

(4) <u>Eating until 80% full</u> is a secret back door to more patterns that represents you are not overindulging on the good things life has to offer.

If someone constantly lives in the pattern of "eating" every good thing they get from life, then it will lead to bigger and worse consequences for life in the end.
Not only is it detrimental in terms of health to eat until 100% full, but also think of it in terms of finances.

You can be poor no matter how much money you make, by keeping yourself poor through making the same decisions to show as if you are wealthy. If you spend everything you have, without planning to some degree for the future; then you will never have money when you need it most or when you desire leisure time.

The same goes for wealthy individuals. If you blow money for no reason, neglecting marginalization, even though you make a lot of money, you will always not have any from over-indulging past the 80% usage.

It is important to let the pattern of not overindulging on anything and everything, become a staple of diligence onto your "sliding door" of wisdom, for all aspects of life.

(6) <u>Drinking ONE glass of wine</u> simply represents the ability to do things carefully when relaxing.

In today's world, wine is easily seen as a commodity, along with being reserved for those who have gone through a long workday or used during celebration. Either way, it is a form of relaxation. But one thing wine has in it, is alcohol.

Alcohol in great amounts can be detrimental to your overall health. So just as you need to be responsible when drinking (sliding door of wisdom for **#4**), you need to be careful in the patterns you develop while relaxing. You can pick up some nasty patterns that turn into impulse habits within your pattern-allistic mentality, once believe you should not put in effort where needed. The result pattern being you losing self-discipline in your purpose.

<u>We as individuals need to practice the saying my grandmother used to tell me:</u>

"It is ok to eat desert every once in a while, but not all the time."

This saying sets into place a mentality pattern to be self-disciplined in not over-indulging on the good things in life, do not take life so serious as to not joke around, and learn to embrace having fun every once in a while; with the knowledge there are still things yet to be accomplished.

That being known, you need to recharge your batteries in an HONORABLE/RESPECTABLE/INTERGRITY filled manner. This does not mean go on a binger of doing bad things, or even do one giant bad thing. It simply means take **A** step back after being self-disciplined for a certain time span to recharge your batteries.

<u>Here's an example of taking **A** step back:</u>

Go on vacation for a weekend or marginalize your time better to take PTO. Another way is to buy <u>(within reason)</u> something that makes sense for you to have *dopamine*.
Understanding relaxation/leisure is important. But you have to be diligent as to not become so overindulgent, it becomes a staple that bleeds into everything you do when applying new patterns onto your "sliding door" of wisdom.

(5) <u>More veggies, less meat, and processed food</u>. This number actually goes hand in hand with **4** and **6**. Eating less processed foods is imperative to your health, but you can easily burn yourself out by maintaining such a supremely disciplined lifestyle. And eventually (after a while), you determine that is just not worth it in the end.

Which is why a good portion of sports stars who had to be in incredible shape their entire lives, go off their diets and gain a good amount of weight. (Let's be frank about another topic. Judging if someone eats meat or not, is a waste of time.)

The problem with today's food (especially in America) that bleeds into society, is the fact that people do not recognize the benefits of staying relatively healthy. Because individuals have decided to listen to those who do not understand how to truly love in a way that wants the best for someone else, and that we as individuals should not do whatever we want. Which ultimately leads to individuals not wanting to change themselves for the greater.

Staying diligent in how much you consume into your body is equally as important as what you do with it, because neither can reach its' full potential life greatness without recognizing the requirement of the other. *I want the best and longest life for you. You don't need a 6 pack, but it is imperative to stay in some kind of beneficial health shape.*

(2) Now we get to the number everyone has probably been waiting for……**how to know your purpose**!!!

Simply put…**Drum Roll**…….

..................*I do not the answer.*

What?! Cut me a break. I'm not God. I'm not someone that can determine the purpose for every living being by just using a book. But I can make it semi-fluid for anyone to understand in their own mentality and talents, through patterns.

Everyone is different and I respect that. But what I can say is, take to heart the words in this book, apply greatness patterns to your whole-body life, and discover your hidden messages I put in this book by applying them to your life.

We all struggle or will struggle with in some form/aspect or pattern in this book.

I will tell you this about finding your purpose:

When you have an unshakable feeling deriving from past experiences, feel a burden on your heart to complete, or keep noticing you have a knack for a certain skill set for the real world, and it makes you feel energized during the integrity/honorable filled process of completion...
...*you should pursue the hidden premise of that feeling, as it may become your purpose.*

That being known, finding your purpose can be difficult. Which leads me to my next rabbit hole. The main reason why people commit suicide or become depressed, is the feeling they will never find, nor will regain that one thing...their purpose.

Down a rabbit hole!!

Here's what I have to say about the emotion that stems into suicide:

It's normal to feel that unsure emotion. But just because you have not found your purpose YET, does not mean what you're currently doing will not contribute to the purpose meant for your life.

It's amazing the trials and many lessons we as individuals don't want to have to go through, in order to get to the specified end result, because we as individuals want things ASAP. Yet, even bad things that occur have a reason for happening in the grand scheme of things.

That known, it might take time to divulge the wisdom needed to progress into the next higher level within your purpose. With this understanding, there is no reason to be disrespectful/dishonorable to others about the events, when you can find wisdom to become greater in any and every situation or circumstance.

So, rise above the situation knowing you'll find your purpose using the wisdom gained from the circumstance you are/were thrust into, because it leads to a development of your needed talents/gifts. You will create valuable additions to your pattern-allistic mentality and "sliding door" of wisdom, if you choose for those situations/circumstances to have a beneficial meaning.

<u>One thing to remember about any situation you find yourself in:</u>

There is a difference between standing up for and being disrespectful/ dishonorable to yourself or others, by letting pointless pride/emotion take over because of what happened in the past. (The past can even be 5 minutes ago)

You never know how a situation will affect your future self. So, you need to show respect/honor to yourself by reacting in a way with the greatness of your future in mind.

We are always worried about what is happening in the now, and all need to ask for help in some way. But we should understand, sometimes that help is not how we envisioned it. Yet, in hindsight, the way in which help came, was exactly what was necessary for the development of aiding or rekindling the discovery of our individual purpose.

<u>A story of patterns from the past changing the now:</u>

I was listening to a good friend who had their own successful business talk about some of the things in the past that happened, they were not too fond of before becoming a business owner.

They talked about how right after getting out of college they had the dream of running their own business. But became frustrated in the problem that they did not have the experience of running said business, nor did they know where to start. So, they reluctantly found a sales job. From there, they began to tell me about the worst parts of that former occupation.

When this person finally stopped complaining about the past and moved on to how well they were doing now, I stopped the conversation. I said, "What do you think is the hardest thing to obtain when starting your own business, besides dependable employees?"

To which they replied immediately, "Customers…customers are the hardest to obtain outside of dependable employees."

To which I said, "Do you realize the one thing you are saying is one of the hardest to obtain, is also the one part you worked on developing at the job you just complained about? Because when you start anything like a business, what is the hardest thing to do?…Convince or 'sell' yourself to someone else, that you are capable of benefitting them."

All of a sudden, you could see the shame of time spent hating the necessary pain for the business they ended up wanting to have, being washed away with the realization it was for their benefit.

The same goes for life. We all go through situations or circumstances we don't want to <u>have</u> to go through. But if you only knew the benefit of wisdom it carried for your future self in the end, you would understand that you need to do your best in any situation. Regardless of if you like it or what can come of it.

I personally ask Someone for wisdom and intellect every day. And one day I always wondered while I was growing up, why things happened, why people asked me for advice, and why they told me about horrible things going on or went down in their life? (Do you remember how to gain wisdom and intellect though from earlier in the book?)

<u>You can gain wisdom and intellect to a "sliding door", by either knowing how to truly listen or through learning the hard way.</u>

<u>*Ask and you shall be given pattern tests to receive. But do you know what it means to understand what you're going through?*</u>

Why do you think I introduced you to your own "sliding door" of wisdom, and wanted you to mentally group categories together? I did it to get you to think about the various events of your life consciously and subconsciously, through the mental patterns of wisdom. Because all events play into each other according to patterns of the current mentality in that moment.

Out of the rabbit hole!!

Evaluation number

(7) Creating a healthy social network stands on its own, because of the fact it requires the ability to (like I mentioned previously in this book) diligently evaluate yourself, and the people around you.

You are the average of the sum total of who you hang around. So I want you to answer the questions below on a separate piece of paper, because I can't stress enough how important the alignments/people around you are.

<u>*Maybe it's not the world keeping you down, but the people you hang around keeping you mentally broken-down.*</u>

Why might you need to phase out certain people of your life? Do you know if they truly love you? (If no, then you might need to evaluate yourself, and the people you hang around.)

Who should you keep/willing to take advice from? Why? (Outer circle of people who have achieved great things, but are not constantly around)

Who should you cherish/willing to take criticism from? Why? (Your "Inner circle", should be smaller than the above)

What is the type of person you want to become? Why? What does it take (research it, don't be lazy)?

CHAPTER 6: The weight of the Great Journey

The individuals who chase a trophy might see it come to fruition, but at what cost? How do you measure the weight of an achievement? Why gain the world only to give up your soul? **It's not about the destination, rather about the journey it took to get there. The journey you take is what makes getting there so worth-while and fulfilling. In the end, the weight of your soul is what you must bear, because the destination/trophy will always be there.**

There are always things in life that happen to people along a pathway, which can cause a percentage of the albatross mentality to appear in any portion of someone's life. As for this mental pattern of thinking, some of the greatest life advice to combat the weight of the journey (using my sliding door of wisdom) came from the 7th grade math teacher I mentioned in the 2nd chapter of this book:

"Bad things happen to Good people, which is bad. Good things happen to Bad people, which is bad. Good things happen to Good people, which is good. Bad things happen to Bad people, which is 'good'."

What's funny is she wasn't even trying to talk about life. She was talking about multiplication of positive and negative numbers. Which is why I know it might seem kind of confusing when in relation to life, but let me explain.

Here is what I want you to think about:

- What paths do you think you or people took along the way, in order for good or bad things to happen them?

- What was the weight of their journey? Did they lean on shortcuts, thus losing their soul?

- Did they deserve those good or bad things to happen to them?

- What situations were those people in to have that good or bad thing happen to them?

- What mentality pattern did those people who had good or bad things happen to them, create for themselves during previous relatable situations? Was/Is there still honor/respect?

Those who <u>truly love</u> you in honorable, respectable, and integrity filled patterns, will always find healthy ways to be in your presence and will truly love using the way you should be loved, to be something greater!!

Right now, you might be playing out real-life scenarios in your head you have seen or heard of. But this next question is what we have let other people we interact with or listen to, decide for us, based on emotions within the moment. Without questioning whether it was/is beneficial to an individual's life or not.

What does it mean to be a good person?

We as individuals are throwing out our mindsets for what the world says is "ok" to be. Resulting in becoming blind to the fact, most individuals have lost a righteous heart in a sea of the world's opinion.

Though it might seem beneficial for someone to go down a certain life pattern now, in the end, all it does is hurt the person who made such a pattern life choice. But why did they choose to go through with it?...Because the ones they decided to listen to, told them it was beneficial. But whether or not it truly was good for them, can only be determined by the collective pattern-allistic mentality of the previous individuals who used the pattern(s) in the past, and where their heart, mind, body, and spirit ended up...that is what it means to understand both the failure and success halves, of the <u>coin of wisdom</u>.

Here is the world's opinion:

"Nothing BAD should happen to GOOD people!!"
This throws away the fact that when life happens, everything always occurs for a reason.

But exactly what does it mean to be a truly good or bad person today?

Here is my insight on what the world sees as "good" or "bad" in a person:

"Good": You accept everyone, no matter what. You are perfect the way you are, which is why you should be accepted no matter what. There are no reasons why anything considered bad should happen, and no stress should come your way.

"Bad": they have a differing opinion pattern of any kind, from what is seen to be "good".

Both of these worldly manipulated definitions are lies. If you believe in these terms, they will only lead to misery, and the stagnation of your own mind.

Action or reactions between two or more people: There are reasons that lead to situations of why bad things happen to people, both the one's having the bad thing done to them, and the person deemed doing the bad thing.
If you believe you are doing great things, while honor/integrity/respect are lacking in your own life, then greatness will not constantly be associated with your name.

From the opinion of the "Good":

"Those who think differently are trying to take the journey out of life, and don't know the weight we bear as individuals to grow and succeed."

This is blaming someone else for why they can't succeed, instead of looking at their own pattern-allistic mentality, because all they see is

constant failure. Thus, not understanding what it means to be grateful and use all of chapter two's keys for life.

No one is trying to hold you down. The "Good" people who think like this have twisted the meaning of, "You're made perfect". Everyone should be accepted for who they are is true, under the premise God made us **perfectly-imperfect**.

Being perfectly made imperfect beings means, we were made perfect out of the womb to climb the theoretical **Mountain** *of* **Life** *to achieve a higher purpose within ourselves, than the circumstances we were born into.*

Just being acceptable, means being the average of what your mind, and what the world wants you to be. If groups/individuals remain stagnate, ONLY wanting to be "acceptable", it will only lead to frustration, cause cliques to form, and shift accountability from themselves to others. Disregarding the fact, it is not the fault of any one other group/person, but the fault of the group/person who wants to remain average in their respected environment (color of skin doesn't hold you back, especially in America).

"Bad things happen to Good people."
"Good things happen to Bad people."
"Bad things happen to Bad people."

Climbing the mountain using this book's patterns derived through effort in yourself, will help create the momentum needed to become an unstoppable force within your own life, if you stay consistent. So do not be the person on the mountain that believes they deserve to have good things, because they are not inherently bad. Instead, move yourself in the faith that good things will happen once you start to practice healthy and great patterns, in the aspects you want to grow in. **Do not be discouraged when you do not attain exactly what you wanted in that season of your life but use your adaptability to pivot for growth of greatness, in the understanding that you gained wisdom to go higher.**

This life is full of, "that's not fair", moments and there are many fake people in the world who claim to be "Good". Which led to the influence of you the individual and the world, to believe someone is Good and Bad once we determine if they are, "on our side".

We tend to listen without question once this determination is made, because we as an individual want to be inherently good and have good things. So, we listen to those who have not achieved, nor practice what we want, but we tell ourselves, "They know what they are doing! I should be able to do that!!".

So, we as individuals tend to throw out the notion that we are all born into differing situations and develop differing pattern-allistic mentalities. As a result, to go along with these mental decisions, individuals tend to allow fake leaders to lead or influence them in some way in everything they do. And it only became worse with the introduction of technology as a way to influence our daily lives by these fake leaders.

With the internet at our fingertips and the readily available media, the mindset that you can achieve what this person has, has made this craving for something greater, almost unquenchable. But because we do not take into account how doing good things are portrayed in how they were achieved, what it takes to reach our own individual greatness, and/or whether or not that person we see on the screen should be deemed as a truly good individual, or if they just follow the rules for that day's worldly opinion of what a "Good" person is; we do not inherently answer the questions:

- How did they attain or have this happen to them?

    o Is it real? Or am I being manipulated into emotionally feeling, thus leading into a pattern of thinking by what I see?

This craving of wanting so desperately to have what someone else has, is now such a strong pattern in our mind and daily lives; that if personal growth is involved, we can become frustrated in our own perceived stagnation as to why that person has those things and we don't.
But we are not there in person to see what happens to/for everyone. For it is impossible to know every detail of someone's life, when our eyes see a <u>snapshot or glimpse</u>, of what we want for ourselves in someone else.

So as a result, the "Good" are portrayed as **completely** accepting of everyone for who they are, no matter what. Yet, through that pattern, our mind can deceive us if we continually listen to others for everything. <u>Because not everything people do, are a part of, have done, or taken part in, is good for them or necessarily good for yourself</u>.

We all differ in the life we are born into. So simply listening or watching what someone says is good, does not mean it is inherently good for your mentality. And having good things, does not necessarily mean you are truly good.

Unless you personally know the path someone took to get what they have, you need to understand; all people who have good things, are not necessarily good influences for your life. Likewise, you should not judge other's hearts by judging what they do/don't have, because their constant honorable/respectable greatness filled actions will prove it for you. Nor should you determine what someone else is based on a 30 sec to 1 minute clip, because you are going to constantly be pattern-allistically manipulated by the "Good" individuals, who are actually, truly bad pattern influences.

All that being known, certain situations or circumstances do arise in the lives of individuals (including yourself) based on who they (you) hang around, and their (your) attitude towards what is going on around them (you). Everyone messes up from time to time, but those who stay in failure (ultimately deciding not breaking the pattern they know is not good for them), will only lead to even worse situations <u>when</u> life happen.

But we should not intentionally be looking to find fault in others without first realizing there is always fault in ourself, because what goes around does come back around, and pride always happens before the fall.

The types of people who live in failure and want to find fault in others, will eventually rely on others to continue their failure patterns. Which has created groups of people in a society that claim to "care" about others, when in fact, it has done just the opposite.

As a result, it has led to individuals not being able to think on their feet, because their mindset is stuck on the "Good" they perceive to see in the thinking they (you) are perfect the way they (you) are, and in turn, skew the perception of common sense. So, now there are groups of "caring" individuals, believing as long as they live within a certain limit of their group, they have nothing to grow in personally through patterns, or worry about in how they see all life patterns.

We as individuals are not taking responsibility for our actions, and in doing so we are only breeding a more divided society that is subject to greater manipulation of the way we individually-pattern-allistically think.

With this knowledge in mind. The abuse of "caring" is rampant in societies that have the most ease of access to technology of all kinds. <u>Because while it is important in keeping us together, making life easier, and key in the liberty of free speech. Some have determined through that same technology, that if you don't adhere to what happens to someone else deemed to be good, then you are inherently evil.</u> So, as an individual, we need to learn that things happen to others for any certain number of reasons, understand everyone is human and entitled to the liberty of an opinion. (This is why AI will never understand when used by certain media. The gift of allowing humans, to be human.).

- The situation someone is in.

- What have they done to themselves to get there?

- Who are the people they hang around?

- Are they even attempting to rise above the situation they are thrust, or put themselves in?

- What are their patterns of greatness in their totality?

Very few people want bad things to happen to truly good people. But in this life, there is always a chance something bad can happen. Yet, you can mitigate those chances by the pattern choices you make, through gaining wisdom and using the details of a situation you hear or were previously a part of.

<u>For example:</u>

There are drug dealers who deal to kids that have good things but go to jail once caught doing bad things.

Ruthless and conniving people, have what this life considers, good things. So, someone who has many good things, does not mean they know what is truly good for you. For unless you know their heart and the weight of their journey, it is impossible to know if they want what is best for you. **TV, social media, and people you have in your life, all play a role on how you think. Evaluating who wants the best does not necessarily mean telling you want you want to hear. The best thing you can do for yourself in today's world is evaluate. Learn think for yourself.**

<u>Drug dealing is an extreme, so let me impart you with this:</u>

If an understood pattern that is solely your decision (means a pattern choice that does not involve marriage decisions) you participate in, has a history of bad results and history of bad things happen *not of integrity/ honorable/ respectable patterns*, does it mean that pattern is good for you to do? (<u>No</u>)

If you haven't guessed by now, I've gone in a very particular order. Even if it might seem confusing at times. I strategically placed every section and certain statements where they need to be, because I want you to invoke your individual pattern-allistic mentality using your effort.

So now for the part of this chapter that talks about the section that doesn't take much brain power to understand. But like anything and everything…
…something can be hard if you make it!!

<u>Unfortunately, that includes life and the understanding of what should be an easy topic in the world today:</u>

"Good things happen to Good people."

Truly good people who put forth effort into serving others through true love/honor with integrity, and work towards their goals, will find that good things come in time. So, it is good to have goals, but never good to become completely obsessed with any goal, because worldly obsession means it runs your entire life.

Patience is a virtue that everyone needs to learn. Just as Rome was not built in a day, each stone/pattern placed for an end goal takes effort and time. Because (like most things in life), there are no shortcuts when achieving something greater that was meant for you, while maintaining your joy or soul.

- Time, momentum, and constant movement are needed. If you always expect to be handed something, then you are doomed to fail.

- If you take anything by force, expect to create more divisions in your own world that will seek to keep you down.

    o This does not mean once you have the ability to invoke force you should retaliate, because that is not how respect is earned.

- The truth will set you free if you allow it. Lying to yourself will only hinder your growth in where you want to go.

The earlier you learn that how you perceive various personal mountains in life can affect how quickly you climb; the more you are able to understand what you are not inherently great at. Thus, gaining wisdom to overcome those weaknesses, take the higher road in all things, and do all that is great to determine your next steps. Then when those next steps are determined, you sprint to the finish line gathering all the details, because they are the key to wisdom in other races you want to finish as you use your "sliding door" of wisdom.
<u>**No one can stop your growth…but you.**</u>

<u>Evaluate your pattern-allistic mentality and the people around you:</u>

- Are you setting yourself up for failure?

- Do people around you have your best interest in mind? What follow through have they shown?

- Actions or the lack of will, always show the true meaning/intentions of someone's heart. Do they only perform those actions when needing something in return?

The weight of the journey is what causes most to stumble. So, to stay true to yourself in mental patterns that are not saturated in conforming to the ways of this world. And know, over saturation of worldly patterns of the word, hope, is the obstacle course that leads to stagnation, which forms frustration, and the mentally worse beyond.

- Never forget to smile to show yourself that your light can never be taken away. Even when in hard times smile, because you know it will eventually pass, and cherish/remember the good times for when life throws mountains at you.

    - Whether you succeed or fail, you will gain wisdom if you allow yourself to

- Do not seek validation in things or people, especially in those who do not understand how to truly love

- Look to something higher than yourself and help others out in ways that are truly loving/honorable/respectable

- Even when respect is not being shown, be respectful at all times. The greatest strength you can show who you view as enemies, is respect

- o Showing respect in every situation will never diminish a relationship when differences are voiced. Instead, a show of respect will lead to an understanding of differences, which can lead to an agreement

- Show true love unto yourself, so you can show true love to the people around you even if it is not reciprocated

  - o Sometimes tough love is needed to be recognized in yourself before you can truly love someone else. Stay consistent in everything and adapt for truly honorable growth, as it means you stand for something higher than yourself.

- Compliment yourself in things you accomplish, achieve, and overcome as personal self-confidence needs to be fed too. Then do the same for others around you, compliment through seeking the greatness in everyone

All of these listed above, are what is required to become a truly good person, and not what this world sees as "good". What this world sees as "good" is a lie from the devil himself, because he does not want individuals to grow. The devil wants you to stagnate, to become frustrated, and then suffer from the mentally beyond.

Consistency is key.

This is life, so when you are frustrated by a mountain, keep moving towards your goals in patterns you can control, and the rusted wheels keeping you in place, will begin to turn faster and faster.

An example for those who believe they are Good and still wonder why Bad things happen:

Many people feel like they have been transgressed against. But in the end, there are simply situations those people specifically put themselves in, that led to patterns and ultimately contain

circumstances to answer, the why. There are very few instances that are truly "unfair", but you should do your best to not allow the situation to control your emotions.
Because once your emotions are controlled by a circumstance from the past, they can hinder your understanding of how to grow in the present and future.

One such instance of truly "unfair", includes the passing of my Mamaw. My most favorite person ever, went out of this world in the worst way I can think of, and she did nothing in my opinion to deserve it. That being known, there were circumstances that led up to how it happened. But it definitely played a major role in me becoming what I am today.

For those who believe that something bad happened to them or someone they loved/cared about, here is a story that I wasn't going to put in here at first. But in order for me to best serve and truly love you, I need to be as transparent with you as I can be.

Well…here we go…

…I sat in the hospital room, watching as the sun was disappearing behind the hills in the distance. It had not even been two weeks since I saw her looking strong in her old age, joking around, and playing strategy games with me. To now barely being able to talk, let alone keep her eyes open. There was blood coming out her mouth from the cancer she was diagnosed with.

I couldn't utter a word. All I could do was stare out of the window as time passed and try to use all of my mind power to search the knowledge I amassed, to use my sliding door of wisdom, to determine what could be done to get her out of this situation; while occasionally looking in her hurting eyes that were tearing up.

With all of my comprehension and all of my gifts to use my mind to determine patterns for solutions to problems for a wide variety of situations, I tried to find the answer. I pushed my mind as fast as it could go and beyond. So much so, that I ended up causing the nose bleeds she helped me learn to control as a kid (because my mind went so fast), but I couldn't find the answer. After the 3rd nosebleed in 30-45 minutes, I heard a voice tell me, "Put your mind at rest. This is not something any person can control, but there is always a reason for everything."

So, for the next 30-45 minutes (still looking at the sunset, avoiding eye contact), I talked about all of the fun we had over the years. Then I spoke about all the tough times we went through, and what she taught me.

From the work she had me doing and habits she instilled in me to always believe in myself, even when no one else did. I spoke about the wisdom, patterns, and intellect I gained from her and the world over the years. Then I told her about how I applied a pattern of my mind into my sister and how successful she was already becoming, because of what I gained through her (My Mamaw).

After crying through most of the stories and me managing to get a slight chuckle or smile from her for some of them, I decided it was finally time to open up to someone and tell her everything I was scared of.

My Mamaw was the only person to that day I had ever opened up to about my feelings and emotions, because I always did my best to hide them from everyone as to "become stronger". She knew I had worked hard and achieved so much already. But my Mamaw knew from being around me so often, how much I was holding back concerning the true potential I had. She just couldn't figure out the reasoning why. But because of the situation and her being the wisest person I'd met; I knew it was now or never.

I turned from the window, looked in her eyes as the blood dried around her mouth, tears filled both of our eyes once again, and said:

> "Mamaw, I'm scared. I know what I can do, but it scares me so much. I've tried to hide it for so long, because of how people would treat me (how the world will see me). I know I can do it (change the world). I know what I'll have to end up going through (mentally) if I tap into this (my potential). I know the mountains, but I'm so scared that even attempting them will change my heart from deeply caring about people, to becoming selfish like all of the rest." (Because I'll take my heart and mind further than anyone has ever gone, to tap into my one-of-a-kind spirit.)

With tears in her eyes, she slowly wiped the blood from around her lips, and uttered the wisest words that ring in my head today:

"Then don't let it."

I know it seems like a simple phrase, but wisdom is not some super complex thing.

<u>In fact</u>:
<u>Wisdom is the ability to make something that seems complex, simple. Though the words are simple to understand, they carry just as much weight as the task or situation at hand. As a result, the words balance out the mental scale in our mind of what we once deemed as difficult.</u>

Everything happens for a reason. There is no such thing as life being unfair when born in a free world/nation, as there are kids born with special needs, and kids going through terminal cancer. If you refuse to think your life is in many ways fair, then go see those kids, as they continue to smile through the pain that's slowly killing them, regardless of color or gender.

Or you could see what I saw as kid in bad neighborhood nursing homes; the elderly seemingly abandoned by their, "family". I tried my best to talk with them, but their hearts kept searching for ways to make them in some way, still feel relevant and human. So, I could only do so much as they were slowly dying inside, because of what their "family" was doing to them.

God always has a plan in place…even when life feels or seems inherently unfair.
I've been on the short end of the stick of true racism with a principle and teacher in school. But I do not need to hold a pitchfork against those who fit the bill as a way to show I was going to be something greater, and they could never control my greatness in the end.

I've also seen a born special needs quadriplegic (all because the father used hard drugs) in my family have a beneficial impact on the lives of everyone around him.

I've had to give up my dreams for a time period, because of the situation I was born into. But I did not let the anger screaming "why" it/things happened I couldn't control, cling to me.

It is nothing but one giant excuse to say life is "unfair" or blame it on God. Because when in conjunction to the goals you want to accomplish, you need to enact <u>faith</u>, through action (<u>belief</u>), and find ways to rise above the "unfair" situations or circumstances of this world, with <u>understanding</u>. That is where you find success.

FAITH + UNDERSTANDING + BELIEF = SUCCESS

Find the details within the details as to <u>why</u>, and respectfully **understand** *the reasoning of <u>why</u> it happened. Then move forward in* **faith***, adapting as best you can in patterns <u>you</u> can control, to find, then* **believe** *in your purpose. And in return, make the world around you greater by letting your righteous and <u>Good</u> light shine that comes from Him.*

When factual truths are present, there are no such things as coincidence. Our minds and other people skew the fact there is a reason for everything that happens, to try and delete known facts of what is actually beneficial growth, for decision making. Meaning, the decisions you make from patterns carry more weight than you can imagine, and once wisdom is understood, the past pattern should be an aspect of the world we should understand is exactly that...in the past.

We should allow for human error to occur, and not constantly seek to bring up past patterns that since have been changed.

After seeing someone so close to me who never deserved to die in one of the most painful ways possible, I had every excuse to question God. My Mamaw went to church when her body would allow it and helped as many people going through hard times as she could. Regardless of who they were or if she agreed with them or not. I had every reason to question life by divine purpose creation.

Yet, I don't know what would have happened if she were still alive today or had died in a lesser way. It was the first time I ever admitted I was scared in what I could. But I don't have a time machine, so there is no reason to dwell on it. Yet, it was the simple wisdom to a young person that was too scared to show this world their true potential, that led to so many great things, tough times, and lots of people served already (with so many more than I can fathom to be served in the near future).

I wouldn't have been a quarter as intelligent or wise today (and still growing in every aspect), if it were not for her. My Mamaw was my best friend and the only person I trusted at the time, because she was the only person I could truly connect with on a mentally intelligent/wisdom/understanding level.

I do not see myself as being on a pedestal above the world, but it's my mindset of patterns that always set me apart from everyone else. It's a pattern mindset, that I want to impart on you. **A mindset that I've proven to work for the benefit of those intentionally around me, after simply being around them.** *A mindset that I believe, knows the true way to <u>show</u> the lock of true-life greatness potential in everyone (more than I believe any run of the mill life coach will ever give you). But it is up to you to find the keys that unlock your own greatness inspired pattern-allistic mentality within.*

I traversed through the mental pain, the failure, and the adherence to all the hurt I've seen or been a part of. I traversed the very slippery slope that are the details of patterns of the human mind as filtered through a life of reaction for any one mindset, as to benefit you, so I could best truly love…<u>you</u> through this book.

I've simply gathered all my knowledge/wisdom/understanding into one place. But I, nor anyone else, can-do/adhere to life for you.

<u>I challenge you:</u>

Write down your excuses and doubt in yourself on a piece of paper, then burn it. On another piece of paper write, "I will not let (insert that doubt here) be an excuse. I'm going to put in place patterns that strive for my greatness potential!!". Then hang it somewhere you can see it every day as to hold your subconscious mentally accountable.

This is the end of this section. I did not directly define what a Good, "Good", or Bad person is, and why bad things happen, because it is not up to me to set those parameters. We all have individual pattern-allistic mentalities, and all have not lived a perfect life except for One. So instead, I gave you things to spark thought patterns within your own life, and a few insights to not be afraid of the bad, <u>when,</u> it occurs.

Focus on your personal good, because the end result of those who are truly Good, <u>will</u> be great things. But you have to understand life from both the good and bad patterns, in order to acknowledge why good or bad things can occur. Your degree of this understanding will correlate with your potential greatness life factor, causing it to be higher or lower.

You are not what the bad things of the past say you are, if you consistently live in patterns of greatness. So do not let the past define your mental ability to change for greatness today, or become an obstacle for the great life you want to achieve in the future.

<u>*Search for the truly Good in other people, because everyone has greatness in them. When you find it, celebrate it as they live in greatness without the need for you to hear celebration in return. As you do this, you will understand who truly loves, encourages, and celebrates you. Do this even when it seems as though life is hard, thus refueling your drive to keep pushing for greater to prove them right.*</u>

BABY STEPS ARE KEY

Do you consider yourself a good person, or are you conceded, hiding in what this world views as good? Write down what you believe is a good person, as you now know what the world views as "good". Do you agree with the worldly opinion?

Write down situations you were involved in (voluntarily or not) on one side of the space below. Then write down what you did during those situations and how you reacted (or didn't react) on the other side. Is there a trend? (Example of a trend: pride that you had to be right) **Trend or habit is a series of patterns that came together to form a bigger pattern.**

Did any good come out of those situations? In what patterns can you grow in? How do you plan on holding yourself accountable for growth in those patterns? (example: ask someone you know is great who truly loves you, to help hold you accountable)

Why True Champions

Great human patterns at the core in the world today, before all of life's worldly patterns are instilled (giving and caring)

At the core today, we are relationship driven beings, and inherently care for everyone. But what trumps this ability to care, and/or give/serve others is: we are <u>ALL</u> born with the desire for power, due to instinctual, then pattern developed <u>PRIDE</u>.

<u>Giving</u>

<u>Some insight into money/big business problems for the world today:</u>

You look at big companies now, as opposed to when they were created. The owners started them, because they saw a need to be filled in society (a new way to care). But once a compassion for everyone, eventually turned into a passion of money/power as time passed. Thus, ending the pattern knowledge of how to truly serve/give back to others.

Those once small companies now try to find their roots of serving others, through listening to the <u>excuses</u> of those down the ***Mountain*** of ***Life*** and "help". But the patterns in which they tend "help", do nothing in the end for the betterment of the company, employees, or world as a whole, because they lost the pattern-ability to truly care.

<u>Not all big business owners or wealthy people are bad people at heart. Nor am I judging them for their business acumen, and I understand there are always jobs that are not deemed the greatest.</u>

But as money and power comes to pass; the bottom line of those below the very top becomes priority as heard from the owners, stockholders, and others in executive roles, produced through meetings. <u>To which I understand they carry a heavy weight to keep growing the business.</u>

<u>So before I move on to what we as individuals should practice, but have lost sight of. I want you to ponder this question:</u>

What happens when stagnation of the mind of life comes from the top down, and the mid-management that are desperately wanting to be one of the few major decision makers (gain power)?

You become lost in how to benefit those who work for you, lack empathy development in greatness patterns, and solely focus on the fake "empathy" that people tend to practice today; all to show you from the top down..."care".

https://generocity.org/philly/2020/05/21/charitable-giving-are-the-rich-really-stingier-than-the-rest-of-us/

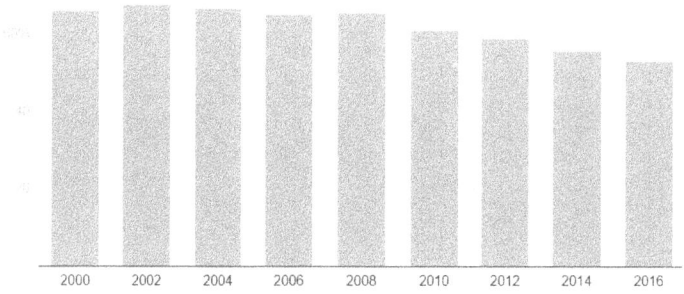

From: The U.S. Department of the Treasury
https://home.treasury.gov/news/press-releases/sm1040

BONUS POINTS: You impose more things like, I don't know…like taxes, or increase of inflation due to increasing the minimum wage, and in the end, you're taking more money away from everyone below a certain level (mainly middle class). Ultimately, taking away the pattern ability for people to give back more, to benefit the mental patterns of a country as a whole. The above sentences play into the factor of a Socialist point of view who manipulates the poor and minority, saying they will "get rid of and give" them things without putting in place a pattern-allistic mentality of growth. In the end, Socialism is only nice for those at the top. Now that we know this rule of, only good for the top. Socialist then prey on the cries of others without doing anything to actually help, and create a type of "middle management" who will turn on anyone they can, to be seen as higher in society (sounds oddly familiar doesn't it, and a little like what a certain evil person invoked with "middle management" from a foreign country to tattle on others or turn them in)? UUHHHH-OHHHHH!!! Still think stagnation of the pattern-allistic mentality has nothing to do with today's world even after this understanding??**

Why <u>True</u> Champions

The graph shows America as a whole. Now you tell me to go along with the statistics of suicide and depression, that the country has been trending in the right direction in terms of mental patterns for growth. Can you see the problem yet? Ever since 2008 we have become a country of, "give me this, give me that", instead of:

What can I do for myself to raise the level of any room I step into?

<u>A little personal story to go along with it:</u>

I will not get too political, there are snakes on both sides of the political spectrum, ignoring hypocrisies, and most people want to be ignorant to their own short coming hypocrisies today.

I'll never forget when I said this very basic statement to a group of friends my age on all sides of the mental political arena, "Don't force the world to conform to you, because you can't. So instead, put in the effort to change yourself towards personal greatness to show why it should see your light and respect it."

I know people might not be able to completely understand the statement, but some of the group tried to argue that someone shouldn't have to change themself through personal growth in order to change the world around them. Which begs the question…

…what kind of "give me" crap are we learning from patterns of media, parents, schools, and everything in between of those around us, to think we shouldn't change ourselves in some way for the greater?!

I understand there will always be people that abuse the "give me system". But that doesn't mean it is a format to be followed, because all it does is make you weak minded, and unwilling to reach the greatest version of yourself in the end, via not pattern-allistically giving back to others (selfishness).

As a result of this pattern becoming rampant, we have become a nation of weak-minded pattern-allistic people. Which is the reason why a true champion is so hard to find, or so hard to fathom existing now a days. I have been asked too many times why I think the way I do, how I can care about people so deeply, or why do I give back so much of my money/time but will not condone people doing certain things that make them "happy" in the now. And to put it simply for those around me…

…I cannot and will not, condone a pattern without consulting about said pattern, that will result in the hurting of themselves in the end; just because it is their life to live, and it makes them "happy" in the <u>now</u>.

I will never give into a way of thinking that simply allows people to be fine, with being perfectly fine, due to it causing stagnation of the mind, because it will only hurt them in the end, when it could've been avoided all together.

When it comes to patterns and pattern-allistic mentality: <u>*It's never a matter if, but a matter of when, when practicing a failure life pattern.*</u>
I want the best for everyone, which is why I talk about this concept that has everything to do with anything……pattern-allistic mentality.

The world may come to hate my guts, but I will do everything in my power to give back as much as I can. So, I will not become the embodiment of what the other person thinks about me if it's in a bad light (if without sound reason), and I will continue to try my hardest to live up the light others see me as.
This is what it means to turn the other cheek. This is what it means to rise above. This is what it means to give back.

<u>Important life lesson and something we should all practice:</u>

In the Bible, it says to give back <u>10% of what you make. Why is that?</u> Well in simple terms, it for sure causes a pattern of giving back while looking to something higher. But it also acknowledges God is the One whom supplied you the ability to earn that money, and trust Him with what I call, "the greatest stress relieving tool of all time" *money*.

Money can't buy complete happiness but is rather, the greatest real-life-personal-scenario-problem-solver when used within margin to relieve stress.
<u>Now let's take a look at the benefits of the giving back pattern:</u>

If you can give your money, it's the first step in giving back many other things for a bigger picture, such as your time, and possibly the greatest gifts you have (shout out the person I mention in the Truly Love/Honor section). If you grow the giving pattern, it will create more beneficial patterns in your personal life than you can imagine, and I say that from personal experience over the course of many years.

Such as the ability to "plan money" (marginalization), because it gives you the mental pattern to be more conscientious with <u>your money</u>. (Hmmmm...I wonder where you might've heard that pattern of <u>not completely consuming a good thing</u>, thus leading to a better longer life before?)

You know what else is crazy?
What happens when you learn to give your money in any capacity, then you slowly start to give your time, and then your gifts?

All of a sudden you practice your gift => it leads to you being better with it/them, and you use it to serve others => all of a sudden you have a sense of accomplishment, validation, and confidence (natural dopamine) => in the midst of that, whether you realize it or not, you can potentially find an adaptive purpose as you find energy through what you do. (As others see your value, you potentially create alignments to reach greater heights, potentially to monetize a gift...crazy right?!)
You just...never...know...so why not <u>give</u> life your all?

<u>A family dream of money currently that **will always be** fulfilled through my kids and generations to come:</u>

For a long time, people around me stated that they would like to have the ability to give large sums of money towards a random person. My father, his father, my uncle, cousins, my mother, her family, my friends, my parent's friends, and everyone around me.

I would constantly be told by my father the dream of, "If I ever have the money to give thousands of dollars to someone who deserved it in an envelope, then I would do it in a heartbeat."

I heard the pattern to give constantly, with little follow through. But there were some who did in serving and giving back, that gave me the possibility to have the pattern to see/understand the benefits of it from an early age.

Which led me to ask myself in high school, "Why does it have to be some outlandish amount? If I'm giving God 10% of what I make and am supposed to be wise with money. That means I can give back extra after the 10% in any amount to someone random, whether it be something small or large, because it will benefit their mentality regardless. So, making the extra solely about an amount, means in your pattern of thinking, you are doing it for selfish reasons of you wanting to believe you're a 'great' person."

One time (at the age of about 12-14), I remember my father and I were in the living room watching football one Sunday, when I felt bold about the topic. A commercial for donating to hospitals just ended, and I asked him why someone was wearing a specific article of clothing on their head during the duration of it.

To which he replied, it was to represent an association of people I never heard of that give money to hospitals (and still today only know of, because I see this association obviously still represented in commercials).

So, I told him how I thought that was a weird concept, because anyone who needs to join an association to feel represented, in order to give back extra in any way, only gives for selfish reasons within their heart. They didn't truly individually care, and these types of people just want to be involved with a group who want to "show" they care. Unfortunately (as a result of my comments), my father became frustrated and said it was just the way things were.

As a kid it was/is hard to explain anything like that to someone older, because (from personal experience) most would smile, ignoring what was said, or take offense to it, even when true. So, I did not push the envelope and just internalized my greatness pattern of how my spirit would do it one day.

Looking back at it now, I understand my comments might have been (worldly opinionated) conceited. Not everyone understands how to give extra back by themselves, so they participate in certain group ventures. But the joining of an association to feel obligated to give, stems from the pattern that we as humans want to prove to each other we have power in some degree. And others believe, until they get the means to give some in some absurd way, there is no reason to give extra as an individual. Which is why some individuals join groups that give back in large amounts.

As a result of the pattern, "<u>only when I reach this level</u>", it builds a lie in an individual's mentality to cover up their convinced mental pattern, they believe they are not yet good enough until they reach that certain level in the eyes of other people. So, in their heart and mind, until they reach that level the individual will not see themselves as being "good enough" to give extra. Because they are so worried about others validation, when the only validation they (you) could possibly need, is within your own actions with the understanding, they represent the greatness inside yourself. While <u>giving</u> a reason why your heart can be trusted with more.

*For some, this need to reach a higher level in order to see themselves as great, creates a moving finish line in their mentality. It is not until they realize the pattern of giving/ serving starts with intentional **baby steps**, will they understand the hidden greatness patterns within themselves. And ultimately not seek validation in others, but rather, validate through their own actions.*
You can only hope to change patterns when you address them with intentionality. Because they slowly create a new internal subconscious impulse pattern, which results in even greater outward impulse follow through patterns, as time goes on.

Fast forward a few years from that chat with my father and I can confidentially say, ever since I received a constant paycheck, I have given my 10% in tithe. On top of it all, I've given extra back to people I have been led in my heart to. Individuals that include the "rich", poor, black, white, tan, man, woman, kid, and everything you think of in between.

I gave even before I had the ability to give some astronomical amount at any one time, and I don't even report the extra cash to individuals on my taxes either (I know there is more than likely some kind of form out there for this, nor am I telling you all this to pat myself on the back).

Giving/serving back extra can be as simple as a buying a random person or someone you know, coffee or lunch. That small pattern just gave someone else a new greatness pattern to potentially also take on, then display. (Plus, do you remember what I said about dopamine and physical energy within your life?)

Giving extra for tax purposes, to join some association to feel representation, or give extra towards a designated type of person, doesn't mean you are great. It means you are trying to prove through the validation of others how great you are. When in reality, you just prove to yourself how great you are not.

You might be wondering why anyone and everyone I feel so inclined to give to?
I know it is my money, but it is not actually my money at the end of the day. So why should my heart differentiate between whom I bless in any capacity? (Keep reading on to chapter 7 and 8 to see whose money it really is)
Whether we realize it or not, we have all been given so many great things in this life so far. But we as individuals might have just forgotten how to truly listen, and truly open our eyes, because of how selfish our individual desires have become.

<u>*It is not until you truly understand there is more to giving than just money, will you understand, the heart to serve and your current natural pattern-allistic mentality towards serving. Until you truly understand this within yourself, you will not understand your true untapped potential within.*</u>
Excuses to not serve, give, or give extra in any capacity with maybe only a smile from someone to show for it, means you are wasting the opportunity to achieve the greatest version of yourself you <u>could</u> potentially attain.

<u>What to know what happens to you mentally when you give in general?</u>
Search this for yourself:
https://greatergood.berkeley.edu/article/item/5_ways_giving_is_good_for_you

---

<u>*The giving pattern also develops a sense of marginalization patterns, and creates a pattern of thankfulness in your subconscious, that spreads into all realms of life.*</u>

Patterns build patterns.

Caring

Become the controversial kindness that stands in fields of integrity/honorable reason, hard work, and excellence. Then give it back in any reasonably honorable/respectable way you can, without always expecting anything in return.

It might be hard at first to change patterns that have been set in stone for so long. But this book presents the ability to think for yourself about a new pattern, reversing what was once set in stone through your own mentality to be greater, and how to practice true greatness in your life. We all want to **care**, *but the manipulation of such a potentially powerful word needs to be addressed:*

To truly care for yourself, others, and to not be manipulated or offended in the process, is the ability to know when a pattern is meant for righteous greatness. Thus, meaning you stand firm when the world can't fathom why you have chosen to not condone certain patterns around your life, that lead to an even worse harmful pattern in the very end.
This.....is a part of the weight of the great journey.

Here is one very blunt example (You should know me by now, I am not afraid to point obvious things out with sound reasoning):

There were protests (riots) in the streets of America that caused billions of dollars in damage, and innocent people within the situation to be killed (2020-2021). Yet, you could not get certain officials to not condone the blatant rioting, destruction, and violence, out of a need to maintain a good standing in the public eye to show they "care" (hypocrisists).

Let's take a little in-depth look at the situation drawing such attention (Remember, you don't know what I look like and the name I created is made up):

You have a situation in which a group of people are claiming to want respect, but then go out to destroy, steal, and commit violence. Now I'm all for protesting, but does being associated with violence really impart a reason to deserve respect? (Remember, respect cannot be forcefully taken, because it will drive a wedge that creates further division in society.)

<u>Now let's look into the tragedy that caused all of this commotion:</u>

Remember when I said there are always a set of patterns that lead to a reason for situations/circumstances to happen in every individual's life?

It is tragic someone passed away, but there are certain patterns that led to the tragic result.

<u>There were copious amounts of drugs in this person's system, and the area in which everything took place, is one of the worst in that state from an aspect of criminal activity.</u>

<u>Then you factor in the need for everyone in the vicinity to want to capture what was happening with a phone, resulting in the creation of a crowd in a crime ridden area.</u>

<u>All to go along with the fact, the person who did tragically die, was known to be a very violent criminal. (This person who tragically passed away, was prosecuted for holding a loaded gun to a pregnant woman's belly while robbing her. It doesn't get much worse than that other than murdering a child, let alone threaten to kill a pregnant woman.).</u>

<u>Then you have someone of the opposite race trying to get said person in a squad car, because it is their job to hold people accountable for their actions.</u>

Of course, when everything came out, all we saw was a small portion of video from the media (Compared to the bodycam video as a whole, but what do you expect from a business run by how many eyes it gets for money.). Which as a result, only ballooned up emotions that led to the riots, and more harm than good, thus further dividing a nation right before a <u>political election </u>(Remember what I said about Saul Alinsky's book and the manipulation of emotion?).

Set of events and patterns:

- Person known to do bad things, with hardcore illegal drugs in their system

- In an area known for doing bad things

- With people who want to be a part of everything going down, gathering around someone doing their job

- Someone trying to do their job and make it home at the same time trying to ensure his safety

- Made a mistake while helping as much as they could (see full body cam video, they were trying to reason with said drugged person who tragically passed away as much as they could)

- <u>Media</u> of all kinds who blow up the situation trying to <u>get eyes to make more money</u>

- Riots, looting, destruction, more death led to more media eyes to play sides for money

Are you getting the gist yet? Was it a tragedy? <u>Absolutely, 100% yes</u>. But when people choose to react without knowing the full set of events, nor have all the information; sometimes they will react very poorly within pure emotion. It proved the exact thing **true freedom** *can't exist in…<u>manipulation of actions and perception</u>.*

Today, we have people who see this bad person as a martyr. (A martyr who did not lead a great life, whom was a bad person in terms of character. Not the color of their skin.). Which takes me back to this point:

Anger based emotion, followed through by an action, will more than likely not lead to anything beneficial.

If you say you care about someone, a concept, an opinion, or anything, but are quick to feel anger; then act on that anger in the human matter at hand…<u>you are a fool.</u>
<u>There is a difference between calling out hypocrisy with emotion, and choosing to act based on an emotion, that leads to hypocrisy.</u>

<u>It is not just on a country wide individual scale in which this "care" is shown either:</u>

People tend to act in anger in everyday life, because they feel like they are not being cared for enough. Yet given that anger stems from pride (the root of all evil), how do we know that we care for people, when we do not understand how to truly care for ourselves?

If we cared for ourselves, then we would understand the ability to respect the failure this world and individuals have, and know it/they are not perfect. If we understood this concept, we would not allow the world (anyone) to lead us in anger, which causes an action that is not respectable/honorable/righteous, no matter how many times we as individuals feel "not cared" for (disrespected).

<u>There is a difference between standing up for yourself or anyone, in a manner that is honorable/respectable for a truly righteous cause, and immediately acting in anger, aligning within the reach of what could be deemed the hypocrisy you believe needs to be solved.</u>
<u>You will not receive that which you seek, if your first action is from a spirit of anger and disrespectful or dishonorable pride.</u>

Quickness to anger will only lead you on a path of <u>when</u> the choices you make to be angry seem beneficial now. But <u>when</u> the potential life factor kicks in (and it will), it will <u>only hurt you even more</u> in the end, by outweighing what you believed started it all.

The only type of person who is more asinine than someone who chooses not to adhere to wisdom, is the one who has an anger pressure plate so sensitive, it can pick up the drop of a grain of sand.

You can't always choose the actions that happen to you or someone you care about, but you can choose how you react to all actions.

<u>Greatness is consistently doing things at a high honorable level, and a morally righteous life, is the greatest indicator of that consistency.</u>

What triggers do you have for anger?

Does acting on anger in a disrespectful/non-honorable manner truly show that care for anyone?

<u>The difference between reacting in anger, and rising above the anger you see being performed, are patterns that prove you're not a fool.</u>

BABY STEPS ARE KEY

Do you serve in any way? (Serving is not some ginormous thing, serving can be as simple as holding a door with a smile on your face for someone.) Answer yes or no, below.

What does serving mean to <u>you</u>? How can you serve if <u>you</u> do not already?

Does being quick to act in anger serve you in any way, or does it control an individual more in the end?

What did giving back and giving extra, mean to you before you read this section?

Whether you believe in the Bible, God, or are not religious in any way. How do you feel about giving back? Would you be willing to give now that you know the patterns of the mind it can give you? (If you're not a believer in God, the Bible developed all of the patterns for how to truly love and have a great/successful life.)

Part 3

The results of the Great Journey.

Preparation of the pattern-allistic mentality you need to achieve in yourself, and how/what to expect in this walk of greatness.

The final key of becoming the True Champion you were meant to be.

CHAPTER 7: The result of the Great Journey is a True Champion

We've been on such a long ride, and you've done a great deed to yourself in reaching this point, but we are not done yet!! There are still some things that must be clarified to truly understand the details within the details, of why I only mentioned the word, "Champion", twice within the chapters of this book until now. In fact, I'll go as far to say, without these last sections:

You will never be the unfathomably impossible person this world never knew existed and will never be a true champion without these last sections.

Instead, you will become another statistic, with a unique number of life in the grand scheme of things.

Would you rather me tell you the factual harsh truth or a beautiful lie?

Think about it for a second before moving on. Here's an example of a beautiful lie people who murder themselves are told or tell themselves, because they find a type of poetic mental freedom when times are tough:

"If I (you) died, this world would be better off."

This is a freaking lie implanted by the devil himself, using your own mind or others who are insecure in themselves.

The devil knows every angel, Biblical passage, parable, and he knows how his story ends. And he wants to pull as many people as possible down along with him, so he does his homework. He knows what lies in the details, and how to twist them in the minds of humans, because there is always the other side of a coin.

<u>The coin that has the face of wisdom, also carries the tail of deceit</u>.

Deceit twists wisdom, manipulating it for the darker emotions of the heart, mind, and ultimately is given the decision to be followed through in action.

That being known, do you think the prince of darkness, chaos, and evil doesn't know the greatness in each individual? Do you really think that piece of crap won't do his best to knock you down, and keep you there using the deceit in your mind and the world?

<u>The devil of all beings knows what it takes to change the hearts of humans and knows better than anyone, that perceived stagnation leads to frustration, and the mentally darker beyond.</u>

This book was created to potentially show how anyone can beat that perceived frustration of stagnation. But even someone as mentally capable as I, understands simply reading a book will only take anyone so far.

<u>**So let's keep the ball rolling!!**</u>

True Empathy

You're probably thinking, "Why wasn't this mentioned in chapter 2 or chapter 6? Why introduce this new section now?"

This topic needs to be in the final chapter, because it is the ultimate glue that holds all of this book together. Everything I put in here was given to me in order of understanding I gained over the years. But I know for a fact, this topic cannot be practiced properly in everyone until a constantly adapting growth mindset is understood, and most of the patterns that potentially can happen discovered (the previous chapters).

Today, after simple conversations with VPs, Professors, and business owners, they all tell me, "I didn't expect this. You're actually a <u>true</u> genius, and you carry yourself unlike anyone I've ever known or seen. You somehow said it better, told me, or reworked the concept of my realm, towards a better view or how to fix something. All without fully comprehending the totality of my experience, while breaking my thought process."

I DO NOT <u>PERSONALLY</u> BELIEVE I AM THAT. I should've walked in faith and hope that God has me in His hands a lot sooner than I did. Since fully giving into faith, I have not felt such a peace and a tranquility, learning to let go of things and simply working to become my greatest self. It wasn't until I understood where all gifts come from and how I created nothing, but was merely pointed to discover many things, did I discover pattern-allistic mentality.

I didn't tell you the above to pat myself on the back. In fact, hearing it still makes me uncomfortable, because compared to Him, I am nothing. I told it to you, so you could understand that not even someone like myself knows everything and I'd be the first to tell you, I don't deserve the amazing gifts I've been given.
Yet, if we all got what we deserved, life would not be half as enjoyable as we <u>can</u> make it.

I've always known the rules of how to be good at relations and understanding, but never knew the true meaning of empathy until just recently. In fact, it's not a topic that people inherently know how to put into practice properly, until they understand what it means to know what empathy truly is.

True Empathy – **is whole heartedly understanding not only what problems exist for anyone or yourself in any situation without being directly told, but also deals with the reasoning/understanding for your own pattern-allistic mentality, and how well you can connect to any other person/groups pattern-allsitic mentality using your personal "sliding door" of wisdom to discover the greatest pattern possible for any individual or group, for them to become something greater within their self(lves).**

True empathy is very much a learned trait that must first be understood and exercised constantly, or it will go away. So had I of known true empathy earlier to go along with the knowledge I already gained, I'd have been where I'm currently at years ago. But everything happens for a reason, and this concept is a lot for any one person to understand.

True empathy was the final component to unlocking the true champion within MYSELF and can be more than likely, one of the final keys in understanding the true champion within YOURSELF.
When used properly, true empathy is one of, if not the most important key to emotional intelligence.
EQ…just the most direct factor that determines SUCCESS in anyone's life according to studies. But even the definition of EQ has been manipulated.

As I've come to learn, true empathy plays a role in all aspects of life and in becoming a true champion. Once you gain this component in its truest form, you will become un-offend-able; no longer even thinking of playing the victim, and you will understand what it takes to truly lead yourself and others. Not only that, but you will slowly learn to look at things from a different perspective. And ultimately, relate to how you can truly become a leader of others using your light, without forcing someone else to notice that you deserve respect.

Like I said, true empathy is the glue that holds everything together. It determines the connections/alignments you have, the problems you see, and at the end of the day, validates the patterns you have/don't have. But be careful in your understanding of empathy. Use what I gave you in the previous chapters, because they are the foundation to true empathy and beyond.

MAKE SURE TO APPLY THE PREVIOUS CHAPTERS WITH THE TRUE EMPATHY DEFINITION. BECAUSE IN LIFE, YOU MUST LEAD YOURSELF FIRST, BEFORE YOU'RE GIVEN THE CHANCE TO LEAD OTHERS.

This is the last section of this kind in this book for a reason, because today it is the ultimate manipulate the world uses to turn people on each other.

This manipulation is called, "Empathy", and it can be used in a very dangerous way if you do not first apply patterns in yourself to becoming a truly great person. "Empathy" can not only hurt you, but the people around you, and those who will interact with you in the future too. (Patterns build Patterns)

The sense of "empathy" is what is being used to manipulate/control the public with the media, social media, and politics on all sides. But I believe this book embodies the true way to change a nation for the better, because starts with the individuals themselves wanting to become something greater FIRST.

Most people do not realize the division this "empathy" has caused in ourselves, our relationships, and the individuals that make up this world.

So it must be addressed:

"Empathy" = the world's opinion of what should be considered great or empowering, but ultimately proves to be detrimental to the individual themselves in the end. Thus, impacting the body as a whole (mentally and physically) for a worse pattern in the end.

"Empathy" is what is telling young kids that they were made perfect, instead of perfectly-imperfect. Leaving horrible influences in this life to throw the impressionable, pattern options of drastic life changing decisions, that will affect them the rest of their lives.

"Empathy" is what telling people of race and gender, that they are systematically oppressed (especially in America). Then are told that there is no reason to grow in why you should be respected, so you have "empathizers" joining a cause without rhyme or reason, claiming to care for them. When in fact, what is mentally practiced, only hurts everyone in the end.

"Empathy" is the media and politicians, distorting numbers and facts. When still lying and attempting to cancel those who do not agree with them, while they as individuals live in hypocrisy they call, "care".

"Empathy" is what is making the gray area of making it ok to kill innocence in the womb, but saying it is not ok for someone to not want to take participate in putting something in their body. Thus, getting rid of accountability to be more responsible, and further construing the lines of what truly great liberties people should have.

"Empathy" is what is telling men and women in a relationship that when a little pressure is on them, they need to run to someone else, instead of working towards fixing the problematic pattern towards an understanding.

"Empathy" is what's causing people to turn on each other, due to the fact someone may have a differing opinion on a subject (shows a lack of self-respect that someone cannot be allowed to think the way they do).

"Empathy" is turning a blind eye to the factual truths, and instead going with opinionated truths someone living in failure wants to hear.

"Empathy" is believing that you do not need to be reasonably greater than you were the day before. (In anything and everything, the healthy value of, competition, is life.)

"Empathy" is what is causing schools to fail in the ability to help provide or find a purpose for kids. Thus, playing a major role in suicide rates to continue climbing.

"Empathy" is what parents call not wanting to discipline or talk to their kids in a truly loving respectable/honorable manner, to show them a greater way to live.

"Empathy" allows others to say individuals shouldn't like someone, because they are providing correction in a respectable/honorable manner towards a greater pathway (though it might take time and effort).

"Empathy" is what is telling men and women in a dating relationship that even though their significant other has done bad things to them, "That person will change because I love them…". This "empathy" has done nothing but show that other person, it's ok to do those bad things, because you'll still be there through the hurtful patterns in the end. When a change of pattern-allistic mentality is a necessity for true love to occur, when in a romantic relationship.

- <u>Sorry</u> means to do your greatest to never do something ever again.
- <u>Repentance</u> is to change your patterns to help <u>ensure</u> you never do what you did before.

"Empathy" is continually listening to the lies of worldly opinions, and those who do not truly care.

"Empathy" is believing you should not/cannot do life with anyone.

"Empathy" is believing/telling you, you deserve (blank), but you go out and practice disrespect/dishonor as a way to achieve it.

I'm not saying that the circumstances or life that happens behind these topics of "empathy" are not real. But at the same time, each person lives a unique life full of circumstances they do not want to go through. (There's a difference between pity for attention and money/eyes and testimony.)

So, to play out the 1% of the 1% and apply it to the rest of the 99%, saying "if you don't empathize with these people, then you're a terrible person", is the opposite of helping anyone. Especially after manipulating facts and playing on the emotions of others, because that is the definition of manipulation at its core.

You must first learn to truly empathize with yourself, before showing empathy to anyone else. I do not hate people for thinking differently than myself, but I cannot fully condone someone that continually chooses to disrespect, dishonor, and blatantly manipulate.
There is a difference between standing up for yourself in a righteous way, and doing something that is dishonorable/unrespectable, claiming it to be filled with integrity.

If you feel emotion to a situation because of what someone else says, there is no reason to make yourself look like a fool in order to get your point across. Those types of people will not know true empathy, and they will never grow into a true champion, no matter how hard they try, unless a change in patterns is first recognized.

So if you perform, or are on the side of destroying liberty that leads to someone else believing another to be evil based on manipulation you subjected yourself to, just know……..you are on the wrong side of empathy.
You want to know what happens when you're on the side of the "empathizers"?
One day you'll realize, you have a different mental pattern, and they will turn on you, ultimately trying to destroy your name. So why even think that way, or give these "people" any kind of control in your life?

Stop living in fake empathy with those who constantly live in subtle, but blatant hypocrisy. For only the person who intends to show disrespect/dishonor does things in a subtle manner. Like a snake laying in the tall grass of life, coiled and ready to strike.

BABY STEPS ARE KEY

Write down the definition of empathy. Then look up the definitions of the 3 elements mentioned below.

Empathy-

Cognitive-

Emotional-

Compassion-

What areas/mental patterns can you get better at when it comes to other telling you how to feel?

Why <u>True</u> Champions

The <u>*GRAVITY*</u> of the situation

One day, as you seek patterns in how you can be great, you'll either stumble, be humbled, or know the direction you are to point your greatness in. Then, as you grow in that aspect, you'll teach, meet, see, and learn from others higher up that are willing to share the pathway paved from their own climb on the **Mountain** of **Life**. You will be able to tell they completely understand what they went through, because they are humble, yet stern in how they do things. And all the while, maintain a consistency of greatness in themselves as they choose to impart on you.

Trust me, from someone whose been there and done that. You have no idea the level of striving I have personally experienced when encountering people higher up who've helped me. So I'll help you with what you might/will endure within yourself.

When you get mentor or get mentored by these individuals who have accomplished so much, you will quickly want to mimic the patterns they perform. Then as you relate your talents/gifts to the type of great person you know you can be, the <u>need</u> to achieve/have things your mentors or mentees have, will suddenly start to feel like a heavy weight on your shoulders.

In fact, a new type of perceived stagnation will creep in. This gravity to achieve your greatness will serve as a catalyst for a fast-approaching frustration. Then there soon in the beyond, the mental fatigue stemming from the need to grow fast, with a hint of jealousy, could become placed on your mind. Resulting in the albatross percentage I spoke of, to potentially spread in your mind, as you want to have success or greater success now.

This new feeling and the potential fast spreading infection of the albatross mindset percentage is, <u>the gravity of the situation</u>, as you understand your potentially vastly greater/more successful life.

This <u>gravity</u> on your life is the pressure of a growth mindset, that stems from the understanding of what you could potentially be. Which derives from your own pattern-allistic mentality, as you comprehend the great heights you know you can reach, even when they feel so far away.

From what I've learned, the easiest way to not be crumbled by the bone crushing, back breaking, and brain rattling weight, is to do the exact opposite mental pattern of what you put yourself through, to have the ability to be mentored or instruct someone you see as great(er).

You have to learn to stop moving for short bursts at a time, to mentally work through the gravity itself, and remember the progress you've made, no matter how significant or insignificant you believe it is. Which results in your pattern mentality to find ways to <u>be thankful</u> for the things, or people you currently have around you.

<u>**Don't let the frustration of what you perceive is stagnation, get in the way of your determined greatness imagination**</u>.

Just as every muscle needs rest to get bigger. Your mind, heart, and soul need a little rest from time to time, so you can divulge in your own technique of how to be thankful. (Example: tell others you love something about them, give, and serve) (Patterns build on patterns)

Remember, just as no two people are alike. No two ways of achieving greatness will perfectly lineup for everyone. So be thankful in the understanding of the greatness you can achieve and use it as a motivation to continually develop/hone your greatness patterns.

Once you come to terms with the fact that the level you want to achieve must start with <u>your</u> first step. You must continue to be thankful for your current position. The faster you understand this, the quicker you will adapt to any kind of gravity you throw on yourself. From there, it is on you as the individual to adhere to wisdom, apply it through patterns, and then put it into action in your own way using the true empathy you've gained about yourself and the world around you.

Do not be afraid to talk about this gravity with someone you know truly loves you, because no one can become a true champion by completely shutting out everyone in their life.

I've defeated many personal demons and conquered many life mountains that seemingly can't be overcome. Yet, (to me personally) the GRAVITY of the mind in the midst of preparing the fields knowing the soil is rich, the seeds are healthy, and understanding the climate, is one of the biggest mental demons you can face. Because you're battling a demon of the mind that lives in your mirror…..BUT YOU CAN BEAT IT USING THE PATTERN I GAVE YOU.

Patiently waiting for the rain to fall on your fields can be most terrifying.

But why worry about:

Will the rain come? Will there be a drought?

To those questions here is the perfect quote:

Matthew 6:34 - "Therefore do not worry about tomorrow, for tomorrow will worry about itself. Each day has enough trouble of its own."

Now repeat this mental pattern out loud:
I will not worry about whether the rain will come, because I have prepared the fields today. As someone who hates wasting their time, I can confidently say that at the end of the day, no matter what happens to the fields I've prepared…I've done what I could. But will always look to learn, then apply action patterns where needed. So, in the meantime, until the rains come, I'll set-up other crops and till other fields. I'll keep growing myself. I'll find ways to bring water to my fields and keep believing the monsoon rain will come. So, by the time the monsoon occurs, all of my fields are ready. And even then, there will be A LOT of work to be done to reap the massive harvest I have sown. Yet, I know I've already conditioned my mind to be disciplined towards the patterns of work/doing what needs to be done. But one thing is for certain,,,,I was very well prepared to reap what I sowed!!!

<u>Patience</u> is very much a lost art, because even in patience you need to keep working towards the goal you want to achieve. Yet do not spend too long in patience, because a pattern in yourself <u>might</u> need to be changed in order to break the patient time you are in.

<u>Too many times people give up in times of patience, thinking it is stagnation. When in reality, there are a few more patterns someone needs to adapt in, in order to reach the level of greatness they want to achieve. Always keep working on yourself or in whatever you do, to make sure when the rains do come, you are well prepared for the bountiful harvest at the end of the season.</u>

<u>Faith</u> in <u>Patience</u> is the ability to <u>trust</u> something <u>will happen</u>.
*For something that is **<u>truly</u>** <u>honorable</u>, <u>respectable</u>, and in <u>integrity</u> you must <u>trust</u> it will happen, through consistent effort in <u>patience</u> with the mentality of not if, **but** rather <u>when</u> it happens.*

If you don't have <u>trust</u> in <u>patience</u>, then that something you are <u>believing</u> for will not happen in accordance with the highest life greatness level within yourself.

You might be able to force a square peg into a round hole on the cube named life, but how damaged is the square peg in the end, due to lack of <u>understanding</u> timing through patience. When the square hole was on the other side of the cube, and all that was required was a simple <u>faith</u> or <u>trust</u> <u>in</u> <u>effort</u>, of the <u>patience</u> in the time it takes for you to simply turn the cube.

<u>Description of Faith</u>:
Derives from action/effort patterns with the comprehension that a patience of greatness is the understanding that the patterns you are honing, comes from the understanding that you were meant to achieve greater things. As a result, the individual is not afraid to always practice greatness patterns and cannot be stopped when they feel so moved to act in true integrity/honor/respectability. (Patterns build on patterns)
<u>Faith + Understanding + Belief = Success</u>

Anyone can become a Phoenix % wise in any and every aspect of life, if they so choose

Remember when I said the types of people most likely to be a phoenix are ones from poor back-grounds, based on the driven poor mindset I described (not to be confused with a poor mentality), and how a phoenix needs to have good mentors/leaders around them, or they will end up burning their environment, resulting in doing more harm than good?

Even though a phoenix is the most powerful mentality or embodiment to have, it can be the most easily manipulated, because of the background it is mostly found in (poorer background).

A true phoenix, mixed with a driven poor mindset, knows how to best increase themselves from a life standpoint. Which means, they know how to handle themselves, treat people, and have an already instilled faith-based mindset, due to having to trust their odds of success from an early age. They also know what it means to make things happen in the most efficient way (wisdom).

Patterns of a Phoenix with a driven poor mindset:

- The pattern of knowing what needs to happen, and how to accomplish tasks in a timely manner is the best solid base pattern to build off of. Efficiency is a staple in life.

- The giving/serving back to the people around them in any way the phoenix can in that moment without hesitation, is backed by the street-smart pattern of, "I don't know who this person is, but I respect them, because I don't want to hurt my possibilities of what can happen in life." So, when the phoenix does succeed, they give back even more when they can, in ways that are important to them.

- They seemingly make connections in many different ways, providing many angles of insight. But the key to leveling up fast as a phoenix, is to increase your knowledgeability factor. So, it is imperative to search for things that can apply to the life pattern wanted and build the necessary patterns of understanding through their newly acquired knowledge in application through their life.

- Mix knowledgeability of the understanding mental pattern to be humble, in that they know they will never know everything (but know enough to be dangerous), with the swagger to understand how to change a situation from bad to good and good to great, and you have someone who can raise the level of an entire group all at once.

    o When in addition to the "sliding door" of wisdom, in conjunction with efficiency of getting things done. The pattern ability above (when it comes to fruition), will attract experts in various realms to help put various complex patterns together. The phoenix will use this knowledgeability, and when done correctly, the individual will have one of the most adaptable greatness pattern minds on the planet.

<u>I hope these pattern dots above help spark the mental process in your driven poor mindset Phoenix mentality.</u>

<u>Here in lies a problem with a Phoenix and everyone today:</u>

When a high greatness level is reached, the type of people mainly around this person is just as integral as discovering the subconscious technique of your phoenix. Because the good old saying of, "birds of feather, flock together", will come to life.

Personal respectable greatness will put you in rooms where success can happen, with people of all types. Some people may be like a phoenix personality (yet most aren't), but all will recognize the hidden potential of a phoenix/person they just encountered. So, mindsets will then be thrust onto that phoenix/person, and if those influences do not have great applicable values, they naturally will (like everyone else) become the sum total of the patterns they spend the most time with, are around, or have thrust upon them.

Which ultimately, can potentially lead to the phoenix giving up on giving back, in the most beneficial ways that truly help from a life perspective, because their pattern-allistic mentality is now majorly flawed.

From there, the balance of where the phoenix came from, who they want to be, and what they want to do, becomes unevenly balanced toward what they can achieve. As a result, they will lose the driven poor mindset that put them in the possible success environment in the first place.

The only way to combat this possible mental pattern change, is to understand the right alignments, through recognizing the greatness patterns others display.

What some of you reading might be thinking:

"What if I'm not, or was never born poor? How can I attain the driven poor mindset? What patterns can I hope to instill at this point that will turn me into one of the greatest mentalities anyone can have?"

Well, this book puts everything into very simple patterns, to drive your complex mental thought patterns of how to attain a greater mindset. Via accessing your subconscious, through conscious intentions, to instill personal pattern applications for your life, and displays the possible obstacles you will face on your personal greatness journey. But once again, simply reading a book can and will only, do so much.

So, if you apply a new life pattern-allistic mentality to yourself and remain consistent, the **Mountain** *slope of* **Life***, will not be as steep from shock factor when real life occurs.*

Obviously, you can't change every mental pattern at once and that's fine. In fact, very few, if anyone really can change a pattern almost immediately (Unless it's a drug, violence, or alcohol problem. Those need to be dealt with in a very cold turkey stoppage manner). So, the more you practice greatness patterns in your conscious; the more your subconscious will have an impulse pattern (habit) for a great pattern-allistic mentality when using your personal "sliding door" of wisdom, to develop the phoenix you were meant to become.

<u>Discovering how you can be a driven poor mindset Phoenix mentality, is like working out for the first time. Start with **baby steps**, then work your way to higher pattern levels as greatness comes along.</u>

Great pattern **baby steps** to start (if you do not already do so):

Set an alarm to wake up 30 minutes earlier in the morning than needed (do not press snooze on the alarm, waking up at a consistent time is vital for daily routine and sleep schedules), set a part time to train yourself mentally by creating plans and practice patterns in aspects of life you want to achieve those plans in (hang them on the somewhere you can see as a reminder), create time to think to regain focus on what you can control, and set aside time to give thanks for what you have (it develops a subconscious pattern of gratitude in life).

Can you imagine the capabilities of a driven poor mindset phoenix mentality, and the giving back of someone who isn't or wasn't born poor? It's a good thing this book was written right?!?! It can be applied to anyone and everyone. It's like Mr. Scrooge on Christmas morning after seeing his future type of stuff (changing his patterns for greater)!!

Do not forget to express thankfulness in honorable/respectable ways to yourself and others around you. Such as giving back extra <u>when</u> you can and developing patterns of recognition, through the complimenting of others around you, by finding the great in anyone/everyone.
<u>**DO NOT SEARCH FOR THE FLAWS OF OTHERS EITHER.**</u>

<u>A GREAT JOURNEY **ALWAYS** STARTS WITH **BABY STEPS**</u>

You know the best part about this book? It comes from the disciplined mindset of a phoenix who has gone through or seen every stage of mental classification in this book and gone through <u>**A LOT**</u> to pave a path higher up the *Mountain* of *Life*. Therefore, this book provides the very mindset and blueprint pattern for an ever-changing world. But the changing of your pattern-allistic mentality will be required. If you want to develop this phoenix mentality you can, or if you just want to learn how to climb to higher levels of greatness, it's all here. Either way, this book provides a greatness mental pattern shift through the subconscious, in way that (unlike most) presents lasting change, as long as you stay consistent in greatness patterns.

Write down baby steps you can practice today on a separate piece of paper, using aspects of life you want more greatness in.

True Empathy, Sliding Door of Wisdom, and Biblical Understanding of real-world Patterns

An example of a pattern of true empathy for growth in greatness ***Warning: you are going to be told factual truths and not opinionated statements this world has to offer***:

Too often Christianity is considered a very "judgey" religion, because of all the various differing opinions located under the Christianity umbrella.
That being known, I say the reason for such a word, stems more or less from an aggressive response to the world trying to impose things on Christianity, that it would not do to other "religions".

America specifically, was literally built on religious freedom, liberty of speech (whether people agree with it or not), consistency of greatness in leaders, the words "In God We Trust", and has shown to still be the greatest country in the world up to this point. Even while in the midst of the greatest mental civil war it has ever known.

Since the rapid decline of "Christian" speech that started close to 20 years ago, the exponential rise of technology, and the "care" factor stemming from the human core creating division; America has become an entire nation of judges through labels, with problems that seem to be formed in our minds. So much so, that Americans would rather elect people who have done nothing beneficial, in close to half a century for the country's civilians as a whole. Which is all due to following labels and "caring" more about fictional made-up ideals, that stem from their own twisted imagination, for manipulation, to garner power.

These types of people elected, have put in place policies that have hurt more than help, and continually adapt their opinion to fit any narrative. They live in a life of hypocrisy to fit what the worldly opinion of the day is, and use carefully manipulated wording, to represent the "care" they show.

As seen in patterns of the past (to become more well known in the future), those who helped/help these people get into power, wonder why things happen the way they did. And wonder why it seems as though their life only became worse but ignore the answer right in front of their faces (literally most of the time). Today, the media of all kinds produce narratives saying they are, "the good guys". But how can you be good, if you live in a hypocrisy web of lies, spun through division that causes people to choose a side, all in the name of, "care".

The individuals might not be bad people at heart, but when someone uses this tactic of patterns to garner eyes, and to split nations as deeply they could in every major way, how can you call yourself good while producing and living in hypocrisy, to ensure your benefactors are met? How can you say you are producing for the people, if you continually push the hypocritical agendas of those who own you?

This book will either heighten your sense of those people or cause you to see the hypocrisy. Despite this understanding, if I were to meet these people who look to manipulate, and anyone who did not agree with my viewpoints, <u>I would still treat them with respect.</u>

If controversial topics did happen to come up, I'd do my best to keep things civil and have an educated chat. Because as long as the person across from me can see the greatness in my heart, and the true love in my eyes, who knows…maybe that connection will subconsciously do something to change their heart or mind for the greater.

I would try to understand their views and where they are coming from, without a place of judgment. **Because who am I to compare one sinner to another**. *But if that person asked for my advice, I would not come from a worldly pattern-allistic mentally standpoint.* <u>***It would be from a biblical one. Whether you realize it or not, this book is riddled with Biblical mindsets that have proven to work in achieving greater things in life.***</u>

People should not tolerate condoning a pattern-allistic mentally that <u>sacrifices</u> integrity, righteousness, intellect, true common sense, true empathy, and respectable honor, for deceit of the heart, lies to the mind, and promotion of stagnation.

There is a difference between condoning and condemning a pattern. To condemn, is to judge. While to not condone, is to understand that a pattern is not beneficial for the human mentality in the end, because there is more harm than good that can come from performing certain patterns.

This book are my words to the world, and these statements are words to those who will hate this book:
Take your faces off the screens, and you'll realize how closed your eyes and ears truly are, to the truly great details for a greater life.

The below are my insights from time conversing with the elite of this world:
Do not trust in the world's opinion of how someone else should give back to you. Even cracking that door of worldly opinion, creates division and manipulation.
There are snakes on both sides of political patterns. But today, only one majority side's pattern mentality truly partakes in the combination of the Latin and dictionary definitions for SINISTER.
I challenge you to look up the definition for the Latin and everyday definition for SINISTER; then combine them.

"We wrestle not against flesh and blood, but against principalities, against powers, against the rulers of the darkness of the world, against spiritual wickedness in high places."
-Ephesians 6:10-12

We should all learn to be a brother or sister meant for adversity, instead of a "yes" person (condoning), or someone who consistently condemns the way someone lives, without knowing how to best truly love that person according to the definition of true love in this book.

<u>An example of detrimental pattern-allistic mentality of worldly opinion, in conjunction with the sliding door of wisdom:</u>

Down a rabbit hole!!

<u>Abortion</u> – the killing of a fetus

Bonus time: I've had conversations with lawyers and family friend lawyers, regarding the definition of, "killing", and how the word, "murder", can't be applied to this scenario. Why does it matter which word is not applicable? Why converse with lawyers at all you might be wondering? Well…because lawyers are the greatest manipulators of definitions, words, and events. Which is also why people call them, snakes. **But everyone on this planet has unique knowledge in some way, based on their gifts, and their own pattern-allistic mentality. So, keep your true friends close as you learn to love their unique patterns/gifts, and keep the ways they are better versed in that you are not accustomed to, closer. Understand the tactics they use in their realm, because you never know <u>when</u> life hits and another from the same realm will come along to try to bite you, and you'll need to understand the antidote (wisdom).****

*Let me say this first, <u>I do not **condone** the killing of a fetus</u>. But I will not condemn/judge you if you have, because it is not my personal place. That known, <u>I understand what that pattern leads to, and with my gift, I want to be there for you as a true friend who truly loves you</u>.* **The controversy with many people's viewpoints regarding this topic is; at what point does a fetus become a being that deserves to be protected under the right to live?**

Some put a time period on it, some say not until it leaves the mother's womb, others believe upon conception, and some believe the power of life to kill the unborn belongs with the mother under the tag line, "My body, my choice!! No matter what!!". (**cough cough** Except for what the government declares you need to have in your own body. So maybe stop condemning other people for what they don't want to do with their bodies, when that pattern doesn't actually benefit when destroying fear. Especially when the problem does not warrant it and when the good of not following the pattern as a country, outweighs the bad **cough………cough……**)

Clears throat Where was I? Oh yes…

…after conversing more than anyone should with lawyers concerning the topic of abortion, I believe I found the only line in the sand that can be drawn to reconcile both sides within the legal system today. Although subjective it, is still viable, because it uses the objective details within facts.

In lawyer talk, the reasonable decision to kill anything is in itself……subjective, so it requires objectivity to set the line, destroying the gray area of the nation.

Yet, you could make the case all court cases are subjective in some way given how facts are presented, as they depend on the word play of the situation(s). Which is why lawyers will tell their client not to say a word until they get there, because word play can affect the outcome of a situation (you should be adding word play with integrity to your "sliding door" of wisdom).

Soooo…what is the one thing that separates the words "killing" and "murder"?
Easy…it's <u>motive</u> which constitutes the reasonability pertaining to why a certain set of events happen. Murderers kill with no reason other than an urge or ability to do so. Murder can either be used in the context for someone's own benefit, or not. The topic of urge (reasonability) of ability is subjective, and evidence is what makes the justification of words, objective.

I am not a lawyer by any means. But **<u>motive</u>** is the only foreseeable way to overturn the legality of abortion with my insight. Or at least, make it harder to have one from a legal-leeze standpoint, and finally at least draw a line in the sand:

- <u>That is a whole new being with the ability to have a life of its own. If we are going by the rule of the fetus can be killed, because it is not self-sufficient or out of the womb.</u> Then a human being out of the womb younger than a certain age should be legal to kill, because the parents should not have to be burdened. So, by that standard, we should also kill everyone on government funding younger or older than a certain age, because they are not self-sufficient either, because their mother is the government itself (aka everyone else's taxes). But we are called to help the poor and needy. You simply wanting/needing to end another's life, shows why you shouldn't…awkward huh?

- Moving onto the definition of, "my body, my choice". There are literally two beings involved in the abortion procedure inside the womb. So, unless humans can all of a sudden universally biologically form double the vital organs necessary for life, there are two separate entities in pregnancy (the heartbeat forms around 6-8 weeks, look it up, start discovering unbiased moral truths for yourself).

- The motive of killing a fetus that is going to be born with defects. If the defects are not detrimental (subject to killing the fetus or mother) to the fetus or the mother's health, then the subjective opinion of objectifying a motive to justify the killing goes out the window. (Did you not see the comment of how my family members changed for the better because of the responsibility of taking care of a paraplegic? There is always a rhyme and reason for everything, whether we see benefit in the situation or not.)

- **Best case pattern scenario for the opposition against the line of motive: hard line in the sand of heartbeat, with various practical and reasonable scenarios of life or death, for either inside of the womb or the mother becomes the only factor that could change the situation.**
    - The topic of a mother's health is a tricky one to gauge and must be monitored before a decision should be made.

Once again, I'm not lawyer, but I believe I made valid points to build patterns off of. There are very few motives I can even attempt to wrap my head around to warrant such an act that include: rape, incest, or detrimental to the mother's health. **To those still not agreeing with me, couples across the country want kids, but cannot have any and are looking to adopt.**

Motive might be subjective, but unless it involves: rape, incest, or detrimental health of the mother (very small percentage of abortions fall under these categories). The killing of a fetus has no objective viable reasonability, other than having the ability or urge to kill. Which is by definition, murder (lacking reason in the action of killing). An act that is very much against the law, especially against someone with a heartbeat, once it is formed.

As for the ways to determine motive, I know they are hard (but this decision like the thing that led to the fetus/baby was/is an adult one too), but if a clinic wants to perform an over the 6-week rule of heartbeat nationwide abortion, then the basis of discovery for investigation into someone's motive is warranted, with stringent rules for violation. I leave the rest of the legal-leeze to the lawyers and lawmakers who read this book, if they find the pattern viable.

Here are some stats as provided by the CDC, and another abortion stat site whom uses the CDC:

https://www.cdc.gov/mmwr/volumes/69/ss/ss6907a1.htm,
https://abort73.com/abortion_facts/us_abortion_statistics/

The factual numbers:

As of 2018, the link says abortion has decreased, but the pattern-allistic mentality of 20-29 accounted for 57.5% of abortions and have gone up. From 2014-2018, abortion ratios only decreased in the age group older than or equal to 35 years. Surgical abortions past 9 weeks accounted for 61.4% (100% - 38.6%) of the 614,820 reported in 2018, with 85% being unmarried women. With only 1.5% of those 614,820 (9,222) accounting for rape, and incest (2004, if stays consistent to 2018 *https://www.guttmacher.org/sites/default/files/pdfs/pubs/psrh/full//3711005*). <u>**So the total unwarranted non-reasonable abortions in surgery is, 362,128 innocent killings for 2018 alone.**</u>

Subjective opinion based on pattern-allsitic mentality of the nation according to the facts:

The decision to settle down (in other words, maturity age for understanding responsibility in women and men) and the time span of those who've had abortions wanted, then had kids resulting from the average of a decade of mentality patterns lost, resides at the "old" age(s) of, 30-35 (20-25 being the median for abortion age ocurred). Pair abortion numbers with the knowledge that the birth rates of the USA are down to 12.001 in 2021, from the 16.031 in 1972 (a year before abortion was put into place in 1973, https://www.macrotrends.net/countries/USA/united-states/birth-rate, and also post WW2 scare of not having a family), and now you have a trend in the wrong direction. It seems since we as a nation have decided its ok to kill innocent gifts that derive from responsibility or lack thereof in self-discipline, that something or Someone, has decided to weaken the ability for new gifts (babies) as a whole for the nation.

Children are a gift from God, and they have limitless potential for making a better world overall. But how can that chance be possible, if irresponsibility keeps them from having that ability?

The scary thing is our grandparent's average married age was 23 for men and 21 for women. Now the average married age of responsibility and maturity of their grandkid's (millennials), is 28 for men and 26 for women. Given what I said of the greatest generation (millennial's grandparents) in knowing what they've got to do and understanding responsibility in adaptability, the rise in age of maturity and responsibility goes hand in hand with abortion numbers going down after the age of 35 and increasing in ages below that (20-29). This correlation screams one obvious pattern:

PEOPLE TODAY DO NOT WANT TO ACCEPT RESPONSIBILITY FOR THEIR ACTIONS, BECAUSE THEY BELIEVE THERE ARE NO REPERCUSSIONS TO THEIR HEART, MIND, AND SOUL PATTERNS.

(Patterns build on patterns to pg.336)

Marriage stats: https://www.pewresearch.org/social-trends/2011/03/09/ii-comparing-millenials-with-gen-xers/

<u>Now for the mental patterns approach of the example (the bottom line of the detrimental pattern):</u>

It is very much illegal to kill a human without reasonable causation (Also known as: <u>murder</u>). Which falls directly under what abortion unproportionally is used for.

But why is the obvious rule of, "Do not murder" without <u>reason-ability</u> in place, within law everywhere for civilians?

Do you know what killing a person with or without reason does to a person's mental patterns? (Even in terms of war, when killing might become a justifiable reason, it changes the mental patterns in someone, and effects people around them as a result.)

Murder creates a false sense of entitled power and/or free will, that we as humans should not be allowed to possess in a range of situations. Even taking away someone's ability to perform daily life is an evil act, because the moment you take away the ability to even perform life, you are killing the soul of a human being, which is just as bad as killing them physically.

<u>Veterans should be treated with the utmost respect, because not only did they put their life on the line for you to live the life you do, they also sacrificed a portion of their mentality for you to have the ability to tell them they don't deserve respect (liberty of free speech).</u>

If as a human you want to justify having power by killing innocence, due to a lack of responsibility. Then as an individual, you will not be <u>as</u> respected, <u>as</u> honored in the end <u>as</u> you could've been, or <u>as</u> favored in the grand scheme of your own life.

Upon murdering, there is a numbing of the mind to people around you. Empathy can/will become a thing of the past, as you've already set a precedence of one of the most detri<u>**mental**</u> patterns any one person could develop in their <u>mind</u>. You took away the ability of life.

This is why therapists, psychiatrists, and council become a necessary for people to have in abortion scenarios. <u>It is a mental pattern that can become extremely difficult to navigate with as they isolate themselves, and specifically</u>

prefer to be around others who will not question their decision making, in any way or aspect. Which leads to more mental irresponsibility from said person, because of the mental pattern set in place that has now become a corner stone in their life for their pattern-allistic mentality.

Acting as if responsibility of actions is out of context for you is also called, self-righteousness. Which is believing you are better than anyone else who tries to correct you, which gives you a false sense of entitlement that goes past even God.

End of example (out of the rabbit hole of mental patterns)

Just as I do, you must understand that it is someone else's life, and you can't control what someone can or can't do. But in the context of condoning versus condemning, why even give the option for someone that leads to so much more pain and misery; whether they realize it in the now or not? (Chapter 1 life factor of happy in the now)

The mentality of no repercussions leads to riots/looting/hate being called peaceful, massive manipulation with no concern for objective non-manipulated facts, and those not wanting to adhere to people who truly want the best for an individual's personal life. Which all lead to the death of greatness from the inside out in an individual, then overtime, a nation.

All things being known, I will not personally judge someone for doing anything bad in their past. In fact, someone very close to me had an abortion. Now, I was not in her life when it happened, but I could see the pain, remnants of hurt, and sorrow no matter how confident she seemed in front of others.

The ability to see patterns of sorrow is coming from a person who used to pray that I could go through pain instead of someone else, because I knew I could handle it. Having personally gone through so much pain, both personally and using true empathy, I now know/understand why it's selfish to feel other's pain.

Hindsight is 20/20 and growth can be found in the pain. But that doesn't mean I can't help people navigate all types of pain or help avoid it, using my extremely unique gifts along the way.
<u>I will help anyone tap into their hidden potential if they give my King and themselves the chance.</u>

<u>You should take this statement below to heart and develop it within your own pattern-allistic mentality by saying it out loud. Thus, applying it to your "sliding door" of wisdom:</u>

"In the end, I know I personally cannot control what someone does with their life, and I know I'm in no place to judge anyone. I know I need to respectfully-honor or help anyone; forgive when difficult and even pray for those who have hurt me intentionally or not, because I know…<u>I'm human as well</u>."

Even nations have a pattern-allsitic mentality, and just like individuals, there is a choice to truly listen or live in ignorance of what will come to pass. That being known, some national patterns have been changed, and certain individuals don't realize it. They choose to live in <u>PERCEIVED STAGNATION, THAT LEADS TO FRUSTRATION, AND THE MENTALLY WORSE BEYOND (more specifically: stop thinking there is still widespread racism or gender inequality keeping you down)</u>. Which then leads to contempt based on their lack of responsibility for their own life, so they blame it on others (mountain section), and they adhere to those who agree with them (failure section). Because there is always a rhyme (<u>pattern</u>) of reasons why things happen in your life, when you look inward FIRST (2nd chapter).

If you think I left out what men can do that is bad for mental patterns. Trust me, I don't want to type for that long, and gender equality is there on all levels where it's needed. Guys, do you think committing violent crimes makes you a man? You think hurting women or people makes you a real man? You think walking away from your family is what a real man does? You think not taking responsibility for your patterns makes you a real man?...IT DOESN'T, AND GOD SEES ALL.

<u>Give me a break…just as males say women act like girls:</u>

<u>BOYS</u> who are supposed to lead themselves, have not shown why <u>GIRLS</u> should act like <u>women</u>, equally as much as <u>GIRLS</u> have shown there is no reason for <u>BOYS</u> to act like <u>men</u>.

<u>Pattern-allistic mentality…learn to truly see it in yourself first.</u>

That being known, there is greatness in both genders still out there, it's just even more hidden, because the patterns of the world have made it that way.

**Bonus time for both genders regarding the statement above:

The ability to swipe right has not helped the overall patterns of maturity. Girls want attention and boys are willing to give it to them. But this destructive pattern is so both can feel less lonely in the world, as neither knows how or where to find greatness pattern driven individuals. So, those of all ages who use these platforms to find attention, are stunting their growth without knowing it, as they will take swiping into the real world too. As for the individuals trying to find something serious in these particular tools (I hate to say it, but it's true); you are left trying to find gold in a garbage can that **mostly-full** of wishy-washy people who do not know what it means to grow up and become something greater, because of the life patterns they've taken to heart (for relationship patterns in these people: pg.146, that's why lack of commitment). It's not until maturity is thrust upon them do girls who have a kid out of wedlock want to grow-up all of a sudden, and why great guys as a whole, find it hard to take on such baggage at an early age so early in their career (hence another reason marriage age is going up). As for great females trying to find something serious; it's even harder because real world males see wanna-be kings getting "great girls". They also do not succeed in the trash can of relationship platforms or in life, because "women" who are now used to media, tend to believe there is something better, so they ignore the good ones. And so, the good ones in turn stop believing in doing what made them a great in the first place. This swiping mentality is also what has led to many other detrimental patterns in this book too.**

Forgiveness

Understand that no is perfect and that includes yourself. So mental and actionable forgiveness is a necessary.

In any type of relationship forgiveness and acknowledgement is a necessary. So why wait to communicate it in a respectful, yet bold manner, to come to an understanding, if it means moving forward to grow greater in the end?

If we all understood forgiveness and compassion in regard to respect and integrity, actions displaying respect through honor by both parties through/during a situation to achieve greater things, would not seem as full of hate in this world.

Forgiveness is very much needed to unlock the patterns of a true champion. Along the journey you decide to take, you will encounter people of all kinds. Like I said earlier, some will love you, some will aid you, some will hate you, some will encourage you, some will applaud your setbacks, and some will applaud your greatness.

A lack of forgiveness leads to perceived stagnation of the mind.

<u>Forgive and you shall be forgiven:</u>

- Forgive those who helped in your setbacks and **<u>pray</u>** great things over them

- Forgive yourself and **<u>pray</u>** for wisdom to learn from your shortcomings

- Forgive those who applaud your setbacks and **<u>pray</u>** for great things over them

➤ For all, show reasonable actions of forgiveness:
  ❖ Patterns
  o <u>For yourself:</u>

- <u>Mental</u>: Say out loud, I forgive me for (blank)

- <u>Conscious</u>: Understand you can't change the past, but write down how you could be greater

- Follow through with **baby steps** of greater in consistency

o <u>For others</u>:

- <u>Mental</u>: Say out loud, I forgive (name) for (blank)

- <u>Conscious</u>: Understand you can't change the past but write down how you could have been greater. Then write down the adjective you believe (name) and yourself could've been greater

o <u>For those close to you</u>:

- Tell (name) you forgive them out loud, but you wish (adjective) would've happened. Then ask them how they wish you could've been greater.

- After the conversation, tell them you love them, give/serve them in action (within reason)

- Follow through with **baby steps** of greater in consistency

o <u>For those not close to you</u>:

- Tell (name) you forgive them out loud

- Give/serve them in action (within reason)

- Follow through with **baby steps** of greatness with consistency

*Also, do not forget to **pray** great things over those who truly love and help you. <u>Pray</u> and give thanks to the many things you have accomplished, want to accomplish, and have yet to accomplish, while achieving higher levels of greatness. Then adhere to the wisdom being given in life <u>when</u> understanding comes.*

The one constant in the list above, is prayer of great things for all. Doing this sets a precedence pattern in your life/mind, that no matter what happens, you will not let the situation stop you from growing. And also, that you want the greatest you, you can be for yourself, and be towards everyone around you, no matter what. But as you can tell, they all require action of some kind.

<u>Me personally</u>: I will give back to those who don't like me. Even if it means only in prayer, because I understand everyone battles something when they reach a perceived stagnation, that leads to frustration, and the mentally darker beyond.

<u>Forgive, but remember the wisdom gained through the lesson someone provided.</u>

<u>Here is the greatest example I can think of for forgiveness and how far we should be willing to forgive:</u>

The story of Jesus dying on the cross for our sins.

<u>Remember this when reading below</u>: **Even Jesus became emotionally (humanly) angry** *flipping over tables and telling the people how the mental patterns should be, when He caught those in His Father's house doing things they shouldn't. (The people ripped off (stole from) outsiders and became a "den of robbers", while not allowing the court to be what it was promised to be…a place of worship.)*

True love for another is not, never showing emotion, but knowing when or when not to apply emotion to truly righteous actions that honor yourself and others around you, as you look to something higher.

As it says, you have the Son of God who committed no sin and truly loved others. Sometime later after this emotional incident, Jesus was beaten, spit on, slandered, and crucified by the very same people who were cheering His name as

He entered the city only days before His death. But He went through all the pain, so we didn't have to. (Remember what again?)

*Jesus could've called down the heavenly realm to save Him and destroy those who did these terrible things to Him, but He **chose** not to. Even hanging on the cross, on the verge of death after all the pain He said, "Father, forgive them, for they know not what they do...".*
Who the heck says that on the verge of unjustifiable earthly death?!?!?! Some of us can't even forgive the fast-food worker for forgetting our sauce. *There is only one reason why He said this...He and His Father truly loves and wants a relationship with us, via the Spirit.*

Say this out loud, "Jesus loves me, and I am made for greatness".

Because even after doing bad things He will guide you to a great and wonderful life if, you'll allow it. All He wants you to do is ask for forgiveness, then repentance (recognizing your patterns aren't perfect and will work to be greater), ask for Him to come into your life, then truly listen to the Word (the Bible), and apply the patterns of wisdom to your life (heart, mind, soul).

Why those simple tasks for a life of greatness?......because this is all due to the true love He showed us, by dying on the cross.
The Bible and the Biblical pattern-allistic mentality, will aid in unlocking the hidden potential inside yourself of becoming a true champion...it's a place that provides insight into patterns for true greatness.

If He can forgive those who killed Him with no strings attached, provide a pathway to a greater life, and ultimately eternity with Him. Then He can forgive you, so you should be able to forgive those around you who have hurt you, regardless of if it was with words (or lack thereof), physical nature (or lack thereof), and/or in any way someone can.

I understand tragedy is not something anyone wants to go through, but physically your body is not the same after a certain amount of time, due to the shedding and disposing of cells. Which leaves the patterns in the wake

of the trauma to linger in your <u>mentality</u>, then into your future, as the situation of the past becomes ever so distant.
To find out how often simply research it:
<u>https://science.howstuffworks.com/life/cellular-microscopic/does-body-reall-replace-seven-years.htm</u>

<u>Here is another example through my story in how we as humans need to perceive the ability to forgive, and how we should perform forgiveness mentally, from one human to another:</u>

I was a part of a church group, and we were on an outing. I was I believe in 9th grade, and I wasn't able to make it on time to ride with the main group. But a few people were kind enough to pick me up, along with other adult leaders.

I can't remember how the topic came up, but someone asked the van a question about what could be reason why the world thinks Christians judge the way we do, and how to potentially fix the perceived problem. As a kid, I wasn't very talkative when it came to these types of situations, because from an early age I learned people don't like to hear staggering truths that combat what they actually think is Biblically correct.

But low and behold after going around the van, they decided to ask some 9th grader who just learned about the in-depth knowledge of World War 2, and the Holocaust (this is where you should possibly start chuckling or have your mind blown, because of the writing on the wall).

Me being me (and as anyone normally does at such a young age), before answering, I thought to myself, "This is a safe environment, semi-free of judgement, so I'll answer to the fullest extent." So, I proceeded to tell the van about the in-ability we have as humans to whole heartedly not judge, and forgive people or one's own self, for things that happen. Then I said how it is human to think like this, but just being a morally correct person is not the needle for a Christian's compass, because that is how the world thinks.

Aiming for a morally correct life, not in conjunction with a desire to achieve greatness, leads to an eventual perceived stagnation of the mind, then frustration, and eventually the mentally worse beyond. We all have *the ability to be normal. Yet, without leading a pattern of life that creates patterns of personal growth, we all will find ourselves in perceived stagnation <u>when</u> life happens. So why not unlock the hidden greatness patterns within yourself to project your light into the world sooner? Why wait for perceived stagnation?*

After I described the mental problems associated with a lack of understanding, forgiveness, and Christians. I then proceeded to list off the number of people who died in World War 2, the estimated number of Jews/others who were brutally tortured and killed in concentration camps, then said:

"People will not like this…but if Hitler really asked God for forgiveness and repentance, truly feeling sorry for everything he did, asked for Jesus to come into his life acknowledging Him as King, truly wanted to change his life turning his eyes and heart towards God, and ultimately did not kill himself, because suicide is murder. Then God would've allowed him into heaven."

When I tell you that was the most awkward 45 minutes I have ever personally experienced. You could hear a pin drop in the midst of a few head-bobs from the adult leaders, and on the way back, they did not talk much, just letting the radio play pretty loud. (LOL)

But as I grew older and better versed in the Biblical mentality. The more I understood that statement and the pattern mindset behind it, to be a hard factual truth we as humans need to understand within our own pattern mentality of life.
The Father sent his only Son to die a shameful death after living a perfect life, taking <u>EVERY</u> transgression/sin ever committed upon Him in death, and whomever believes in that truth and acknowledges Him as King (thus changing their heart patterns) will have ever lasting life in heaven.

This means, <u>LITERALLY</u>, every sin that was or has ever been committed, has been taken into account. All you have to do is ask for repentance (meaning you will change the very heart pattern that you are asking forgiveness for), and you will be wiped as white as snow, no questions asked, and be given what everyone today craves…HOPE.

Even though after you acknowledge this, it is not Biblical for YOU to judge, lest YOU be judged. We are all sinners and have come short of the glory of God.

There is a difference between judging and <u>allowing for honorable discipline through a righteous means</u>. When your parents, parents of choice, or authority try to discipline you <u>through righteous means</u>, it is not judgment of your life. Rather a self-discipline pattern they are trying to instill in you to become something greater than you were/are in that pattern moment.
That being known, those who fear the Lord should not be afraid to point out <u>true</u> injustice or evil. But there is a time, place, and how for everything.

Now that thinking of God and Hitler might not be what people or Christians may think is moral-judgmentally correct, but who are we to judge when sin is sin no matter how big or small in the Lord's eyes?

We are all human in the end, and if we got what each one of us truly deserved while alive, then <u>no one's life</u> would be even remotely enjoyable.

If you still can't seem to believe someone so evil whom changed deserves something as amazing as to enter heaven. Look at it this way. If you so badly want judgment to be brought upon someone like that. Today, it is talked about how the number of jewels on your crown when you enter heaven correlates to deeds.

So, think of it like this, had Hitler truly and whole heartedly changed; once he passed away (based on the given the amount of time left of his life to perform great and honorable deeds) he probably would've never received a crown in the first place. In fact, instead of a mansion, Hitler would probably only have a tent just barely inside the pearl gates. But guess what?

<u>He'd still be there, and the Big Three (Father, Son, and Holy Spirit) would love that he was.</u>

That is the power level of forgiveness we are individually called to have and practice. We need to wrap our mentality around the crazy thought of arguably the most-evil man to ever live, getting into heaven because of forgiveness/repentance; then reciprocate that mental pattern, through respecting we are all human as to not judge, we would all treat each other A LOT better than we actually do.

Don't get me wrong, obviously there is a law in place to deal with people who commit wrong doings in today's society. But I'm not saying forgiveness to the point of letting criminals walk free, because there is a worldly condemnation that will more than likely need to occur. But whomever believes injustice is being done to you. Simply and wholeheartedly forgive (but not condone using evil in your heart patterns), just as Jesus forgave those who murdered Him.

*Remember the situation and gain wisdom from it, but do not hold on to it, because it will only become an albatross around **your** neck in the end.*
Understand the difference of righteous, honorable, and integrity filled discipline, compared to forcing someone to adhere to a way of living that has historically proven to lead to worse patterns.

<u>Something even more mind staggering:</u>

I want you to think about this for a couple of minutes. For every coin, there are two completely different sides. And the battles you fight through represent the higher levels of greatness you can potentially achieve in life, because they cause a strengthening of the mental pattern muscle needed for conquering.

Hitler performed some of the most evil deeds that will influence the world for generations to come. But what if what I said came to fruition, and he did change his life? Can you imagine the greatness he could've achieved?

He could've provided the template of how to avoid regimes like his, potentially completely eradicating those types of evil views, and manipulation from spreading ever again (socialism/communism). In fact, some of the things going on today might not would be happening. Many people's thought patterns in politics would have been completely changed if what I said happened.

It's just something to think about. But then again, I don't know what would've happened. We might still would have a world that doesn't like when people put thought to the patterns going on in life or call out false truths, and/or have hypocrisies or fake leaders, of all kinds in the world…(did you make the connection yet?)

A true champion knows how to use the keys to find themselves, give back in many ways, show consistency, forgive, understand, use the bad for good, want the best for everyone around them, see the greatness in everyone, and ultimately, keep their eyes up towards heaven for direction through <u>every</u> situation. No matter how stressful the uncontrollable(s) seem to be.

Hard times of Forgiveness prove Leadership

I found myself in the bathroom behind the college basketball gym, crying in one of the stalls. That year, I pushed through all the pain from the injuries to my ankles and feet. Injuries so bad, that at one point the trainers nicknamed a tape job I needed to even run, "the cast".

Before a grueling 6 months of pain, it started with the severely sprained, possibly fractured ankle, in a team open gym. When just a few days prior, one of my fellow teammates said I was one of the top scorers on the team but wasn't given a proper chance.

And it was roughly less than a year when teammates told me I was the vocal leader during games and in timeouts, in the conference tournament, where we were the bottom seed; but made it to the conference semi-finals, losing in overtime.

After a grueling six months, it was about a week before senior night when the coach said it looked like I was moving as if healthy again. And I told him my ankles and feet finally started healing a couple weeks prior.

I didn't give my body time to heal, because I wanted to play due to me feeling like I had more to prove to a coach that seemingly didn't want to respect me.

When I would get playing time, I had various adults tell me I should get more, and I even had fellow college students (some who used to tell me I wouldn't make it) tell me the same thing. I knew what it was, because I had seen it before, yet conquered it. But I didn't want to make the excuse that it was due to a coach who didn't want to respect me, because I wasn't "chosen" by him to play there.

I sat there on floor of the bathroom in a locked stall, crying from not playing at all, and having the crowd beg the coach to put me in on my senior night in front of my family. While there, I was visited by many people who told me that not finally getting the chance to really show my talents was wrong and disrespectful, because they had seen glimpses of what I could do if given the opportunity.

After 45 minutes, I finally decided to wipe my tears away, stand up, and change out of my jersey one last time.

The next day, I was told by teammates and parents apart of the senior party after the game, that the room was close to a tipping point, as they were fuming as the coach made paper-thin excuses for his actions. That whole day, I had a big life pattern decision to make as a young man. Do I show up for my last practice ever the next day, or do I not, because of the disrespect that was displayed?

I had teammates text or tell me not to show up, saying they would understand. That is what got me thinking about them and their future though. What good would it do as someone who went through so much, to give up on the greatness in myself now? What example would that set for them in the future in relatable emotional pattern situations?

How can the world expect unique greatness, if it keeps giving up because someone loses hope <u>it can be great</u>?

So, I said a prayer of forgiveness in myself for not allowing the proper time to heal my body first and forgave the coach for his egregious and disrespectful actions. Then decided to show up for my last practice ever in college.

As I stepped onto the court and sat on the sidelines after warming up waiting for practice to start, the coach pulled me aside. He said he was sorry for doing what he did, and I told him I already forgave him. Then he thanked me for coming to practice, and I looked him in the eyes and said:

"I didn't do this for you. I did it for them (my teammates). I did it to show what it means to be leader in yourself."

After I said it, all he did was nod his head, shake my hand, and walk away.

During that practice, we ran a scrimmage type drill for 20 minutes where the winning team stayed on. I hit the first shot of the drill, then I hit the next. I bet I hit 90% of my shots. And every time I brought the ball up, I would shoot it from deeper, until I was hitting shots from the volleyball line, and on all sides of the court with a defender in my face. After dominating for 10 minutes, he stopped looking me in the eyes, and looked at the ground.

For 20 minutes, he watched my show against his "chosen". And in the locker room when practiced ended, a good portion of my friends and teammates couldn't believe what they witnessed.

The ability to truly forgive yourself, gives you the potential to serve yourself in greater patterns through self-leadership.
The ability to truly forgive others, gives you the potential to serve the world in greater ways.
<u>The usage of both abilities, in conjunction with the pattern to continue to rise above in faith of the greatness bestowed upon your life, gives you the potential...to lead nations.</u>

Before David became king, he could've killed the current king wrongfully hunting him twice. Instead, he chose to rise above in faith because he understood the greatness he could achieve.
The ability to judge or condemn others lies solely with the One who created it all. But condoning patterns of failure lacking in honor, integrity, and respect in truly loving ways, is as if you dug a deep trap hole for yourself on your pathway of greatness.

The next section is the most important key this book has to offer in reaching your potential greatness. It is where you will decide on many things, and even has the most important decision you will ever make…

The Bible

Keep in mind up, until these past couple sections, this book does not hit you in the face with a Bible (Even though some of you reading this need to be from time to time, myself included LOL).

Don't worry, this section will not do that either. But whether you realize it or not, some of the stories and parables you read, came from the Bible. Successful people or companies in every facet of life, practice Biblical principal patterns. But some if not most, just don't realize it.

I could have gone on and on…and on…and on…bringing upon you the amount of wisdom the Bible contains. But then this book would have been over 1000 pages long (Not even joking, there is a file in my computer filled with sermons, and notes developed from a singular verse in some cases. I'm doing all of this while running multiple businesses, writing curriculums, and books. If I can do all these things, then you can do just as much!!!).

Fun Fact: The Bible is the only religious text/book that has been traced back as being historically accurate and is the best-selling book of all time!!

The Bible tells people to be weary of what you hear, see, do, and people around you. What do all these things have in common? Something from way back in chapter 1…OH YAAA!! A pattern-allistic mentality!!!

Simply put, pattern-allistic mentality is once again:

Everything we say, hear, or do can subconsciously, or mentally affect us on any given level, depending on how many times we see or potentially emotionally associate ourselves with that thing (marketing, media, and people around us).

But inevitably, without a concrete pattern foundation of some kind, that starts at the core of our mentality values, and works its way out for the benefit of oneself and others; those things we associate with can hurt any individual, including ourselves in the end (patterns large and small we develop from a young age, after becoming cognitively-abled to apply to our "sliding door" of wisdom).

So, without this concrete value driven pattern base, in conjunction with a Bible/Biblical mindset, we are setting ourselves up for failure.

Faith + Understanding + Belief = Success

Knowing you have the freedom to do anything, while forgoing it is not good for you to follow certain patterns, will only hurt you in the end. As doing those certain mentally detrimental patterns, will ultimately affect your mentality in any given range of events, as you associate yourself with the opinions of this world.

Worldly pattern-allistic mentalities will only bring you pain, and eventually the people around you, when life hits you in the face. So, the Bible and having a Biblical mindset, will provide the pathway for all patterns. But that means following the pattern-allistic mindset that comes with it. (As I believe was presented in this book, because it helps with the patterns of the mind, for the heart and soul.)

"Whom the **Son** sets free, is free indeed" – John 8:36

Patterns, **The Father, Son, and Holy Spirit** (The Big 3) explained:

My section on patterns everywhere in the first chapter can have the ability to spark the debate that every event is set in stone, or that at the end of the day, there is no such thing as free will. But it really doesn't. In fact, it normalizes free will built from purpose driven design. Yet, derives an additional layer where predictability, numbers, and percentages come into play.

Everyone has a very specific pattern-allistic mentality. Think about the "random" ads that pop up in someone's feed on social media. Life, free will, and God's great plan, work in the same way, except for the ultimate benefit of your life. God knows the absolute greatest patterns for you in any and every situation, and what you personally want to achieve in life. So He then guides you, but waits to see what avenue you are going to take, and to be frank, sometimes the greatness avenues require pain, heart ache, and time. (As is what might be required in certain steps of gaining a particular wisdom/knowledge of life. Remember the businessman, turned owner, who hated his first sales job for so long? *Faith in patience*)

The Big 3 know the percentages of what you will do in any given moment, in any range of life choices, and God lives in the unknown percentage that is dependent upon faith. So, in the midst of it all, your current faith level can also affect you in any number of life choices, but its' the angle that faith comes from in terms of your heart and mind patterns, is what gives you the free will to choose.

But if you so choose, you can ask for guidance from The Big 3, and depending on the level of your faith, you can/will decide what is wisest for you to do in the end (This is where free will comes into play). You have the right to choose any variety of pattern options, but it's on you to subconsciously weigh the pros and cons for them all, in the understanding of <u>when</u> you suspect life to hit you for the worst.

God lives in the unknown as a multiplier effect. He guides you to higher levels of mental patterns, which at the end of the day, guides you to reach levels of greatness in any and every situation (Even if the situation seems bad, or is something that only occurs <u>when</u> life hits you. Even when life seems unfair **read the story of Job in the Bible**.).

All you have to do is have <u>trust</u> in the <u>patience</u> through consistently great growth effort (Faith). Then when it's time to reap the rewards (potential life factor), He multiplies what could happen within the growth pattern mindset even further than what would have happened without Him.
All you have to do is give every pattern aspect of your life to Him.

You see? Patterns are where omnipotence and free will live together in harmony. We can choose to do any number of given things…

…but a matter of how many times a pattern has been placed in front of you or performed, and how well your spirit/emotions connect to that pattern through other life patterns, will narrow down the percentages of either: <u>performing greater future actions from your personal finite list via faith or have worldly opinion patterns become the driving force of the finite list of patterns you partake in.</u>
Meaning, you can choose the failed worldly opinion pattern or the proven (but not as widely acknowledged as it should be), Biblical pattern mindset.

<u>How the Big 3 work example:</u>

You're at a used car lot trying to decide on what car you should buy. The salesman (the world's opinion) shows you a car, downplaying the various odd sounds after turning the ignition on, while saying the car is amazing, but he actually has no idea how cars truly work.

In fact, you know the car lot has a reputation of selling lemons where the buyer(s) couldn't even drive the car across the street. And you also understand that at the end of the day, the buyer(s) signed the papers and have to take full responsibility for that lemon car in the end (most just won't admit it).

On the other hand, The Father, the Son, and Holy Spirit are the mechanics, with cars for sale everyone talks about as being really good, but you've heard they require you to help out (action/application) so you can learn. You also heard; they tell you exactly what's wrong in ways you might not like (wisdom). Heck, you've also been told the Big 3 Mechanics will even show you another car for you to have, but you need to completely give up the piece of junk you spent money on.

Yet, most unbelievably, for all the good they offer, for some reason they always charge the same price for their abilities?! So why don't people always use and learn how to have a working relationship with them?

Well...people naturally don't like the thought of being wrong. Let alone put in effort to admit they were wrong, for potentially long-lasting correction in what caused the bad outcome for them in the first place.

"It's crazy, that's preposterous!! I don't care what someone charges, as long as I don't have to put in effort. Just fix what needs to be fixed with what I have, so I can move on."
–Some people in their minds when the Big 3 Mechanics offer their services
(PRIDE)

But little do potential customers know, the effort needed from you is to only find the nuts and bolts (pattern mentality through action/application), because the mechanics will provide the parts. And the only price they charge is the acknowledgment of their ability, tell more people about the work they do, bring in your other cars (aspects of your life) for them to fix or replace, and have a genuine relationship with them.

<u>**Unfortunately, some owners of the lemon car will **pride**-fully have the car towed to be worked on by other, not as great mechanics (people). Or will try to fix the car themselves in an attempt to maintain a sense of pride. To be honest, it may work for a time before the problem rears its ugly head once more, and they have to fix it again. So why not take your car to the finality experts?**</u>

The only "problem" with the Big 3, lies in the ability to find these nuts/bolts, in conjunction with the limited effort people want to put in nowadays. So, I ask again; why not use the mechanics who've proven how great they are already, and ask them to help you locate the nuts/bolts?

Some bolts are heavy, so when you think you truly can't pick them up, all you have to do is ask the Big 3 for strength, and they will provide help. And in the process, will ultimately provide patterns for you to get stronger in the end as well.

Some bolts require leaps of faith to get, but even if you fall, the mechanics will catch and help you back up to try again.

Bolts are found relatively easily, and some might be found in areas people might fear. But the Mechanics literally have anything you might need to help find them. And on top of it all, provide a manual for anything that could go wrong (Bible/Biblical pattern mindset) when fixing your car.

<u>Let's recap:</u>

You have the salesmen (worldly opinion) who talk A LOT, trying to get you to buy something when very few of them have any real insight on what they are selling. Then you have the Big 3 Mechanics, who will do as much as they possibly can to give you amazing things. But you just have to put in effort for growth, and they will never steer you wrong.

<u>*Who are you going to choose?*</u>
Do you want to listen to how the world does life, not knowing the terrible things, or what you'll have to repair after making life that much harder (The proven horribly rated used car salesman)? Or do you want what's known to work, proven to help, and will level you up as a human being, when in conjunction with a pattern growth mentality (The Mechanics who will fix anything and will even give you a brand-new car if you want)?

<u>End of Example</u>

A True Champion knows where their faith lies, the patterns within themselves, and knows even if things go wrong, God works all things together for their good. Then above all else, knows God will help them rise up from the mat to keep fighting in the boxing ring of life.

<u>Remember chapter 1?</u>

<u>*Example*</u>

<u>Even by just reading this book guess what happens to your pattern-allistic mentality with a growth mindset, then allow the Big 3 to take hold:</u>

1. Decision that seems beneficial now, but is bad for yourself => **Life factor** for right now = **+5** => **Odds of doing it** = **30%**

    a. But could lead to something bad later causing an increase in problems in any way => **-15 to -50** for <u>when</u> it happens **(potential life factor)**

2. Decision that is <u>good</u> => **Life factor** for right now = **+10** => **Odds of doing it 35%**

    a. <u>Could</u> lead to something <u>good</u> causing => **+15 (potential life factor)**

3. Decision that is <u>best</u> => **Life factor** for right now => **-5** => **Odds of doing it 25%**

a. <u>Could</u> lead to something <u>great</u> if you apply yourself => **+75 (potential life factor)**

Unknown factor that could change the mental percentage, that could change the **odds of doing something good and above (always above just the growth mindset version) = **+10% * ??% (always above 1)** => **(+20) * ??% (always above 1) (Potential life factor additions)****

Now that we've come full circle together. I want you to take a look at the major difference(s) between the pattern-allistic mentality growth mindset you have for yourself. Use your own background, gifts, etc in chapter 1, and the biblical mindset pattern-allistic mentality for growth above.

*Do you comprehend what could be done when you add Them in one aspect example of life? Now try to translate it using your Sliding Door of wisdom into **every** aspect of life.*

Write down the difference(s) in the examples below.

The Lord will provide opportunities to become greater through actionable patterns that **Honor** *Him.*

Yet do not expect those opportunities to always be in ways that are <u>conformitable</u> (<u>my new word</u>: conform to your patterns of comfortableness). Because patterns for growth are meant to stretch your mentality and greatness capabilities; through understanding the wisdom needed to develop patterns for growth in greater actionable ways, that will honor The Big 3.

Meaning, ask and you shall receive. But receiving greater starts with developing your greatness patterns first. To then produce in your household, family, and world.

Joy, Peace, Favor, and Blessing

You've seen from the example in the previous section what happens when you apply the biblical mindset into your pattern-allistic mentality of growth, into your life. So, when you give the entirety of your life to God a favor is bestowed upon you that will create a peace in your mind, heart, and soul, as long as the pattern is shown through heart consistency.

As this peace takes over, giving in many areas and serving others will be as easy as breathing. The results being as you serve and give, you will find yourself receiving favor on your life that will guide you to make greater pattern mindset decisions, and in the end, you will attain a multiplication factor of blessing that will only rise as your faith (confidence in the Big 3) builds even more. On top of it all, you will develop true friendships, fully understand true love, take joy in learning to understand/perceive, and be provided alignments on levels you could not possibly imagine, that could lead to greater things in life if you prove consistency in action.

The gravity of the situation will not feel heavy anymore, as you live to trust the effort through patience, and understand the gifts you were given. Which results in more faith in success, through knowing how to hone your skills to a higher degree through developing your new pattern-allistic mentality. Even looking back the past, you will recognize you never climbed the ***Mountain*** of ***Life*** through your power alone. But rather had points of stoppage for understanding to discover patterns for your purpose.

But it's when you refuse to understand in patterns of life you can control, does stagnation turn into frustration, and the mentally worse beyond.

All of that being known, when you change your pattern-allistic mentality to one of a growth biblical mindset, you will be tested by the worldly opinion in ways you've never seen, because the devil himself knows of your potential greatness within. So, he will do everything in his power to keep you from reaching that potential. Which will lead to the deceit via twisted wisdom causing a perceived stagnation, then frustration to possibly start to form. So do not find it uncommon for trials to come as you look to achieve greatness in the name of the Lord, through righteous actions.

Yet, it is on you to decide how to pull yourself out of the stagnation, then the frustration, and the mentally darker beyond. I have done my best to prepare you for that perceived stagnation, by you recognizing your pattern-allistic mentality for everything that has or has not occurred, over the course of your life.

You need to create or change patterns in your pattern-allistic mentality to pull you out of the perceived stagnation, then frustration, before you reach the mentally darker beyond, <u>when</u> life hits you.

For example: stop moving, pray, and give thanks for what you do have (write them down if needed). Then ask for understanding of the perceived stagnation you're in.

<u>Bonus time</u>: When you've experienced the mentally worse beyond, and don't want to go back, there is a tendency to take on patterns that might keep you from the gifts the Lord has for you to experience His blessing, favor, and joy He has in store for your life. I understand that sometimes, people need time to take a step back to work on themselves in understanding to become greater, in order to receive. But let me challenge your thinking with this: <u>What if the things or events that led up to a certain circumstance or meeting a certain someone, was meant for you as the gift from God? For He knows what your heart has been searching for and needs after those storms of life are over.</u> That is why it is beneficial to look to Him for answers, and not solely rely on your own mental understanding. Do not stay in what's left of the worse beyond patterns that cause you to mentally experience doubt that you are not currently worthy of the great future husband/wife, or other great gifts that might have recently come into your life. Do not rely on mental patterns that you believe everything has not led up to a point; from trials into the blessing was meant for you. Thus, causing you to not seize the right now gift, meant for you. *One day it could rain, the next it could pour, for a week it could flood, then one day you notice the sun is out.* **But you do not go outside, because you believe there's no way the water could be gone. Yet, little do you realize, the surface is dry and now has become a gift for you to receive. That is how God <u>can</u> work. He can turn all of the worst events meant for you to develop greater patterns in understanding and change it all in an instant for a blessing of joy and favor the very next day. **So, you must <u>always</u> be mentally and pattern-allistically willing to receive a gift when given.****

AAAAND NOW!!!

Why True Champions Don't Seek Trophies

True Champion's do not seek trophies, because they prefer to validate themselves through their own actions and accomplishments. Trophies and accolades are ONLY nice prizes that come with being a True Champion. That being known, True Champions will always receive the trophies they desire in accordance to the personal greatness goals they have.

True Champions let the light of every aspect in their life become the only validation they seek, and let others compare their life to determine the greatness at which they themselves should yearn for.

Meaning, True Champions care, but do not care about what others think, because the True Champion is acknowledged by great pattern backed individuals and others, who from the heart, tell them they are great. They also rarely take offense to anyone or anything.
True Champions do not boast of having a bright light, but they do not allow it to be hidden in the darkness of world.

If you claim yourself to be a True Champion, then look at where you've been, what you've accomplished already, and the people you have encountered along the way (no matter if they agreed with you or not).

If you hold yourself in such high esteem without the proven patterns to show for it, then you are not a True Champion. True Champions in a room of individuals, see themselves as someone who serves others, and sees hidden potential greatness within everyone.

No True Champion looks at their life saying they have accomplished everything they wanted already. Though we acknowledge we are good at

<u>many things, we reasonably understand that we can be better in everything.</u>

What is the point of reaching for a low bar, grabbing onto it, and being satisfied? Especially when the high bar of a beyond normal life in greatness, is made of up easy low bars that make up the ladder of success.

Take it from someone who knows what makes up the most complex systems known to man in my background of engineering, psychology of the mind, finances, definitions/words, how the human body works, and so much more using my sliding door of wisdom, to make complex things into easy relatable patterns:

The most sophisticated programs, machines, beings, and sciences are made up of A LOT of simple parts. But if you're missing a key component in the pattern, the sophisticated thing(s) will not work as great as they were intended in the end.
There is no short cut to life.

Let me tell you right now who alone, has the ability/potential to access the vault of the components in becoming a True Champion:

YOU AND YOU ALONE

<u>Not your…</u>

- Mom
- Dad
- Sibling
- Friend(s)
- Coworker
- Government (Stop depending on those idgets to do everything for you. You're being lazy. They don't care about you. Someone who cares, wants you to be the greatest person you can be. Saying they'll give you things without the intent to stay consistent, will only lead manipulation. Start using your head and make something of yourself.)

- School
- Media
- Social Media accounts/friends
- Not anyone who is, can be, or ever will be associated with you
- Not your skin color
- Not your gender (male, female)
- Not what you have, see yourself having, or what someone else has

This list and the fact you must make the decision to become greater in yourself alone now understood, you also need to understand; True Champions know life was not meant to be performed alone, and greatness in all aspects of life cannot be achieved solely by an individual. Which is why a good portion (if not all True Champions), have a Phoenix or strong Lion mentality, in conjunction with their designated gifts/talents.

As I stated earlier in the book. You can control yourself in all situations and circumstances to some degree. But blaming an individual's personal inadequacies is something of the norm today, so this needs to be reiterated again:

You alone have the choice to use the keys of success.

<u>Faith + Understanding + Belief = Success</u>

(Especially in America) No one can take your greatness from you, unless you allow them to. That being known, there is a right and wrong way to do things. If you want greater, then hold yourself accountable, and in doing so, greater will come start to come with consistency.

<u>*As you consciously practice greatness patterns, your subconscious world will become that level of greatness, until you so decide to relinquish or level up your greatness pattern mentality.*</u>

<u>True Champions rise above in a respectable/honorable/righteous way, regardless of what the crowd around them thinks they are. A True Champion will continue to smile as the darkness closes in, because they will show everyone the greatness of their life; through the unbreakable force that is their shining mirror, by showing exactly where their unstoppable light comes from *Him*.</u>

True Champions can easily determine the fakes from the real, because the real want what is best for people, but also understand it takes effort to get anywhere in life.

Meanwhile, the fakes will attempt to give you something with the knowledge that what they say, is not how you as the individual rise above to be seen how you want to. In fact, the fake will not be consistent in themselves, and change what they say in order to accommodate their good standing in the room. When the fakes do this, they are a lie unto themselves and everyone around them. Because they only prove the subtle, but blatant hypocrisy of their life.

<u>Hopefully this book shows you the fake from the real in yourself and the world around you, by unveiling consistent patterns of hypocrisy within yourself to be changed for greatness patterns:</u>

- Own up to your short comings, and failures as they happen, then learn from them. Understand you are not perfect, and neither is anyone else, but look for the greatness in everyone.

- Speak your mind with the knowledge you can back it up through greatness of consistency whether the world's opinion agrees or not. But do not judge, condemning others for their patterns in life. Simply and respectfully, try to help in ways that are righteous.

- Truly love and respect yourself first, to truly love and respect someone else.

- Stay consistent in everything, for being consistently as great as you can be in all aspects, is what sets the developmental patterns of a True Champion.

- Never stop growing in all aspects. Being comfortable is understandable for a time, but after a while don't let being comfortable stop the uncomfortable change needed for growth.

- Stay calm in the fire. There is a difference between being content in all things and understanding that there is wisdom to help you become greater.

- Move and perform actions in faith and do good deeds.

- Put educated and efficient effort into everything no matter what you think the outcome will be, then learn from both success and failure.

- Respect is not taken by force; it's earned by respectful actions even when it seems hard.

- Use the knowledge in this book to your benefit and tell everyone you know about it.

<u>True Champions let their life of greatness shine without recklessly needing others validation.</u>

Chapter 8: My final incites to you (using this book)

Effort and individual pattern of thought through a righteous/integrity/honorable sliding door of wisdom, are required in everything you do, in order to make a wide variety of life practices, business, and political choices more educated/understood.

That being known, we as humans were created to do life together. But it's on us to be weary of who we hang around, what we consume mentally, and who our hearts listen to. As it can connect mentally to affect us in life changing ways, whether we realize it or not, without the correct understanding.

<u>This world will always look for ways to keep you down, and we can be our own worst enemies in MANY areas.</u>

Everyone has their own unique gifts from patterns that have been built and have developed within themselves over time. Yet, it's on us as individuals to learn what kind of patterns we go through, then cultivate, and adapt where necessary.

Some say it's ok to be fine with being perfectly fine. Some people want to live a simple life. But after a while, no matter how long you think you might be able to prolong it, we as humans will always crave something greater in ourselves.

So, if you have been living in consistently being fine, the stagnation, then frustration will only be harder to break, and the mentally darker beyond will seem to be apparent at every corner, until the subconscious pattern level of being fine is broken with new patterns.

Upon birth, we are all given a certain level of faith, and are all tasked to develop our abilities of patterns using patterns, in order to transform abilities into gifts. From there, it is then on us to use them to attain the level of greatness our hearts desire to know Him.

Perceived stagnation will always lead to frustration, and the mentally beyond. So, change starts with your state of your pattern mentality first, then applied action, to forever change your subconscious patterns of impulse.

We all have untapped hidden potential given to us from birth based on our gifts/talent's quad-locked behind the combination of these doors:

Door of Life, Door of Pattern-allistic Mentality, Door of your Heart, and Door of The World.

But the only one who has the keys to open <u>ALL</u> of those locks in the <u>end</u>, is the <u>One</u> who created it all in the <u>beginning</u>.

I'm not saying you can't reach the level of champion (true champion is out of the question without the One) or do great things using this book, because of the pattern-allistic mentality blueprint it will cause you to develop within yourself. But you risk falling within no one to catch you, as you put your faith in worldly views that are proven to let you down, and then you ultimately risk your salvation. Not only that, but you choose to not use the complimentary manual, lifestyle, and mentality that shows you how to deal with patterns when "bad gas" (known as uncontrollable worldly situations), go into your specific life aspect cars.

All understanding of patterns and who you are, come from the Father, Son, and Holy Spirit.

I understand without Them I am lost in the darkness of how the world thinks. But with Them, I can become a light so bright, anyone can see it reflecting off the great mirror of my heart, mind, and soul through action.

Even more to ponder:

Do you believe when God created the universe and spoke everything into existence, there was no energy exerted? (The Big Bang)

There are things even science can't explain, and if you ask the people performing the real scientific research, they will tell you there has to be a God, because of the unique, well thought out, and perfect design. I could also go on and on about how to relate God's design for all living animals to thrive in His creation, and how He gave every living creature/being the ability to adapt to their surroundings (Evolutionist's theory).

But even the creator of modern-day physics as we know it, Einstein, said:

"The more I study science, the more I believe in God…"

In this creation, the difference that constitutes us as humans having souls and animals not; are animals do not have the ability to gain new patterns to differentiate situations that constitute pattern-allistic decision making, unless domestication occurs. That, and humans also have cognitive ability regarding how we choose to break our own patterns at any given moment.

So, it is our obligation as people made by design to learn the truly empathic emotionality of repercussions that can harm the soul; in order to fulfill our capabilities mentally, of becoming more powerful than any supercomputer. Thus, ultimately meaning, we have the ability to determine how our individual story goes, based on understanding truth. So, that means we should not listen to hypocrisiests (new word: people who practice hypocrisy and know they do) in high places, causing manipulation through worldly opinion. But instead, look to on higher that created everything, Who wants the greatest for each of us, while standing up for true integrity/honorable/respect-based justice for ourselves in the process.

I believe I gave you the blueprint of all blueprints, in accordance with the most influential and important historically accurate book ever written about life, liberty, and the pursuit of happiness. All of which were not man-made concepts, but proven to be first conceptualized in the <u>Bible</u>, for all humankind. The Bible and Big Three are all about true love, so a manual of how to live the great life we all want was provided through the living Word.

<u>Do you get it now?</u>

The flip side of the coin of stagnation that leads to frustration, then to depression, anger, and the mentally darker beyond, are Newton's 3 laws of motion in physics used for growth, then applied with a Biblical mindset to your pattern-allistic mentality of life, through a sliding door of wisdom.

1. A body at rest, will remain at rest, and a body in motion will remain in motion, unless acted upon by an outside force.

2. The force acting on/through an object, is equal to the mass of said object, multiplied by the acceleration.

3. For every action, there is an equal and opposite reaction.

(1) Some people can't even get past the first law. So, they think someone else is keeping them down, rather than looking inward of how to become the light their world needs to prove patterns need to change. Most people do not want to recognize their subconscious impulse problems first, because it requires change via momentum and acceleration in patterns, to become an integrity/righteous/honorable filled force.

(2) People can't gain the acceleration, traction, motivation, momentum because they do not know <u>how to move</u>. But little do they know; it starts with their <u>intentional conscious pattern applications</u> to provide a <u>lasting change in the subconscious</u>.

(3) Regardless of being visible in the now, all of the action, effort, and hard work patterns an individual puts in for greater, causes a reaction in ways they can't even imagine, that are meant for their potential success.

Meaning, through the effort of *understanding* the problems in your initial subconscious impulse and intentional application (1), to change your consciousness (2) *Beliefs*, results in (slowly but surely) your subconscious patterns being changed towards impulses of greatness, but consistency is required for you to notice any change as time goes on (3) *Faith*.

<u>Faith + Understanding + Belief = Success</u>

The Sliding door of wisdom I have attained that you can too:

I just translated the patterns of physics, to the patterns of psychology, in order to attain a greatness pattern of the mind (I slid my door across the bar of life).

I know from personal experience that having the relationship/deep connection God so desperately wants to have with you, the Biblical mindset He wants to establish for the greatness of your life, and the people around you, is so incredible, you can't even imagine until it happens. **He is the One who works in the background to help establish patterns for the betterment of us all as individuals. That is why certain things happen. He's trying to increase your <u>understanding</u> of <u>faith</u> to <u>believe</u> He can do all things. But unlike the other two, faith comes from relationship and giving all patterns to Him and His understanding.**
<u>He wants the greatest for you, but you need to want to have greater patterns for yourself first.</u>

The wisdom of cutting an apple and greatness patterns we all subconsciously understand in ourselves but must call forth into reality from our sliding door of wisdom.

We've all seen it, and if you haven't, then there are other wisdom patterns I know you've witnessed before. The cutting of an apple carries the more weight than you realize.
The apple is a fruit that represents redemption, wisdom, and all patterns of life.

There are 3 ways to eat an apple:
- Biting into it
- Cutting it with a knife
- Using an apple cutting tool

Biting into an apple represents the need to always perform patterns your way in life. It might be quick and easy to "cut" compared to a knife. But leaves the apple jagged and ugly in the aftermath. There is no understandable logic, because the pattern of the apple is hypocritical unto itself, as the "cuts" changed constantly and were inefficient.

Cutting the apple with a knife takes time, and you doing it on your own means there is always the possibility of cutting yourself. You try to follow a pattern in cutting you've seen, but it is still not as greatly efficient as it could be. Some slices are bigger, taking more time to eat than others, and take more time to understand how to cut through, as you lack faith/understanding in your abilities for greater cutting efficiency. (This can also be compared to watching great intentionality parents.)

Using a tool, means you follow a pattern that does not lean on your own understanding of patterns. The cutting is more efficient, and you get the most out of the apple in the shortest amount of time. But you have to trust the tool as you put in the effort. When you trust the tool, you get nicely cut pieces, void of hypocrisy in the pattern as you avoid cutting yourself, and get the most of apple.

Doesn't everyone want to be more efficient and get the most out of life?

Applying the Biblical pattern mentality to your driven poor mindset for growth, in combination with your pattern-allistic mentality into life; is the same as using the tool to cut the apple. It's efficient when cutting and you get the most from the apple itself. Not only that, but you show kids, family, and others around you how to be more intentional in how you cut the apple for greater.

In all those scenarios, there is one simple variable that remains constant. <u>Effort and intentionality in yourself,</u> to get the most out of the apple called, **Life**. No one can "cut" it for you. You must apply effort in all forms of action, but (though it might be difficult at times) there is only one mindset that is proven to never steer you wrong in the patterns it presents…the Biblical pattern mindset to honor Him.

Now check out this one last thing from my sliding door of wisdom. (A little portion from my business book, but is applicable here because why?...<u>All great life patterns translate into business, but not all business aspects translate into life.</u>)

Wisdom is pattern comprehension. But to see how your patterns can benefit someone else to increase time, efficiency, and blessing through honor for the benefit of both sides; is the gift of pattern recognition <u>for</u> wisdom.

What happens when you want the Lord to increase what you have?

Just like using the apple cutting tool, you must recognize the patterns He is trying to instill in you, and give thanks with all your heart, mind, and soul. Because those patterns create the mental pattern of understanding <u>you can't do it alone</u>.

In life or business, guess what you <u>cannot do alone</u>?
Reach your highest level of greatness.

Guess what lies in the center of the apple?
Seeds.

Guess what those seeds are made of?
Greatness growth patterns of life.

Seeds can be planted in soil and potentially multiplied. If you are able to recognize the patterns in others, you can see their seeds that lie at the center of their apple as well. From there, you can determine if their seeds can then be used in conjunction with yours, and put into the field called, "The potential in the world…".

Using the chapter 2 keys of life, you can implant patterns of your greatness into the world for the benefit of others. But it takes effort to live in consistency for the benefit of both parties. That is why pattern recognition in others is imperative. Because without consistency in great patterns, the benefit both parties could've had, now becomes pattern-allistically detrimental to each side.

Next, the patterns from chapter 3-6 come into play. Because they point out most (if not all), points of failure in achieving life greatness through growth in understanding. As for these final chapters (7-8), they present patterns that should/need be followed, because the future is unknown.

*The sowing of **Seeds** are your patterns in action.*
*The potential of the world is the **Soil**.*
*The **Sun** is the blessing through effort.*
*The **Water** is the favor of effort, through your greatness patterns from Him.*
*The **Reaping** is the blessing from serving others through your patterns of greatness in action.*
All those things combined, makes the saying, "You reap what you sow", a factual harsh truth.

The crazy part is, in terms of controllability, you have very little except through honorable action patterns. So, if you can't control most of the bigger pattern in terms of what happens to you or in your lifetime in the world, who can?

The only one who can, is the One who created it all. The same One who presented to you the pattern of cutting the apple for a wholesome great life, presents a bigger pattern of how to become great in the world through Him.

Faith + Understanding + Belief = Success

Why?

Because He <u>truly loves and wants the best</u> for you and <u>everyone</u> and wants all to let their mirror shine as bright as His light can for the world to see. So go forth, live in the seeds of a poor driven growth pattern-allistic mentality with a Biblical mindset, and praise Him with all your heart, mind, and soul. As you give back to the One who created it all, regardless of the human mistake pattern examples you see in the world today. Do it for yourselves and live it for your wives, children, husbands, fathers, mothers, and your world around you. Hope lies in Jesus alone. God is not done working in the world yet. His Temple has not been rebuilt as it should be yet...

...So, praise the Alpha and the Omega, and become the beacon of light representing why He should be praised in all corners of the Earth.

One last thing

I didn't put a section of drastic redemption in here for a reason. That is a topic I cannot write fluid enough to represent everyone at once, to raise an entire person, group of people, nation, or world, because everyone's redemption story is different. We are all individual souls existing in a human world.

Yet, in a way, this book is about redemption...a redemption of the mind within every individual, based on the book they're individually writing called, "My Life", using the ink from their heart.

God on the other hand, is all about redemption, living in greatness, and wants you to grow from glory, to glory, to glory!!!!

Living through another human's "why" or walking in someone else's redemption shoes is boring, normal, mundane, and/or is a pity contest that can be used as fuel, but is bottom-line, temporary.

Living for your redemption story...that......that motivation to no matter what, keep rising off the floor when life happens..........lasts forever.

That's all for this book. Applying what's in here will do wonders for you. But only the truly wise will learn of God's grace, give their life to Christ, and do their best to live life as He intended. Keep growing in great patterns, keep standing up, serve/give back as much as you can, do life with people who live in greatness, and when you fall...RISE FROM THE ASHES LIKE A PHOENIX!!

Now go live life like a TRUE CHAMPION that humbly let's their life become the trophy for everyone to see!!

Now that you've finished THIS book. I have only one more question...
<u>**BABY STEP** PATTERNS ARE KEY...SO WHAT ARE YOU GOING TO DO NOW?</u>

<u>HINTS:</u>
A good place to start is by committing your life to Christ, reading the Bible, going to church, giving back, serving others with a smile on your face when you can, and applying the Bible mindset to your life. At the same time, write out various patterns you see in yourself you might need to change or build upon.

<u>A simple **baby step** pattern is changing your vocabulary:</u>
Consistent cursing might mean you are being yourself or is your excuse to say your human. But in terms of changing towards patterns of greatness in the mind, words are absolutely key. Constant cursing is an <u>insult to intelligence, is a desecration to a consistently great pattern-allistic mentality and shows why you shouldn't be followed *life and death is in YOUR OWN words*</u>.

<u>Pattern vocabulary of money</u>: Never use "can't afford", or "not enough...", because it builds a mental pattern of failure. Instead, use "I choose not to...". Everyone has a choice, and I learned growing up the very integral ways money can be used as a tool for stress, so I never followed the same patterns of those who saw it as the end all be all. It doesn't necessarily mean you're not capable of great acts. But once the understanding pattern of money is a tool is firmly in place, understanding great money patterns, and the knowledge of how to get money to work for you, are not far ahead on your pathway. But you must stay consistent in becoming greater.

SEE PAGE 17 HINT

The End...for now...

MAKE SURE TO READ THE LETTER FROM ME TO YOU, EPILOGUE, THE GREATEST TRUE CHAMPION OF THEM ALL, AND THE NEXT PAGES TO LEARN EVEN MORE.

Dear my friend,

- There is greatness in everyone, so truly love all people. Yet, be wise in understanding we are all human.
- In courageous filled integrity, honor, respect, and truly loving ways; do not lie down in submission when the matters of the greatness of the world are at hand.
- Do not be fooled by those who seek to make money from your emotions of anger or pride, because they are false prophets.
- No one knows when your time or the world's time, will end. So, live your life in great patterns with the honorable fear of the Lord as guidance, and there will be no need to worry about timing in any way.
- I'm in no way an accredited doctor of the mind. Though the typing was from my hands, the mental patterns of events, and personal stories are of my life, this book was not for my honor or glory, but for the glory of my King amongst kings.
- Punishment for all bad patterns not of the Big 3 will not go unchecked. So, change them before <u>when</u> life happens, to at least have a higher potential life factor and salvation.

I'm tired of seeing the world/people doubt my King, when examples of His greatness are everywhere. You just have to truly open your windows and ears towards the Son…

(I'll leave that next step into a pattern from that sentence for you to understand)

Your truly loving friend,
Joshua Rose

P.S.
Ironically, this book was finished on the same day after my heart was ripped out by the person I "loved" most in the world at the time and was told it is too big, as if there is something wrong with it (the plate story *the crazy part is I'm not even joking about the date**). I've been told I'm worthless or been heavily doubted by many people, but that one hurt the most.

What was once told was weak and worthless, turned out to be a one in a generation type gift the person could not see. I guess they were right though. My heart is pretty big, because I'm not looking just to love or change someone's life...I'm going to change the world for His honor. Whether is hates me as a result or not.

To share this book with other people have them follow this QR code:

If you would like to have Joshua Rose speak at any of the following:
After the approved conditions

All Personal Life Coaching (*for all economic/financial status*)
Small, Medium, and Large Business Coaching/Consulting
Player Pattern Evaluation (Sports)
Team Pattern Evaluation (Sports)
Leadership/Life Conferences
Church

I have my hand in many areas of business, but my personal favorite was the helping hand in the life curriculum for high school students, young adults, and even adults. To put it simply…it's amazing!! I worked closely with the creator of this new pattern concept. It was looked at by a variety of specialist/doctors after completion; to further ensure there were no hypocrisies and could be used for anyone. In fact, I was in the room with the creator and the specialists, and every time each one said, "It's pretty impressive that the concept was originally developed by one person." Even I have to admit, in terms of fluidity to make all involved greater in the end; the curriculum is second to none.

For a session near you, to have it potentially implemented in your school, church, or area, or to get certified to become a TWT instructor, use the camera on your phone to follow this QR code to learn more:

There is a reasoning letter from the original creator and I on the next page about the creation of the much-needed curriculum for today's world.
For 100 Fold Publishing (Book editing, creation, and design):
jrose@lifeofpatterns.com

The reason for this simple 7-step curriculum and presenting it to the world

We are tired of knowing what could have been. The potential of everyone is greatness. Everything in the curriculum is to help ensure that the youth, young adults, and people of all ages are given a strong foundation to build themselves on. Not only does this curriculum do that, but it also opens ways of thinking in one's personal self, without providing a set-in stone template of how to live.

Seeds of greatness are in everyone, but the ability to notice them is different in everyone. The reason why in the real world most successful business owners are older, is the trial-and-error method is the preferred method of someone finding themselves.

Schools, parents, media, or life consultants are not intentional in teaching how to find your seeds of growth:

School's take the approach of training for a test so they can receive more money. Parents have taken on the belief that they want the best for their kid but forgot that some adult patterns cannot wait until you become an adult. It is important for people to have a childhood, but instilling values and discipline patterns into a person, is just as important.

Media has portrayed a flawed way of lifestyle, and marketing is targeted at a younger age than ever before. So, what we watch on a screen has become that much more influential and caused many to stop searching for the reasoning of why they act. As a result, the seeds of other people have become more influential than ever. And many follow that template, believing that is how you should lead yourself, no matter how good or bad the pattern template actually is.

Now for life consultants or life coaches. It seems like today we as a people are all about changing ourselves as quickly as we can, and many have taken that way of thinking into personally helping others. To that we have this simple question.

Can glue stick to a surface if not given a certain period of time to mold proteins to a molecular pattern?

No, time is always necessary to change the patterns of those molecules.

No coaching in a matter of a few weeks or days can modify the patterns any one person has developed, for long lasting change.

Thus, being successful is not simply following the steps of someone else. Rather taking their wisdom, patterns, and values, then adjusting them to conform to what you want to achieve. This curriculum was designed with that in mind. We are not providing someone all the answers to their seeds of potential. Rather, causing them to develop thinking patterns conducive for each individual's success. These thinking patterns are better known as knowledge and wisdom from a more developed sliding door of wisdom, for action. It is a curriculum meant for developing wise and humble prosperity; centered around discernment in action, while driving patterns of how to be a greater individual over the course of life.

Wisdom is the soil to a seed of potential. However enriched the soil is, it greatly improves the potential of the seeds chances for success of growing, sprouting, and multiplying itself when patterns help germinate the seed. This curriculum is that soil. It adds all of the natural ingredients a seed needs to grow. Everything down to the very words needing to be portrayed, have a reasoning for being heard and seen by the curriculum provider.

But there is a third and fourth component of what causes a seed to be considered to be successful; water and sunlight. The water of this curriculum is its ability to put forth action with words and handouts. Just as action can apply to any situation, water can be put into any object and take that form. And just as nothing is more versatile than water, nothing is more adaptable than patterns in any given situation (via heart and mind).

The homework, meeting exercises, handouts, and zoom calls have been made in such a way, that it benefits any individual (from young to old). They help develop patterns of personal success, and prepare anyone for mountains that might block the favorable rain clouds from moving in. This curriculum causes adaptation through action in present patterns that move or more quickly overcome the mountain.

As for sunlight, the seed must be "seen" by the sun after breaking the surface of the soil in order to grow and remain healthy. The sun is only applicable after the seed has been planted in soil, water applied, and the plant begins to break the surface of the ground.

That ground represents the bar of how successful the average person is. People want to break the surface (plane of average), but they do not know where to apply the action (how to apply water). Nor do they have enriched enough soil to help their seed grow (wisdom how to get started). So, the sun will never see the plant and cause that once potentially great tree to not be seen by as many people as it could be.

We know what you're thinking, "There are some people that do happen to get lucky enough to have all of those things come together for them." To that statement we say, "If they do not have strong enough roots, then the plant will be uprooted by a storm because they were not built to hold themselves down, in the soil of their knowledgeable wisdom value patterns." That is why we want everyone to go through this potentially life changing 7-step program.

If the roots are not deep enough or a lack of sunlight occurs, the plants will slowly wither and die; due to its' inability to keep pushing forward, through gathering the required nutrients, or grow enough to reach the sunlight.

This is where the world has gone astray. We've become too reliant on sunlight (to be seen) to grow to the lengths other plants have. So, we individually put a specific seed in a certain soil, after seeing other "strong" plants and think, "that will work for us as well". But when things don't work out, individuals become broken when it doesn't fit their pattern-allistic mentality.

This curriculum helps someone find their seeds by seeking their true selves. The patterns that are needed to be put action, the ability to be seen after it all comes together, and the most important ingredient to the formula, the soil. The wisdom that would have taken years, if not decades to develop after many obstacles and failures, will be greatly enriched, and be made better prepared for the potential of the seed in a fast-paced world.

So, those who take this course we believe will in fact gain…
…Tomorrow's Wisdom Today^{TM}.

EPILOGUE

I did not write this book to pat myself on the back or to say, "YAY!! I did it!!". If I wanted to do that, I would have put my REAL NAME on the cover. I wrote this with the mentality that I'm going to change the world for the greater.

It might not be today, tomorrow, or even 1 year from now. But I have the belief that one day I will show this world an anointing and wisdom (from God) this world has never seen. I will be a king amongst kings, and a leader amongst leaders, who bows to One King, to change things ON A WORLDY SCALE, All in His name. The glory be to Him!!

This book was the best thing I could think of at the time, to help as many people as I could. I would like to remain as anonymous as I can right now, for the sole purpose of showing the world that anyone can become greater at life using the thing that connects all of the dots all at once…patterns. I also want it to show I could be black, white, purple, brown, any color, or a girl who wrote from the perspective of my brother using his own words and true stories that is living his patterns out.

I could literally be anyone!! ☺

I know my method of patterns provided will work for others, because I enacted the same patterns into my sister. Though younger, she is just as smart and talented as I am, with an even better head on her shoulders, and has more possible doors because of how I was able to truly love her. But she deserves all the credit for the effort she's exerted.

Even though she received or was instilled with some of the concept of the pattern-allistic way of thinking; there are countless others I have met and imparted on using this full way of thinking, and to their credit, most have gone on to achieve great things.

Then there is the matter of the fact I could go on about my friends who have put up with this strenuous, against the worldly grain, pattern of thinking, and the greatness they are well on their way in achieving.

As for my parents, they were not perfect, and neither will/am I (no parents are perfect).

That being known, my parents gave birth to me!!!! Which leads me to know for a fact that the love of a father, and mother who are true believers in Christ will be better than any opinion this world can come up with for a typical/normal family.

I came from a poor family who constantly argued when I was younger, but they disciplined someone like myself who (not to sound prideful) was intellectually higher functioning than most. So, I am extremely grateful for what my parents did for me. Which is more than I can say for others on my street who were involved in gangs, drugs, and even the person who held their own family hostage at gun point.

My parents did their best to try to provide as much as they could and I wouldn't change a thing, because it made me who I am today. I learned so much from them.

In the eyes of this world, my mother was a nothing, a no one, and she was reminded that she would always be nothing every day for years by her boss. Yet, even as kind as she is, she showed a fighter's spirit pattern.

My father in the eyes of the world, was a no one with a small business that would never amount to much. But he opened the pattern door to understand more about business and life than any school, class, or person would be able to.

Obviously, I was not the best kid. I was a very stubborn when I cognitively understood my gifts, because I understood how to succeed (like everyone subconsciously does but chooses not to enact), and how to truly lovingly change hearts around me. But even I would try to get away with not being self-disciplined for long periods of time. To which my family (and what your family or family of choice should do) taught me patterns of how to be accountable through self-discipline in my life. That said, when my father would try to discipline me, we would get to arguing and he took a liking to comparing me to drug dealers, saying I'm not as smart as I think I am and other things that were demeaning.

But after every time, he would tell me he was sorry while hugging me, say he just wants the best for me, and today I understand why people say things in certain ways. Both of my parents' pattern-allistic mentality was one of trying to make it out of the "hood", which is why those words were spoken.

Not imparting or adhering discipline leads to self-righteousness that believes it is greater than the authority at hand, and my parents did not want me to become a part of the environment I was raised in. These specific patterns taught me to be something greater.

I remember the feeling of being left at school by my parents thinking they forgot about me when I was there so late, and I understand why I felt that way back then. But my parents worked extremely hard to ensure food was on the table, a roof was over our heads, and spent a lot of time to make sure to provide the best they could for their children.

It taught me that all good things would not be possible without time, and effort. So, I thank them for their pattern-allistic mentality of application towards greatness, and them instilling in me the greatness patterns I want all who read this, to understand.

While I was at school and even in college, I remember being bullied for wearing the same clothes week after week, not being able to spend money like so many others could, and many other things I wouldn't do. But I understand their patterns. That was all individuals could say once they saw how much things didn't offend or affect me in the classroom, sports, or in my mentality.

I was and still am not a very possession driven person, which is probably due to the pattern I never had many possessions growing up. Then of course, it didn't hurt that I understood how money and economics worked, in conjunction with the mental pattern process before I was 10 years old, through real world experiences.

As long as my clothes were clean and presentable, why would it matter if I only had those clothes?

So, I thank those who were too insecure in themselves for trying to break me, because I gained the wisdom of forgiveness and the knowledge of understanding, that my mentality is the only thing that can keep me down.

I learned the true concept of forgiveness, and how to forgive a long time ago because of them. Which resulted in my knowledge of how that pattern mindset can affect every area of life.

Why would I need to keep up with someone else in possessions if the greatness lying within the details of my growth pattern-allistic mentality, through Biblical mindset, was more valuable than anything this planet could offer?

My close friends who know me, understand that if it were anyone else who would've gone through what I went through; things would more than likely have turned out to be darker, or the light would have gone out by now...

This same drive and pattern mentality is alive in you, but you need to call it forth.

Those who tried to hurt me didn't have what I had growing up:

While looking in the crying eyes of my mother, I decided at an extremely young age to try to not let the world break me, no matter what. Sure, there were times where I wanted to quit, but I deep down knew I couldn't....

...because what would those tears she cried to provide for me be worth if I gave up?

My dad gave me the ability to be more of an adult than most of the people I've encountered. He led me to be man enough to know what must be done and go for it in faith, no matter how much pain or how tired you are in making things happen. And all while treating everyone with respect/honor, and what it means to truly respect/honor yourself.

I look back on where I came from and reflect on what I've done since then. I'll tell you I have achieved very little greatness in comparison to what the world sees as great and failed more times than anyone I know. Yet I am told by someone that was/and still is, admired by many people and many successful large multi-billion-dollar businesses through training the leaders of those companies, that I am a <u>CHAMPION</u>.

The mindset for the key/coin of humbleness/swagger is a cup that pours into all aspects of life. So, I needed to understand the words from this person's mouth in myself, in order to continually raise the level of faith I have in myself, to achieve even greater heights on the ladder of success.

<u>*My parents and everyone whom I have met along the way, are going to witness what it means to grow from glory, to glory, to glory of the highest degree from God above!! (I'm claiming it, because there is power in what you claim over your life. So be careful of what you say over yourself.)*</u>

I am living proof that individuals that are thought to not bring greatness into the world, can bring into it something greater than what is expected. Thus, shattering the perception of what the individual can achieve and so can you!!

And I'm not done growing!! I have not accomplished my visions and dreams…YET. In fact, I may never accomplish them, but that doesn't mean I'm not going to give it my all. And that's what I want to impart on anyone who reads this book…*g<u>ive life your all, for it's the only one you get</u>*.

No matter what you think you're going through, never stop growing, learn of the greatness God has given you giving Him all the praise/glory/honor along the way, and learn to live under pressure.

<u>*For the RIGHT balanced-consistent pressure, makes diamonds!!!*</u>

Why I wrote this book

I wrote this book, because I heard of an 18-year-old killing themselves due to them not knowing what they wanted to do with their life. I'm tired of hearing about the reasoning for performing such an act in people, both younger and older. I'm tired of people giving up on my King.

I know it's selfish to feel other's pain, but had I been there in some capacity; maybe I could've walked them through their blueprint of pattern-allistic mentality. And that's what I believe this book will do. It's the way for me to see everyone's patterns all at once. That's why I wrote it the way I did.

I can't spiritually feed everyone at once, but just as this book portrays; action must be put in. Remember, for every action, there is an equal and opposite reaction. Now it's on you to raise your level using the bolts in this bucket. And the Father, Son, and Holy Spirit are there for you along the way, even more than anyone can/or ever will be.

As for the meat of the book, there are few names in the stories or parables. And I talk through many specific-detailed generalities of the real world, because definitions have been manipulated to the point that strenuous explanations are required for today's world.

Specific detailed generalities and parables are different from definitions of the world, because they are not subject to manipulation, unless the writer is not of greatness intentions. Which is why (I believe) Jesus talked in parables. Parables and stories of wisdom are not subject to worldly opinion, unless a great grasping at straws are at hand. Yet, they are also fluid enough to represent any time period.

In this book, I'm going to let human curiosity of the mind take over, because as the parables/generalities of the world are talked about with the pattern-allistic mentalities of hypocrisiests (people who knowingly live in hypocrisy) in the world, they will slowly be exposed for all to see.

This world needs to know someone out there truly loves and wants the best for everyone, without seeking their own glory, honor, or accolades. I could be anyone or anywhere. But here is a little hint of where I spend most of my time today, when I'm not traveling across the nation, spending time in various places:

You can find me in a church on Sundays in the most wanted place to buy a house in America according to a study from WalletHub™ on 8/25/2021 (WalletHub™ has no affiliation with Joshua Rose or this book)

Here is a special hint/shoutout to someone who I hold in very high regard:

"Why the tears?"

Here is the answer to those tears:

I'm tired of this world looking down on my King. I want the greatest for everyone and want to do something about the darkness this world has seemingly fallen into. Because for every darkness there will be an even greater light. My Father/King is not done yet!!
I want people to know of their untapped potential within and know just how many great things my King wants to give them.

With all the knowledge and wisdom (I was given/attained), I don't even compare to Him who created me. I have a many unique gifts, and this book displays one of my hidden talents I always knew was there. But it's time to access the main lines of royal blood within me to become the warrior king among kings, who only bows to one King, I was meant to be.
This book makes attempted manipulation of the mind known for those who understand.
I'm done with seeing blatant hypocritical manipulation. So, for now using a book, I'm giving you the keys to your mentality, beyond what any <u>one</u> person I've researched, has ever done.

DO NOT WASTE THE UNTAPPED POTENTIAL INSIDE OF YOU OVER PITTY EXCUSES!!

At some point on the journey this book wants to take you on, the world will fight back. You're going to encounter great obstacles on your path up the *Mountain* of *Life*, living to honor Him. Drugs, "friends", "family", people around you, <u>when</u> life happens, yourself, what's considered the norm through worldly opinion today, etc.

But here is one story in the Bible that I recently heard from a good friend of mine, about King David, that has become one of my favorites to help combat the feeling of <u>when</u> uncontrollable **life** hits on your journey.

1st Samuel 21:1-9. **<u>**David was fleeing King Saul who had become jealous of David's (not yet king) favor and blessing, through faith in action. (I encourage you to read those passages with this mentality in your head)**</u>**:

When it came time to anoint a new king, David was not deemed special by his father or brothers. He was a small insignificant shepherd boy. Yet, he, not his older-kinglier looking brothers, was deemed to be the next king of Israel.

As the Word says, even after many great feats performed by David for his good friend, King Saul (the government, media, friends, etc). The then king, did not want to see the fruition of David being the next in line for the throne. So, Saul attempted to kill David several times, so David fled the kingdom (Put into submission, as to keep David in the same place using manipulation).

In fleeing for his life, David sought refuge, and the random place where he found it was harboring the sword of Goliath. There was no sword like it, not only in appearance, but also the freeing power from mental oppression and fear it signified. The gigantic sword also signified a strong light, as it was the first public viewing of God's favor on David's life, and at that moment in time, represented the greatest feat of David many years ago.

Even after putting in all of this effort trying to make himself better than what was deemed of him, and now in what seemed like an insurmountable obstacle trying to keep David from achieving the blessing for his life (as deemed through his pattern-allistic mentality), his promised anointing must have felt so far away. Imagine the human doubt that must have crept in while David was hiding in fear. Then one day, in a place he did not expect to find strength, he picks up the sword that started it all.

What do you think he saw in his reflection? Who was the person staring back at him?

I believe David's reflection was the embodiment of what he went through when he was younger, and the person he once was. A small, unheroic looking young person, with nothing to show for greatness other than unknown miraculous feats only he knew of, and faith by action/effort using a few small rocks and a slingshot.

I believe the young person that was staring back at the older version looking into the sword, had a mental conversation, reigniting the fire deep within. The younger did not worry about the how or <u>when</u>, he only required faith to keep moving forward.

I believe this time period taught David how to have patterns of faith in patience, while staying righteous in integrity, respect, and honor through effort. Because as a king/leader/ruler of others, if you lean on your own or world's timing of understanding, it will lead to stagnation, then frustration, and the mentally worse beyond.

Both the reflection and the person looking into the sword knew their destiny, and what they were going to accomplish. So, why fear reaching their potential because of timing now?

You need to stay grateful and consistent in the hard times, to keep believing you can achieve something when effort becomes harder, and as doubt begins to creep into your spirit. There will always be another ***Mountain*** to climb in ***Life***. But going over a mountain, rather than running from it or waiting for an easy way up to somehow appear, shows how badly you want to get to the top. God will aid you in the desires of your heart. All you need to do is have faith through application of greatness patterns, while asking for His will to be done.

<u>The best part is…**YOU'RE NEVER TOO OLD TO CLIMB THE *MOUNTAIN* OF *LIFE* TO REACH HIGHER LEVELS OF GREATNESS!!!**</u>

THE GREATEST CHAMPION

When did the pattern mindset seem to change in America?

When they began taking the greatest True Champion out of daily life. The One who showed the greatest, most true love, and true empathy of all time.

I lived through it. I saw it happen as the world is took Him out. It is not coincidence that around +20 years ago when it all started, the rise of technology, and now the country of America/world is seen as a dark place, full of hypocrisy, has occurred. Since then, we have slowly become a people of fake winners with a growing problem in mental health, and "cancelling" people we don't agree with.

The greatest True Champion of all time is, Jesus Christ. He did not come to this earth to hate or intentionally harm others who didn't agree with him, in order to gain favor/religious favor. Nor did He come to judge the world the first time around. Instead, He came to show the way and sacrificed Himself to get rid of the obstacle standing between the Father and His people on earth, through true love.

HE DIED BECAUSE HE LOVES YOU MORE THAN ANYTHING OR ANYONE EVER COULD.

Unfortunately, the second time He comes, we as a world will have fallen so far away from Him, that He will be forced to judge the planet. Before then, there will be a period where the one who wants to manipulate the world into belief of "good", but instead are living in false sense of "empathy" reigns. Yet, before the world falls too deep into darkness, He will save His people from that time period and judgment.

In the sense of the thought patterns of the world, it will become good to do evil, and evil to strive for good.

I am not trying to incite the doom of the world, but instead provide a warning to you that the greatest champion will not come back a second time a peaceful King. Jesus will be a Warrior King in order to defeat the evil, and judge those who pattern-allistically follow evil-hypocrisy that is not of Him.

I do not know when He will come, and no one does. But I want the absolute best for you until that time happens. And even though I've never met you, I want to show you true love and not this "love" the world wants to impart on you. The world wants you to be "comfortable" and "fine" with who you are. <u>What a beautiful lie</u>. Jesus wants you to continually grow, so you do not stay in stagnation. He wants the absolute greatest for you. But you need to want greater in yourself first.

Why didn't you know of these deep patterns sooner?

This is a skill (coin), that (to be honest) I and one other person I've met, or researched in my long life, have developed when in conjunction with a Biblical mentality.

This coin derives from a unique ratio of such a deep connection with one's own self in growing, Biblical mindset in everything, a driven personal relationship with God, a massive faith level, and a deep true care for the world, while conquering life's greatest mountains. All despite the feeling of despair, sorrow, grief, frustration, and pain that sometimes feels like they will never go away.

Even now, I do not think this person is aware of this talent, but it is just as refined as mine because of a very obvious factor.

I know this person has the same coin, because I have seen the deeds, and asked people close to them (like family). I can also sense almost the exact same fighter, and a slew of many other reasons I do not have time to explain.

In simple terms of how much I look up to this person.

...**I want 100-fold**. I know the weight that statement carries. But I'm not about doing things in a partial manner. So, as long as I keep adapting and becoming something greater, I'll let the Big 3 guide me to the desires of my heart as I honor Them in greater ways and tell of His will, that WILL come to pass.

Someone like myself and potential people like me, can become the greatest mental builders of a generation. But here in lies a problem. There are very few people (if any) who can actually potentially do, and openly practice this ability to the fullest, because it requires the perfect mixture of a lot of many hard-to-find patterns. And even then, many other aspects need to fall within a certain range of greatness variance.

On top of that, is the ability to live patterns out without being changed by the world. Then on top of those, is the ability to communicate all this info. Which makes the odds of someone to perform this coin to the fullest capacity, insanely low. Then at the very, very top of the pyramid that plays a role into everything, is the understanding of how to best help others, and finally the adherence that the Son shines the light on said pyramid for all to see, is the Biblical mindset, and not be afraid of those who oppose.

A warning:

One day, there is going to be a builder who is just as well formulated as myself, with an ability to adapt their door to fit any shape so fast, it will not seem like this person is even trying. They will have all of the worldly opinionated answers, and those who do not recognize certain patterns, will fall under this person's mesmerizing ability.

Think of my special coin, but this person knows their intentions are the exact opposite of mine. As I told a friend, this person will be Hitler on steroids, because this person will have the ability to unite the world under causes without much push back (on the surface, behind the scenes is a totally different ball game). And this opposite intentioned person will know how to, "play the game", infinitely better than myself.

I don't know when that will be, but those with a certain cement pattern of the house I follow, will know what to look for.

Here's the good news:

By the time this evil appears, there will have been a charge led in the greatest capacity ever known, as a type of warning shot across the bow of the devil himself.

But will you be a part of the house I follow?

What about other influential people who could be like me (the writer, but remember my description of the pyramid and the Son to bring out the coin in the fullest extent)?

Other influential speakers, and those who study the human mentality might know of these deeper patterns if they searched, but most just apply predictability of choice. Also, it seems like they rarely know how to do things from a truly Biblical mindset.

I've been told that I should look into the teachings of extremely renowned motivational businessmen and speakers. But I decided not to, because I've heard how those certain people are at events. And after being told of their back stories, I can sense a spirit of hypocrisy behind them when the cameras are/aren't rolling.

I'm not saying these people have not done great things in the world. Nor am I saying they are not champions to some degree in their own right (different than a True Champion). But remember when I told you a phoenix if not mentored correctly ends up doing more harm than good?

When the cameras aren't rolling for <u>all</u> to see, their mind and spirit switches.
With impressionable people who look up to you, if you are one pattern when the cameras are on and need to flip a switch for other patterns in the same aspect; you are a hypocrite within yourself.
I'll probably end up listening to gain small portions of wisdom here and there after the making of this book, because I still respect what they have accomplished. But I, nor you, should mentally follow someone who needs to constantly flip a pattern switch. That's not what a True Champion should consistently rely on.

<u>Consistency of greatness is the definition of a true leader. So, what about flipping a mental pattern switch depending on who is watching, says you should be mentally followed?</u>

<u>WE HAVE ALL SINNED AND COME SHORT OF THE GLORY OF GOD. YOU WILL NOT LIKE IF THE SAYING, "I WANT WHAT I DESERVE COMES TO PASS".</u>

WE ARE NOT TO JUDGE. INSTEAD, ARE CALLED TO <u>TRULY LOVE</u>. BUT TODAY MORE THAN EVER, PEOPLE (<u>PASTORS MOST OF ALL</u>) ARE AFRAID TO TELL THE TRUTH, OR TRULY LOVE IN CONSISTENCY OF GREATNESS, OUT OF FEAR THAT THE ONES WHO PAY TO KEEP THE LIGHTS ON, MIGHT BE THE ONES THEY COULD "OFFEND".

<u>FOR PASTOR(S):</u>

- GOD DID NOT GIVE YOU A MOUTH TO CONDONE BEAUTIFUL LIES, USE <u>TRUE LOVE</u> IN GRACE.
- YES, PAUL DID SAY THAT HE WOULD CHANGE HIS WAYS IF HE NEEDED TO SAVE A LIFE IN THE LORD, BUT HE DID NOT CHANGE THE TRUTH IN GREATNESS THAT CAME OUT OF HIS MOUTH.
- GOD GAVE YOU A MOUTH TO SPEAK THE TRUTH. IF YOU ARE ASHAMED TO BE A LEADER AS A MOUTHPIECE TO THE BODY, THEN WORK ON YOURSELF OR <u>STOP</u> PREACHING A WEAK MENTALITY.
- JUST BECAUSE YOU ARE A PASTOR, <u>DOES NOT MEAN YOU ARE GREAT A LEADER</u>. TO BE SCARED TO SPEAK <u>HIS</u> TRUTH IS BRINGING FORTH THE OPINION OF THIS WORLD AHEAD OF THE <u>ONE</u> THAT CREATED IT.
    - NEED I REMIND YOU THAT JESUS WAS PUT ON THE SPOT MANY TIMES, BUT CHOSE TO LOVE TRULY; INSTEAD OF GIVING INTO THE OPINIONS OF THIS WORLD?
    - NEED I REMIND YOU THAT IS WHY <u>JESUS</u> WAS SO HATED IN THE FIRST PLACE; BY THOSE WHO FOLLOWED THE WORLDLY OPINION (EVEN PRIESTS)?
    - <u>JESUS</u> FACED THE SNAKES IN THE CORNER OF THE RING AND CHOSE TO SPEAK HIS FATHER'S TRUTH

TO COMPLETION. ANSWERING BACK TO EVERY HAYMAKER THE WORLD THREW AT HIM.
    - IF YOU ARE SCARED TO PROCLAIM <u>HIS</u> TRUTH, THEN SO WILL YOUR CONGREGATION AND ULTIMATELY, THE CHURCH
- YOU CAN NOT CLAIM TO WANT GOD TO PLAY A BIGGER ROLE IN THE WORLD, THEN PROCEED TO ADJUST <u>HIS</u> WORDS AND PUT A SILENCER ON <u>HIS</u> HARSH BEAUTIFUL TRUTH. WHEN THE DEVIL, HIS HORDES OF DEMONS, AND MANY DARK INFLUENCES IN HIGH PLACES, WILL NOT PUT A SILENCER ON WHAT THEY SPEAK.
    - THAT BEING KNOWN, KNOW THE DIFFERENCE BETWEEN SPEAKING <u>HIS</u> TRUTH, AND WORDS OF EMOTIONAL JUDGMENT FROM YOUR MOUTH. USE WISDOM WHEN BACKED INTO A CORNER WITH THE SNAKE AND KNOW THAT IT WILL NOT HESITATE TO STRIKE. BUT DO NOT BE AFRAID TO STRIKE BACK USING RIGHTEOUSNESS IN THE WORD.

<u>TO YOU AND YOUR CONGREGATION THAT MAKE UP THE CHURCH I SAY</u>:

RISE!!!! RISE!!!! RISE AND BECOME THE LIGHT YOUR FATHER BOLDY CREATED YOU TO BE!!! HAVE UNWAVERING FAITH IN WHAT HE CAN DO!!

TURN AWAY FROM WORLDLY IDOLISTIC PATTERNS!! RISE AND BECOME THE LIGHT OUR KING INTENDED FOR US TO BE. FOR <u>ALL</u> OF THE WORLD TO SEE!!

<u>YOUR FATHER'S BUSINESS IS AT HAND!!!</u>

Why True Champions

SOURCES PAGES:

From the website: https://ourworldindata.org/rise-of-social-media (as taken directly from the website)

Sources

MONTHLY ACTIVE USERS (STATISTA AND TNW (2019))

Variable time span	2002 - 2019
Data published by	Statista and The Next Web
Link	Statista: https://www.statista.com/ and TNW: https://thenextweb.com/tech/2019/06/11/most-popular-social-media-networks-year-animated/

Estimates from Statista correspond to yearly averages (Statista publishes monthly or quarterly figures). Estimates from TNW correspond to the first figure provided for the corresponding year (TNW published an animation with interpolated data).

Estimates for Facebook, Twitter, Instagram, Whatsapp, and Pinterest are taken from Statista. All other series come from TNW. TNW does not provide details regarding their underlying sources but our analysis suggests their estimates are consistent with primary sources and reports such as company earnings press releases, official company websites, and published articles.

Statista uses monthly active users to measure social media platform usage. Statista specifies "Facebook measures monthly active users (MAUs) as users that have logged in during the past 30 days. Users are counted separately for Facebook and other apps. Statista specifies "Figures do not include Instagram or WhatsApp users unless they would otherwise qualify as such users, respectively, based on their other activities on Facebook."

Further details regarding the source breakdown for each series can be found here.

Sources

PROPORTION OF PEOPLE AGE 16-24 ENGAGING IN SOCIAL NETWORKING ONLINE (%)

Variable description	The OECD average is unweighted. Data refer to 2014 except for Australia and Israel: 2013 and Canada and New Zealand: 2012.
Variable time span	2012 – 2014
Data published by	OECD (2019), Society at a Glance 2019: OECD Social Indicators, OECD Publishing, Paris, https://doi.org/10.1787/soc_glance-2019-en.
Data publisher's source	OECD, ICT Database; Eurostat, Information Society Statistics Database, March 2016.
Link	https://www.oecd-ilibrary.org/social-issues-migration-health/society-at-a-glance-2019_soc_glance-2019-en

The OECD's Society at a Glance 2019 report provides an overview of a number of internationally comparable social indicators.

Sources

MOBILE (BOND INTERNET TRENDS (2019))

Variable description	Hours per day spent with digital media using mobile. Mobile includes smartphone & tablet.
Variable time span	2008 - 2018
Data publisher's source	eMarketer 9/14 (2008-2010), eMarketer 4/15 (2011-2013), eMarketer 4/17 (2014-2015), eMarketer 10/18 (2016-2018). Note: Other connected devices include OTT & game consoles. Mobile includes smartphone & tablet. Usage includes both home & work for consumers 18+. Non deduped defined as time spent with each medium individually, regardless of multitasking.
Link	https://www.bondcap.com/report/itr19/

Other connected devices include over-the-top (OTT) & game consoles. Mobile includes smartphone & tablet. Usage includes both home & work for consumers 18+. Non deduped is defined as the time spent with each medium individually, regardless of multitasking.

DESKTOP/LAPTOP (BOND INTERNET TRENDS (2019))

Variable description	Hours per day spent with digital media using desktop/laptop.
Variable time span	2008 - 2018
Data publisher's source	eMarketer 9/14 (2008-2010), eMarketer 4/15 (2011-2013), eMarketer 4/17 (2014-2015), eMarketer 10/18 (2016-2018). Note: Other connected devices include

source	(2016-2018). Note: Other connected devices include OTT & game consoles. Mobile includes smartphone & tablet. Usage includes both home & work for consumers 18+. Non deduped defined as time spent with each medium individually, regardless of multitasking.
Link	https://www.bondcap.com/report/itr19/

Other connected devices include over-the-top (OTT) & game consoles. Mobile includes smartphone & tablet. Usage includes both home & work for consumers 18+. Non deduped is defined as the time spent with each medium individually, regardless of multitasking.

OTHER CONNECTED DEVICES (BOND INTERNET TRENDS (2019))

Variable description	Hours per day spent with digital media using other connected devices. Other connected devices include over-the-top (OTT) & game consoles. An over-the-top application is any app or service that provides a product over the internet. For example, OTT providers include Netflix and Amazon Video offering video streaming services.
Variable time span	2008 – 2018
Data publisher's source	eMarketer 9/14 (2008-2010), eMarketer 4/15 (2011-2013), eMarketer 4/17 (2014-2015), eMarketer 10/18 (2016-2018). Note: Other connected devices include OTT & game consoles. Mobile includes smartphone & tablet. Usage includes both home & work for consumers 18+. Non deduped defined as time spent with each medium individually, regardless of multitasking.
Link	https://www.bondcap.com/report/itr19/

Other connected devices include over-the-top (OTT) & game consoles. Mobile includes smartphone & tablet. Usage includes both home & work for consumers 18+. Non deduped is defined as the time spent with each medium individually, regardless of multitasking.

www.ingramcontent.com/pod-product-compliance
Lightning Source LLC
Chambersburg PA
CBHW050119170426
43197CB00011B/1647